✝

What Every Christian Needs to Know About the Qur'an

☾

Books by James R. White

The Forgotten Trinity

The God Who Justifies

Grieving: Our Path Back to Peace

Is the Mormon My Brother?

The King James Only Controversy

Letters to a Mormon Elder

Mary—Another Redeemer?

The Roman Catholic Controversy

*The Same Sex Controversy**

Scripture Alone

What Every Christian Needs to Know About the Qur'an

* with Jeffrey Niell

"The Christian engagement with Islam will be a defining issue for the twenty-first century. Sadly, most Christians do not even know where to begin in terms of understanding Islam. It is absolutely essential that Christians understand that Islam and Christianity represent two contradictory sets of truth claims. James White understands this, and in this important new book he sets out the issues of truth with distinction and clarity. Christians will welcome this book as they seek to understand the challenge of Islam."

R. Albert Mohler Jr. President,
Southern Baptist
Theological Seminary

"This book is magnificent! I believe this is the most thorough and comprehensive book written by an evangelical scholar on the Qur'an. I will surely use it and recommend it in all my teachings! I pray that every Chistian serious about engaging with Muslims would read this work thoroughly. Thank you for your labor of love and scholarship."

Abdul Saleeb
Coauthor, *Answering Islam* and
The Dark Side of Islam

"Dr. James White has written an immensely informative, carefully documented overview of Islam and the Qur'an—rich with fascinating historical, biblical, and theological analysis. In this era of rising Islamic influence and declining tolerance for Christianity, evangelicals must have more than a rudimentary understanding of Islam and its history. If we're going to meet the Islamic challenge to our faith, we need to be informed, intelligent, and prepared to answer our Islamic neighbors in a forthright, clear, and thoroughly biblical way—yet with gentleness and respect (1 Peter 3:15). This book is an excellent model to show how that's done."

John MacArthur
Pastor, Grace Community Church,
Sun Valley, California;
author, *MacArthur Study Bible*

"James White has given the thoughtful Christian a game-changer for Muslim-Christian dialogues about the Qur'an, the Bible, and our claims to truth. For too long, Christians have remained largely ignorant and even reluctant toward one of the world's largest faiths. We no longer have reason for either ignorance or reluctance thanks to White. I know of no other introduction to the Qur'an and Islam that is as technically competent and easy to read as James White's *What Every Christian Should Know About the Qur'an*. This book is my new go-to source and recommendation for anyone wanting a thorough introduction to the thought world of the Qur'an and the Muslims who revere it. For irenic, honest, charitable, and careful discussion of the Qur'an, this is the best resource I know."

Thabiti Anyabwile
Pastor, First Baptist Church of Grand Cayman;
author, *The Gospel for Muslims*

"If you are like me, your knowledge of Islam is probably limited almost exclusively to what you see on the news. Yet many of us have Muslim neighbors, co-workers, and friends. Effective witness to such people requires that we know more about their religion than the television newscasters care to tell us. In this book, James White has done the church a great service by explaining to non-specialists exactly what this most significant religion really believes. A well-written and highly informative volume."

Carl R Trueman
Paul Woolley Professor of Church History,
Westminster Theological Seminary

"Here, finally, is a book that so many Christians have been waiting for: a clear, thorough, and compelling examination of the Qur'an. If Christians are going to engage the Muslim world with the gospel of Jesus Christ, then they need the necessary tools to accomplish that task. And this book is one of them. I highly recommend it."

Michael J. Kruger
President and Professor of New Testament,
Reformed Theological Seminary,
Charlotte, North Carolina

"I am thrilled to see the publication of this much-needed book on a critically important subject, and my friend and colleague Dr. James White is uniquely equipped to write it. He has studied Islam carefully for many years and has engaged in countless dialogues and debates with Muslim leaders. He writes with compassion, respect, and careful scholarship."

Michael L. Brown, PhD
President, FIRE School of Ministry,
Concord, North Carolina

What Every Christian Needs to Know About the Qur'an

James R. White

B E T H A N Y H O U S E P U B L I S H E R S

a division of Baker Publishing Group
Minneapolis, Minnesota

© 2013 by James R. White

Published by Bethany House Publishers
11400 Hampshire Avenue South
Bloomington, Minnesota 55438
www.bethanyhouse.com

Bethany House Publishers is a division of
Baker Publishing Group, Grand Rapids, Michigan

Printed in the United States of America

Library of Congress Cataloging-in-Publication Data
White, James R. (James Robert)
    What every Christian needs to know about the Qur'an / James White.
      pages cm
    Summary: "Apologist uses the text of the Qur'an to explore the differences between Islam and Christianity"—Provided by publisher.
    Includes bibliographical references (pp. 289–292) and index.
    ISBN 978-0-7642-0976-5 (pbk. : alk. paper)
    1. Koran—Christian interpretation. 2. Apologetics. 3. Christianity and other religions—Islam. 4. Islam—Relations—Christianity. I. Title.
BT1170.W45 2013
297.1'22608827—dc23   2012043067

Cover design by Dan Pitts

17 18 19 20 21 22   12 11 10 9 8 7

Contents

Contents

Introduction

Why Study the Qur'an?

The Qur'an is the kalaam of Allah, not created,
and whoever states that it is created is a disbeliever.
    Imam Malik was asked concerning one who says
the Qur'an is created, what should be done to him?
He replied, "He should be forced to repent, and if
he refuses, then his head should be cut off!"[1]

W hy would a believing Christian write a book about
the Qur'an? If he does, why should believing Christians read it? Shouldn't we go to the Muslims to
learn about their own sacred book?

In answering, I hope to encourage you to press forward
through this book with a desire to understand and to make
application. First, a response to these questions, and then a
word to the two audiences I have in mind as I write.

In the three decades during which I have been involved in Christian ministry, I have studied a number of religious movements that are in direct contradiction to and in conflict with my own faith. I learned as a young person that the single best way to honor the truth and to show honor to those you seek to reach is to "hear them in their own language," that is, to enter into their worldview and their theology. I have done this primarily through first reading their own works (not just resources directed to outsiders, but more important, those written for internal consumption) and listening to sermons and lectures designed for their fellow believers.

There is no substitute for original sources, to be sure. But haven't I now argued *against* reading this book by a Christian about the Muslim holy book?

The reality is that there are areas—one being Islam in general and the Qur'an in particular—in which the literature is so vast, and the terminology gap so large, that the resultant task is, or at least seems, too daunting for even the most committed believer. While some of these works are intended for non-Muslims, most Christians who become desirous of learning about Islamic beliefs and of reading the Qur'an find it necessary to obtain the help of fellow believers who already have been led to a deeper study of the field. This is especially true if one wishes to hear "the other side" of the story about the Qur'an, the one normally not included in Islamic sources, about the text's compilation, the differences among the early Islamic community, and so on.

The Christian who writes on this subject must do so first and foremost with a commitment to the highest standards of truthfulness and accuracy. While none of us is perfect, and hence none can claim infallibility in anything we do, our highest goal always must be to honor our commitment to Christ by seeking transparent honesty in all things. Islamic doctrine denies many of the central truths that followers of the Messiah hold dear, and because many today use the Qur'an as a pretext for the persecution of Christians,[2] many Christians are willing in essence to let slide the standard and accept unfair, biased, and distorted counterarguments. While I fully understand the human emotion and motivation, I cannot allow myself to entertain such a temptation.

My study of the Qur'an has been born of a deep desire to fulfill three goals in my work in this field:

(1) To honor Jesus, my Lord, my Savior, my King, through the defense of His gospel
(2) To bless the people of God by providing sound biblical and historical responses to Islamic claims in general and of the Qur'an in particular
(3) To be used of God to bring the glorious message of salvation in Jesus Christ to the precious Muslim people who honor the Qur'an

In pursuit of these goals, I have had the opportunity to debate dozens of Islamic representatives on three continents.[3] This book arises out of that study and preparation, and my sincere hope is that it will bless my fellow believers by helping to better prepare them to minister the life-giving gospel to others.

Everything You Need to Know?

It is not my intention to write an exhaustive compendium of Qur'anic knowledge. Almost no one could, and certainly I could not, even if I wished to do so. My aims are far more focused and modest.

As to focus, mine is provided by my primary audience, my fellow believers in Jesus. This book's title is purposeful: I seek to focus on what Christians *need* to understand about the Qur'an's teachings particularly as it impacts our interactions with Muslims and our thinking on events throughout our world. I operate on the assumption that Christians believe that Jesus is the way, the truth, and the life (John 14:6) and that salvation is only by His death and resurrection.

I will seek to honestly communicate what the Qur'an says about who God is, what His purposes are, and how we are to know Him. I will pay special attention to what it teaches positively about *tawhid*—the oneness and uniqueness of Allah—and what it teaches about Jesus (in its own nomenclature, *Isa ibn Mariam*). And I will seek to consider its teaching on salvation, on the Scriptures revealed before it was written (in particular, the Torah and the Injil [the Law and the Gospel]), and on the vital relationship it must bear to those revelations. In other words, I wish to draw out the Qur'an's teachings on the key issues that separate Muslims and Christians and that form the basis of our dialogues and differences.

I am *not* attempting to write a book that is, at its heart, a refutation of the Qur'an. But I will note the main areas of conflict and point out what I deem to be the best reasons for not believing it a revelation from God. (If I believed it divine in origin, I would not be a Christian.) I believe the best, weightiest, most useful refutation is the establishment of the truth of the gospel. So we will focus upon the issues that directly relate to Christian and Islamic core teachings and hope that this introduction will compel Christian and Muslim alike to look further and deeper into these topics.

We may appear to go a bit beyond this work's educational purposes in chapters 10 and 11 on the Qur'an's history and transmission in comparison with that of the New Testament in particular. This arises from my work in New Testament textual criticism and also my many debates with Muslims, all of which, to one degree or another, have devolved down to the issue of divine authority and the Islamic accusation of the corruption of the Torah and the Injil (in contrast to the Qur'an's supposed perfection). Since this is central to needful conversation between Christians and Muslims, and since the history of these books' transmission through time rarely is an area of strength for adherents to either faith, it's vital that we examine the requisite backgrounds.

The Qur'an is the single uniting factor in the complex study of Islam. From the strictest Salafi[4] Sunni to the most devoted Shiite to the most spiritually minded Sufi, the Qur'an provides the connection, the bridge, that defines the broad spectrum of beliefs and practices known today as Islam. However, in the Christian mind it would be a mistake to make a direct connection to the role of the Bible, for the true parallel between the Qur'an and Christianity is to be found in Jesus Himself, the Word of God. As we will see, Muslims view the mechanism of "inspiration" very differently and have another source of authority (*hadith*) that, at least in function, more closely parallels the Bible than does the Qur'an.

Still, the Qur'an, widely available in English, is the most accessible source of Islamic belief to the Western world. Here we must emphasize that the Muslim normally does not refer to "translations" but to "transliterations of the meanings" and other such phrases meant to indicate that the Qur'an cannot be translated to any other tongue without ceasing to be the Qur'an. And while a number of acceptable translations exist, all suffer to a greater or lesser extent from obvious theological or traditional biases.

The most widely used rendering in English, Yusuf Ali's, is arguably one of the most tradition-bound of all the popular translations (and for that reason is rarely utilized in this work).[5] Even so, hundreds of thousands of copies have been printed in English by the Saudi Arabian government, and it is easily available to anyone seeking to read the Qur'an for themselves.

Lecturing on this topic over the past few years, in Western countries I frequently have asked how many have read the Qur'an. Rarely do more than two or three hands go up, and often none at all. If I were to pose the parallel question in an Islamic context—how many Muslims have read the Bible—the numbers would be virtually the same. Generally, our two communities are abysmally ignorant of the other's sacred texts, so we tend to talk right past each other, assuming nonexistent commonalities of language and definition, which makes for dangerous scenarios (as the headlines bear out).

This is a situation Christians must labor to change, so that we who are commanded to bring the message of the gospel to all can obey our Lord's mandate with reference to the Muslim people. It is my hope that with the material in this book, you will be encouraged to engage in open and frank dialogue with Muslims, who regularly are eager to do likewise.

A Word to Our Muslim Readers

I thank you for taking the time to read this work. I have been in your position many times in spending many hours listening to Muslim scholars and leaders speak on the Bible and the Christian faith, and reading many of their related books. Listening to someone "from the other side" as such can be uncomfortable; I welcome your attention and hope you find this work helpful.

As noted, I am writing primarily to my fellow Christians, but I wish to ensure that, should you desire to know how a Christian apologist, theologian, and minister "hears" your sacred text and religious beliefs, you can do so here.

Also, I ask you to realize that I cannot delve into all the minu-tiae that separate various groups. I know there are differences—sometimes very wide ones, laden with emotion and zeal—that mark off Islamic divisions. I will focus as much as possible on "majority" views and sometimes note when a particular group diverges from the main body of Sunni belief. Often I use ex-pressions like "most Muslims," "many Muslims," or the like to avoid attributing to the entire Islamic world a belief that is not or may not be universal. But should I mistakenly fail to make proper distinction when addressing a particular belief, please extend to me a small modicum of mercy in the matter. If I do not specifically delineate your own viewpoint, please believe I am doing my best to address the topics as fairly as possible.

I have a deep-seated, heartfelt compassion for your believing community. I recognize that we share much in common; the Qur'an speaks of God's sovereign power, His creatorship, His immutability, His essential oneness and divine prerogatives, all truths I confess and believe, even if classical Islamic belief denies that I do.[6]

However, I also realize that our most basic differences—es-pecially seen in our views of *tawhid* and the Trinity, in our understanding of who Jesus was and is, and in our proclama-tion of how one can have peace with God and an assurance of acceptance with Him leading to eternal life—do separate us in matters of confession, faith, and practice. I do not believe I honor God, the truth, myself, or my Muslim friends if in any way I whitewash or minimize significant disagreements. May I suggest, against the trends of contemporary culture, that to ignore our differences or refuse to discuss them forthrightly is itself an act of disrespect to your faith and to mine?

In other words, I respect those who disagree with me enough to tell them when I believe they are wrong. The world today says we cannot openly disagree, especially in the area of religion, without being hateful or bigoted. I suggest that, conversely, it is the world's attitude that is hateful and bigoted. If we will not say that anything is wrong, then at the same time, whether or not we want to admit it, we also are saying there is nothing that is right. Herein we are denying the existence of truth in the realm of faith, and that is a slap in the face of every believer of every creed or background. I sincerely hope you can hear my heart and will keep these words in mind as you read.

The Real Reason

So why read an entire book about the Qur'an's key teachings as they relate to the Christian faith? For followers of Jesus, the answer is simple: We desire to honor and glorify the One who has given us life, redemption, forgiveness, and peace. Redeemed people want to tell others about the Redeemer. We share this planet with more than a billion Muslims, and we should want to introduce them to our Lord.

An accurate knowledge of the Qur'an can help open doors to those conversations. This will provide a foundation of knowledge and insight for communication and understanding. To that task we now turn, beginning where any such inquiry must: the origins of the Qur'an and a man named Muhammad.

Notes

1. See the discussion by Abu Ammaar Yasir Qadhi, *An Introduction to the Sciences of the Qur'aan* (Birmingham, UK: Al-Hidaayah, 2003), 34–45.

2. The level of emotion often accompanying discussion of the Qur'an is well-known in post–9/11 Western nations. On the part of self-professed Muslims, riots and death have followed from even the hint of the possible mistreatment of printed editions. And many Christians who live where they are persecuted regularly for their faith feel no less resentment toward the book always quoted as

the basis of their suffering. In summer 2012, the world was shocked by a video of Muslims beheading, for apostasy, a young convert to the Christian faith. Those who understand Arabic knew well that the words chanted just before and then during this act come directly from the pages of the Qur'an. Many Muslims were as repulsed by that hatred and violence as were virtually all others who saw it.

3. As of this writing, this includes moderated, public debates with Sheikh Shabir Ally, Abdullah Kunde, Abdullah Al-Andalusi, Adnan Rashid, Sami Zaatari, Dr. Zulfiqar Ali Shah, Imam Shamsi Ali, Imam Syed Z. Sayeed, Sheikh Ahmed Mohammed Awal, Sheikh Jalal Abualrub, and Zakir Hussain, among others.

4. Unless you are very familiar with Islamic studies, please utilize the provided glossary at the back of the book as often as needed, for the Arabic language is intrinsic to the history, theology, and practices of all Islamic groups, even those whose majority is non-Arabic-speaking. As Muslims hold the Qur'an to be God's very words, eternally existent in the Arabic language itself, use of Arabic terminology is a necessary if sometimes daunting aspect of studying Islam in all its forms.

5. I am using a far-less-well-known version for its smoothly reading yet consistent and accurate rendering of the Arabic original that avoids many of the aforementioned biased readings. The Christian reader can relate to why I felt it crucial to utilize a Muslim translation; a Muslim has distrust for one rendered by a non-Muslim just as a Christian would distrust a translation of the Bible by a non-Christian. (*The Majestic Qur'an: An English Rendition of Its Meanings*, 4th ed. [note the title as indicative of the Islamic attitude toward "translation"], eds. Abdal Hakim Murad, Mostafa Badawi, and Uthman Hutchinson. Translation committee: Ali Ozek, Nureddin Uzunoglu, Tevfik R. Topuzoglu, Mehmet Maksutoglu [Chicago: Nawawi Foundation; London: Ibn Khaldun Foundation, 2000]. Previous editions were titled *The Holy Qur'an With English Translation*; the first appeared in 1992. It is expensive in print but also available to read online [scribd.com/doc/55420649].)

6. Traditionally Islam has denied that Christianity is truly monotheistic due to the doctrine of the Trinity, which Muslims in general interpret as a form of polytheism. From the start, Christians have insisted that Islam has misunderstood our faith. This leads to the vital question (examined in this book—see especially chapter 4) as to whether the Qur'an understands and rightly represents the doctrine of the Trinity.

1

The Qur'an and Muhammad of Mecca

From the position of Sunni Islamic orthodoxy, the Qur'an is as eternal as Allah himself. It is the very Word of God, without even the slightest imperfection. The finger of man has no place in it, as the book held reverently in the hand today is an exact copy of a tablet in heaven upon which the Qur'an has been written from eternity past.

How did this book, about three-quarters of the New Testament in length, written during the early seventh century in the region around Mecca, come to be viewed by a billion people as an everlasting revelation from God?

While the story is believed to originate in eternity, historically it begins with a man born circa AD 570 in the town of Mecca in what we call Saudi Arabia. Muslims deny Muhammad any role other than passive reception for the Qur'anic text, yet the rest of the human family can be forgiven for considering his importance—his life, his experience, his understanding—as a proper context for the Islamic holy book. Though many long tomes have been written on Muhammad, a brief introduction is a must, as a start, for anyone desiring proper historical and theological perspective on the Qur'an.

The Earliest Years

Putting together Muhammad's story is a challenge, as the sources from which the orthodox Islamic account are drawn come from at least a century after the events of his life. Further, even those show clear evidence of legendary expansion and the influence of piety in the early generations of adherents. Some scholars today actually question the entire existence of such a historical person,[1] and while without applying vastly far-reaching conspiracy theories, it is difficult to conceive of a scenario where a narrative this complex could be fabricated, the fact remains: Most Muslims accept a story that is not nearly as foundationally certain as they think it is. Given Muhammad's centrality to the Islamic experience, the paucity of modern critical inquiry into his life by Muslims themselves is noteworthy.

The story of Muhammad is immensely bound up with the Islamic focus on Mecca, which today no non-Muslim can enter. Located in the Hijaz, about forty miles inland from Jeddah (the region's largest city), Mecca—according to Islamic orthodoxy— was an important center of religious worship all the way back to the days of Abraham. There, it is maintained, Abraham and his son Ishmael established the Kaaba, a site of true worship of the one true God.[2]

Thereafter, a gradual religious decline took place among the Arabs at Mecca. At first, they allowed images to be placed in the Kaaba, and then they began to worship them. This period of *jahaliya*, or ignorance, continued all the way to the days of Muhammad. When he eventually was successful in overcoming opposition there and taking control of the city, he purged the Kaaba of its idols and reestablished the original monotheistic worship.

It was in Mecca, around AD 570, that a man named Abdullah, of the Banu Hashim clan, had a son by a woman named Amina. According to tradition, the child was sent to live with Bedouins in the desert (in popular belief this was a healthier climate than that of the city). His father had passed away shortly after his birth, and at age six, his mother also passed, leaving him an orphan.

At eight, he was taken in by his uncle, Abu Talib, an influential man who became vitally important in Muhammad's life and would even come to have theological significance in Islam. Due to Abu Talib's position, Muhammad had opportunity to travel with caravans up into the region of Syria, gaining knowledge of this vital commercial exercise. Later traditions would narrate an encounter on one journey with a Christian monk named Bahira, who it is said recognized the mark of prophecy on the young man and warned those around him to protect him.

Of the specifics of this time in his life, we have little of serious historical value. However, note that both Christianity and Judaism were present en masse in the areas into which Meccan caravans traveled. Muhammad would have been exposed, at least through the spoken word, to stories told and retold from not only the pagan Arab tribes but also the Jews and Christians. Of course, when hearing marketplace conversations or listening around the fire at night on the long, slow routes, it would be difficult for a teenage youth from Mecca to differentiate between the various sects and groups in both faiths, as well as to distinguish legend and myth from what was based upon historical records. Did the young Muhammad look inside any of the Christian churches in southern Syria? If he did, what would he have seen? We may never be able to answer these tantalizing questions, but as we will see (in chapter 5), we might be able to theorize based on information from later in his life.

Islamic tradition indicates that as he grew older, Muhammad was known as an honest businessman, even gaining the nickname *Al-Amin*, "the faithful" or "reliable" or "trustworthy." His trustworthiness may have attracted the attention of Khadijah, a widow of some wealth, said to be about fifteen years his senior. They were wed around AD 595, and for the next decade and a half it seems Muhammad took his place as a leader in his tribe and clan, for all intents and purposes living a life normal for an inhabitant of Mecca.

First Encounter With Gabriel

Muhammad seems to have been troubled by the polytheistic worship around the Kaaba, though by one story he himself had once been chosen to replace the sacred "Black Stone" in the corner of the Kaaba itself, the one central to Islamic worship to this day. Tradition states that he began to retire for times of contemplation and meditation in a cave on Mount Hira. In 610, at age forty, toward the end of the month of Ramadan, he claimed to experience a supernatural visitation there. In the words of Martin Lings, who wrote one of the most popular biographies of Muhammad,

> . . . there came to him an Angel in the form of a man. The Angel said to him: "Recite!" and he said: "I am not a reciter," whereupon, as he himself told it, "the angel took me and whelmed me in his embrace until he had reached the limit of my endurance. Then he released me and said 'recite!' I said: 'I am not a reciter,' and again he took me and whelmed me in his embrace, and again when he had reached the limit of my endurance he released me

and said, 'recite!' and again I said 'I am not a reciter.' Then a third time he whelmed me as before, then released me and said:

> Recite in the name of thy Lord who created!
> He created man from a clot of blood.
> Recite; and thy Lord is the most bountiful,
> He who hath taught by the pen,
> taught man what he knew not.

He recited these words after the angel, who thereupon left him; and he said; "It was as though the words were written on my heart." But he feared this might mean that he become a jinn-inspired poet or a man possessed. So he fled from the cave, and when he was halfway down the slope of the mountain, he heard a voice above him saying: "Oh Muhammad, thou art the messenger of God, and I am Gabriel." He raised his eyes heavenwards and there was his visitant, still recognizable but now clearly an angel, filling the whole horizon, and again he said: "Oh Muhammad, thou art the messenger of God, and I am Gabriel." The Prophet stood gazing at the angel; then he turned away from him, but whichever way he looked the angel was always there, astride the horizon, whether it was to the north, to the south, the East or to the West. Finally the Angel turned away, and the prophet descended the slope and went to his house.[3]

What followed should interest everyone, particularly Christian readers seeking to understand and evaluate the claims of the Islamic faith. Its sources indicate that Muhammad, deeply troubled by his encounter, rushed home to Khadijah, not to rejoice in his calling as the Prophet of Allah but to express deep concern over what had occurred. Again, he was fearful about possession by a *jinn* (spirit) so as to become spiritually inspired. Al-Tabari puts it this way:

> There was no one of God's creation more hateful to me than a poet or a madman; I could not bear to look at either of them.

> I said to myself, "Your humble servant [Muhammad] is either
> a poet or a madman, but Quraysh shall never say this of me. I
> shall take myself to a mountain crag, hurl myself down from
> it, kill myself, and find relief that way."[4]

In fact, Al-Tabari says that as Muhammad was going to commit
suicide, Gabriel stopped him and addressed him as the Prophet
of Allah.

Khadijah believed his experience was with the divine and
sought to calm his fears. She told her aged cousin, Waraqah
ibn Nawfal, what had happened, and he sent word to Muhammad that the prophets of old encountered the same. When Muhammad met with Waraqah a little later, the elderly man also
warned that the people would treat him badly because of his
prophetic calling. Waraqah did not live to see this, passing on
shortly thereafter.

The Beginnings of the Qur'anic Revelation

Tradition says Muhammad did not control the speed or frequency of receiving the revelations from Allah that would comprise the document we know today as the Qur'an. The classical
belief is that while its entirety was "sent down" in one night—
Laylat al-Qadr, the Night of Power—Muhammad himself received it piecemeal over twenty-two years. And at first there
was hesitation and periods of silence, during which he suffered
concern that what he had experienced was not from God at all.
Al-Tabari recounts one such incident:

> The inspiration ceased to come to the Messenger of God for a
> while, and he was deeply grieved. He began to go to the tops of
> mountain crags, in order to fling himself from them; but every
> time he reached the summit of a mountain, Gabriel appeared to

him and said to him, "You are the Prophet of God." Thereupon his anxiety would subside and he would come back to himself.[5]

In later traditions, Muhammad would liken the inspiration's coming to the "ringing of a bell." Others reported seeing him sweating even on a cold day as he received it. Many have theorized on physical sources of his behavior, but we lack sufficient information upon which to engage in speculation.

In any case, the revelations began to outline the primary elements of the message Muhammad believed he was being called to deliver. Amid the polytheistic worship associated with the Kaaba, he began to proclaim not a new faith but an old one, needing to be reestablished. His was a message of pure monotheism: *tawhid*, as it became known, Allah's oneness and unity, over against the impure worship that had developed over all the generations since Abraham, said to have originally set up the Kaaba.

Muhammad started emphasizing a coming judgment day everyone will face, answering to Allah for all actions. He preached the resurrection of the dead, the joys of paradise for those Allah would favor, and the realities of eternal punishment for those who find their "scales light" (lacking in faith and good works). "Fire" is the abode of those who do not bow, *submit* (the core meaning of "Islam") to Allah; Muhammad's descriptions were graphic. He also emphasized the simple rituals of prayer and fasting, giving to the poor, and rejecting unfair practices that lead the wealthy to mistreat the poor.

Opposition and Persecution

Tradition says, and logic dictates, that preaching monotheism in Mecca, which received so much of its economic activity from idol worship at the Kaaba and from pilgrimages, would engender severe opposition. Muhammad's followers were few in his ministry's first decade, and he often was the object of ridicule, persecution, even plots. After Khadijah, he was joined by some whose names would become well known in Islamic history: his close friend, Abu Bakr, whose young daughter, Aisha, became his favorite bride; Zayd, his adopted son; and Ali ibn Abi Talib, his young cousin who eventually became Caliph (Islamic head of state), but whose name forever would be linked with Islam's Sunni vs. Shiite division. As the numbers grew, the movement was an annoyance and then a threat to Mecca's vested interests. This period was taken up with usually short but frequent revelations, often addressing justice, worship, and the coming judgment upon those who refused to submit to Allah.

The "Satanic Verses"

It is easy to understand how, after years of persecution, few followers, and opposition by the Meccan leaders, Muhammad would seek ways to gain their hearing. The Qur'an is full of examples of polytheistic foolishness, yet many stood firm in their fidelity to ancestral traditions. And so occurred during this time an infamous incident in Muhammad's life.

A number of Islamic sources record what has become an embarrassment to modern Muslim apologists, regarding the "Satanic Verses." This includes two of the most important early sources for Muhammad's life: Ibn Ishaq's *Sirat Rasul Allah* (*The Life of the Messenger of Allah*) and Al-Tabari's massive history. From the former:

> Now the apostle was anxious for the welfare of his people, wishing to attract them as far as he could. It has been mentioned

that he longed for a way to attract them, and the method he adopted is what Ibn Hamid told me that Salama said M. b. Ishaq told him from Yazid b. Ziyad of Medina from M. b. Ka'b al-Qurazi: When the apostle saw that his people turned their backs on him and he was pained by their estrangement from what he brought them from God he longed that there should come to him from God a message that would reconcile his people to him. Because of his love for his people and his anxiety over them it would delight him if the obstacle that made his task so difficult could be removed; so that he meditated on the project and longed for it and it was dear to him. Then God sent down "By the star when it sets your comrade errs not and is not deceived, he speaks not from his own desire," and when he reached His words "Have you thought of al-Lat and al-'Uzza and Manat the third, the others," Satan, when he was meditating upon it, and desiring to bring it (sc. reconciliation) to his people, put upon his tongue "these are the exalted Gharaniq whose intercession is approved." When the Quraysh heard that, they were delighted and greatly pleased at the way in which he spoke of their gods and they listened to him; while the believers were holding that what their prophet brought from their Lord was true, not suspecting a mistake or a vain desire or slip, and when he reached the prostration and the end of the Sura in which he prostrated himself the Muslims prostrated themselves when their prophet prostrated confirming what he brought and obeying his command, and the polytheists of Quraysh and others who were in the mosque prostrated when they heard the mention of their gods, so that everyone in the mosque believer and unbeliever prostrated, except al-Walid b. al-Mughira who was an old man who could not do so, so he took a handful of dirt from the valley and bent over it. Then the people dispersed and the Quraysh went out, delighted at what had been said about their gods, saying, "Muhammad has spoken of our gods in splendid fashion. He alleged in what he read that they are the exalted Gharaniq whose intercession is approved."

The news reached the prophet's companions who were in Abyssinia, it being reported that Quraysh had accepted Islam, so some men started to return while others remained behind. Then Gabriel came to the apostle and said, "What have you done, Muhammad? You have read to these people something I did not bring you from God and you have said what He did not say to you." The apostle was bitterly grieved and was greatly in fear of God. So God sent down (a revelation), for he was merciful to him comforting him and making light of the affair and telling him that every prophet and apostle before him desired as he desired and wanted what he wanted and Satan interjected something into his desires as he had on his tongue. So God annulled what Satan had suggested and God established His verses i.e. you are just like the prophets and apostles. Then God sent down: "We have not sent a prophet or apostle before you but when he longed Satan cast suggestions into his longing. But God will annul what Satan has suggested. Then God will establish his verses, God being knowing and wise." Thus God relieved his prophet's grief, and made him feel safe from his fears and annulled what Satan had suggested in the words used above about their gods by his revelation "Are yours the males and His the females? That were indeed an unfair division" (i.e. most unjust); "they are nothing but names which your fathers gave them" as far as the words "to whom he pleases and accepts," i.e., how can the intercession of their gods avail with Him?

When the annulment of what Satan had put upon the prophet's tongue came from God, Quraysh said: "Muhammad has repented of what he said about the position of your gods with Allah, altered it and brought something else."[6]

Later Muslim scholars and theologians would dispute this story, but they always must face the question: Why would these very early sources, vital for our understanding of claims concerning Muhammad in so many other areas, record such an incident if it were not true? And, in this case, there is a telltale sign found elsewhere that the event was in fact based in the earliest stories about his life.

The most authoritative collection of *hadith* (which we will reference throughout), known as *Sahih Al-Bukhari*, narrates[7] that when Muhammad prostrated while reciting *Surah An-Najm*— Surah 53, the same one in which the alleged Satan-inspired verses were first inserted—"with him prostrated the Muslims, the pagans, the jinns, and all human beings." Why would the pagans also bow down in the very same way mentioned above? These *ahadith* seem to have been edited, with the offensive reason for the pagan prostration later removed out of embarrassment. For Christians, whether or not this incident took place is very relevant to our evaluation of Muhammad's claims, for just as we find it most unusual for a prophet of God to seek to take his own life after his initial calling, so too we would see this as a further significant element in his story and his self-proclaimed role not just as *a* prophet but as *the final* prophet.

The Isra and the Mi'raj

According to Islamic tradition, another event placed in the Meccan period is the Isra, Muhammad's night flight, and the Mi'raj, his visitation to heaven. Early sources differ somewhat in how they view it, but today Muslims in general believe the Mi'raj was not merely a spiritual experience or a dream but happened in reality. In the Isra, he was given a winged steed, the *Buraq*, that he rode, traditionally to Jerusalem, the location of the "farthest mosque." From there, guided by Gabriel, he ascended through the levels of heaven and received the commandment as to the five daily prayers of the Muslim people.

There are a number of versions in the early literature. Given its centrality to belief in the divine nature of Muhammad's prophethood, we must read through at least one. The following is found in *Sahih Al-Bukhari*:

Narrated Abbas bin Malik:
Malik bin Sasaa said that Allah's Apostle described to them his Night Journey saying, "While I was lying in Al-Hatim or Al-Hijr, suddenly someone came to me and cut my body open from here to here." I asked Al-Jarud who was by my side, "What does he mean?" He said, "It means from his throat to his pubic area," or said, "From the top of the chest." The Prophet further said, "He then took out my heart. Then a gold tray of Belief was brought to me and my heart was washed and was filled (with Belief) and then returned to its original place. Then a white animal which was smaller than a mule and bigger than a donkey was brought to me." (On this Al-Jarud asked, "Was it the Buraq, O Abu Hamza?" I [i.e., Anas] replied in the affirmative.) The Prophet said, "The animal's step (was so wide that it) reached the farthest point within the reach of the animal's sight. I was carried on it, and Gabriel set out with me till we reached the nearest heaven.

"When he asked for the gate to be opened, it was asked, 'Who is it?' Gabriel answered, 'Gabriel.' It was asked, 'Who is accompanying you?' Gabriel replied, 'Muhammad.' It was asked, 'Has Muhammad been called?' Gabriel replied in the affirmative. Then it was said, 'He is welcomed. What an excellent visit his is!' The gate was opened, and when I went over the first heaven, I saw Adam there. Gabriel said (to me). 'This is your father, Adam; pay him your greetings.' So I greeted him and he returned the greeting to me and said, 'You are welcomed, O pious son and pious Prophet.' Then Gabriel ascended with me till we reached the second heaven. Gabriel asked for the gate to be opened. It was asked, 'Who is it?' Gabriel answered, 'Gabriel.' It was asked, 'Who is accompanying you?' Gabriel replied, 'Muhammad.' It was asked, 'Has he been called?' Gabriel answered in the affirmative. Then it was said, 'He is welcomed. What an excellent visit his is!' The gate was opened.

"When I went over the second heaven, there I saw Yahya (i.e. John the Baptist) and 'Isa (i.e. Jesus) who were cousins of each other. Gabriel said (to me), 'These are John and Jesus; pay them your greetings.' So I greeted them and both of them returned my greetings to me and said, 'You are welcomed, O pious brother and pious Prophet.' Then Gabriel ascended with me to the third heaven and asked for its gate to be opened. It was asked, 'Who is it?' Gabriel replied, 'Gabriel.' It was asked, 'Who is accompanying you?' Gabriel replied, 'Muhammad.' It was asked, 'Has he been called?' Gabriel replied in the affirmative. Then it was said, 'He is welcomed, what an excellent visit his is!' The gate was opened, and when I went over the third heaven there I saw Joseph. Gabriel said (to me), 'This is Joseph; pay him your greetings.' So I greeted him and he returned the greeting to me and said, 'You are welcomed, O pious brother and pious Prophet.' Then Gabriel ascended with me to the fourth heaven and asked for its gate to be opened. It was asked, 'Who is it?' Gabriel replied, 'Gabriel.' It was asked, 'Who is accompanying you?' Gabriel replied, 'Muhammad.' It was asked, 'Has he been called?' Gabriel replied in the affirmative. Then it was said, 'He is welcomed, what an excellent visit his is!'

"The gate was opened, and when I went over the fourth heaven, there I saw Idris. Gabriel said (to me), 'This is Idris; pay him your greetings.' So I greeted him and he returned the greeting to me and said, 'You are welcomed, O pious brother and pious Prophet.' Then Gabriel ascended with me to the fifth heaven and asked for its gate to be opened. It was asked, 'Who is it?' Gabriel replied, 'Gabriel.' It was asked. 'Who is accompanying you?' Gabriel replied, 'Muhammad.' It was asked, 'Has he been called?' Gabriel replied in the affirmative. Then it was said 'He is welcomed, what an excellent visit his is!' So when I went over the fifth heaven, there I saw Harun (i.e. Aaron), Gabriel said, (to me). This is Aaron; pay him your greetings.' I greeted him and he returned the greeting to me and said, 'You are welcomed, O pious brother and pious Prophet.' Then Gabriel ascended with me to the sixth heaven and asked for its gate to be opened. It was asked, 'Who is it?' Gabriel replied, 'Gabriel.' It was asked, 'Who is accompanying you?' Gabriel replied, 'Muhammad.' It was asked, 'Has he been called?' Gabriel replied in the affirmative. It was said, 'He is welcomed. What an excellent visit his is!'

"When I went (over the sixth heaven), there I saw Moses. Gabriel said (to me), 'This is Moses; pay him your greeting.' So I greeted him and he returned the greetings to me and said, 'You are welcomed, O pious brother and pious Prophet.' When I left him (i.e. Moses) he wept. Someone asked him, 'What makes you weep?' Moses said, 'I weep because after me there has been sent (as Prophet) a young man whose followers will enter Paradise in greater numbers than my followers.' Then Gabriel ascended with me to the seventh heaven and asked for its gate to be opened. It was asked, 'Who is it?' Gabriel replied, 'Gabriel.' It was asked, 'Who is accompanying you?' Gabriel replied, 'Muhammad.' It was asked, 'Has he been called?' Gabriel replied in the affirmative. Then it was said, 'He is welcomed. What an excellent visit his is!'

"So when I went (over the seventh heaven), there I saw Abraham. Gabriel said (to me), 'This is your father; pay your greetings to him.' So I greeted him and he returned the greetings to me and said, 'You are welcomed, O pious son and pious Prophet.' Then I was made to ascend to *Sidrat-ul-Muntaha* (i.e. the Lote Tree of the utmost boundary) Behold! Its fruits were like the jars of Hajr (i.e. a place near Medina) and its leaves were as big as the ears of elephants. Gabriel said, 'This is the Lote Tree of the utmost boundary.' Behold! There ran four rivers, two were hidden and two were visible, I asked, 'What are these two kinds of rivers, O Gabriel?' He replied, 'As for the hidden rivers, they are two rivers in Paradise and the visible rivers are the Nile and the Euphrates.'

"Then *Al-Bait-ul-Ma'mur* (i.e. the Sacred House) was shown to me and a container full of wine and another full of milk and a third full of honey were brought to me. I took the milk. Gabriel remarked, 'This is the Islamic religion which you and your followers are following.' Then the prayers were enjoined on me: They were fifty prayers a day. When I returned, I passed by Moses who asked (me), 'What have you been ordered to do?' I replied, 'I have been ordered to offer fifty prayers a day.' Moses said, 'Your followers cannot bear fifty prayers a day, and by Allah, I have tested people before you, and I have tried my level best with Bani Israel (in vain). Go back to your Lord and ask for reduction to lessen your followers' burden.' So I went back, and Allah reduced ten prayers for me. Then again I came to Moses, but He repeated the same as he had said before. Then again I went back to Allah and He reduced ten more prayers. When I came back to Moses he said the same, I went back to Allah and He ordered me to observe ten prayers a day. When I came back to Moses, he repeated the same advice, so I went back to Allah and was ordered to observe five prayers a day.

"When I came back to Moses, he said, 'What have you been ordered?' I replied, 'I have been ordered to observe five prayers a day.' He said, 'Your followers cannot bear five prayers a day, and no doubt, I have got an experience of the people before you, and I have tried my level best with Bani Israel, so go back to your Lord and ask for reduction to lessen your followers' burden.' I said, 'I have requested so much of my Lord that I feel ashamed, but I am satisfied now and surrender to Allah's Order.' When I left, I heard a voice saying, 'I have passed My Order and have lessened the burden of My Worshippers.'"[8]

This event has become central in the later traditions for proving the divine approbation of Muhammad's prophethood. The discerning Christian likewise notes his unusual exaltation and especially his being placed in privilege above Jesus (and Moses). It is hard not to see an element of apologetic in the story, as it coincides with the Qur'anic argumentation that Islam is the natural, but purified and exalted, continuation of Judaism and Christianity.

The *Hijra*

The Islamic calendar is based upon one of its history's most important events, the *Hijra*—the pilgrimage of Muhammad's followers from Mecca to Yathrib, a city 210 miles to the north, later renamed Medina, the city of the Prophet. According to tradition, this exodus was necessary for simple survival; not only were plots against Muhammad a clear and present danger, but in fact one was hatched the night he fled, just missing the mark. By now Abu Talib and Khadijah had passed away. The Meccan situation had become unbearable.

Upon arriving, Muhammad found a city divided, major Jewish tribes mixed together with various Arab clans. He soon was looked to for leadership and began the process of consolidating his position over Medina. In the next decade, inexorably, while primarily in conflict with Meccan powers, he would establish himself as The Prophet, also by a new and growing aspect essentially unknown in Mecca: political power. Elements of his teaching that in Mecca had been present but not emphasized, now came to the fore as new challenges faced the growing Islamic faith and indeed the growing Islamic state.

Military Conflicts

We will briefly mention Muhammad's major battles, mainly because they figure prominently in the Qur'anic revelations received during these years, and because Christians, in discussing the relationship of Muhammad and Jesus, point to these as an example of the differences between them and the faiths that look to them. Entire books document Muhammad's military career,[9] and his followers treasure the stories of his exploits. Christians need to realize how deeply these accounts have entered into the hearts and minds of Muslims.

In Medina, shortly after arriving, Muhammad instructed his followers to begin raiding Meccan caravans. Today we are told this was a just response to Meccan seizures of Muslim property, and of course caravan raiding was a way of life, a normal part of desert existence for Arabs at the time. Rare was the loss of life in such adventures, but still there was more to it than regular tribal clashing, and both Muhammad and the Meccan leadership knew it.

Three major conflicts between them flared over a relatively short period: the Battles of Badr (AD 624), Uhud (625), and the Trench (627).[10] In each encounter, the Muslims faced superior forces. Prevailing at Badr was seen, as one would expect, as evidence of God's blessing of the movement. Brave exploits of the Muslims there are told and retold to this day.

At Uhud, victory was imminent when certain archers Muhammad had installed abandoned their posts to get some war booty, causing a disastrous turn and then defeat. However, the Meccans did not capitalize, partly because at first they thought Muhammad was dead, though he had only been wounded.

In response, a revelation came down that is now part of the Qur'an:

Allah fulfilled His pledge to you when by His leave you defeated them, until [the moment] your courage failed you, and you disagreed about the order and you disobeyed, after He had shown you that for which you long. Some of you desired the world, and some of you desired the Hereafter. Therefore He made you flee from them, that He might try you. But now He has pardoned you; Allah is gracious to believers. (Surah 3:152)

The third major Muslim-Meccan engagement essentially was a brief siege. Taking advice from a Persian, Muhammad, informed that the Meccans planned to come against him with overwhelming force, introduced something of an innovation for the time in having a trench dug to protect the vulnerable approaches to Medina. This allowed the smaller Muslim forces to keep foot soldiers at bay, with the enemy cavalry unable to cross the crevasse. Once again revelation came down, normally associated with Surah 33:9–27.

Following the Meccan withdrawal, Muhammad turned against the Jewish tribe of the Banu Qurayza, who allegedly had entered into negotiations with the Meccans, betraying their allegiance to him and the city. After a few weeks' siege, the tribe surrendered. According to the earliest sources (disputed by later writers, for obvious reasons), all but a few men (who converted to Islam) were beheaded, and all women and children were enslaved. Normally, his role in this event is explained as purely political, but again the intermixture of state and religion, General and Prophet, is troubling.

Muhammad's Wives

As Muhammad's political power increased, so did the number of his wives. Though the Qur'an had limited legal wives to four (Surah 4:3), it was not long before a new revelation allowed him, as the Prophet, to exceed this number. Modern Islamic apologists explain this in light of his political alliances, and surely that could be part of it but, as we will see, was not always the issue.

Entire volumes also have been dedicated to discussion of Muhammad's ethics and morals regarding human sexuality, marriage, and the resultant impact on family and culture. We will limit our review to the two major issues directly related to the Qur'an: his child bride, Aisha, and the matter of Zaynab bint Jash. We will step out, briefly, from a recitation of the Islamic story, per se, for "Muhammad's wives" is one of the most controversial aspects of Islamic history and continues to engender strife even among Muslims.

Aisha, Daughter of Abu Bakr

Without question, the harshest denunciations of Muhammad have been based upon his marriage to the young Aisha, who was betrothed at age six. Islamic sources are almost unanimous in saying the marriage was consummated at age nine (one major source saying ten). The idea of a fifty-three- or fifty-four-year-old man together with a child of nine is the basis upon which many have denounced even Islam as a whole. Add to this the scandal of Islamic child brides around the world today, and related horror stories associated with Taliban-like violence toward women and girls, and one can see why this conversation can become most strident.

But the Qur'an gives no evidence of any embarrassment or apology as to Muhammad's taking of Aisha. Unlike the Zaynab situation (see below), where a clear cultural taboo was broken, no such concern comes into the text here. Life spans were considerably shorter, and child brides were common. In fact, the Islamic literature's emphasis on Aisha's youthfulness may well be related to defense of her obvious virginity and purity. The denunciation of such marriages in most societies is fairly recent, and though modern sensibilities recoil at the image, people then plainly did not consider it strange or odd.

This brings us once again to the problem of setting up Muhammad as the paragon of moral virtue *for all people and for all time*. He was a man of his day, deeply influenced by the mores and traditions of seventh-century Arabia. It's when those mores and traditions are made *specifically normative* for all cultures and all times[11] that conflict is sure to result.

It is not Aisha's age but an incident in her life around AD 627 that figures prominently in the Qur'anic text. As with so many other aspects of the Islamic story, the many versions vary in assorted elements, but the gist is clear.

When accompanying Muhammad in a caravan, the still-young Aisha had her own attendants and would ride in her own *howdah*, a covered carrier that afforded privacy befitting a wife of the Prophet. The story is that at one time the entire army had to stop so that she could look for a prized necklace that had disappeared. Many were displeased, for their location was inhospitable.

When Aisha's camel stood up, the necklace was found underneath it. They all moved on, and they came to a nicer spot where they made camp. In some versions, the necklace became lost again due to a faulty clasp. In others, the string broke and spilled the beads or stones on the ground. In either case, she went once more to find it, and this time she felt sure of where to look. When she found it, she had to restore the beads, which took some time.

Meanwhile, Aisha's attendants came, found her *howdah*, and, assuming she was in it (she being just a girl and very light), picked it up and went on their way. When she returned with her necklace to the camp, she found it abandoned and the caravan out of sight. So she sat down on the ground and waited for them to realize their mistake and return for her. And she fell asleep.

Meanwhile, a young man named Safwan happened by, having fallen behind the army. When he saw Aisha, he recognized her as the Prophet's wife. He offered her his camel and strolled along on foot, bringing her to the army's next camping location. When the wife of the Prophet came in on a camel led by a young man, rumors began to fly. Aisha, only a girl, was unaware of this for a time. Shortly thereafter she became ill, and it was during her illness that she learned many were accusing her of infidelity.

When word reached Muhammad, he was greatly troubled by the accusations. He inquired of one of Aisha's maidservants, whose sole word of complaint about Aisha was that being a young girl, she often fell asleep while kneading dough, which then allowed her pet lamb to consume it. But Ali, the future Caliph and Muhammad's cousin, made the fateful decision to suggest to him that there were plenty of other women he could marry. This would result in major strife in the coming years between Aisha and Ali.

Eventually revelation came down, exonerating Aisha and condemning those who had spread the rumors about her. This is found in Surah 24:11–15:

> Those who brought the slander are a group of you. Regard it not as evil for you. No, it is good for you. To every man among them shall it be done according to the sin he has committed. As for him that had the greater part of it among them, his shall be a formidable torment.
>
> If only when you heard of it had believing men and women thought well of their people, and said, "This is a manifest slander."
>
> Why have they not brought four witnesses? Since they failed to bring the witnesses, they are the liars in the sight of Allah.
>
> And had it not been for the grace of Allah and His mercy on you in this world and the hereafter, a great punishment would have befallen you, because of that which you spread abroad.
>
> You received it with your tongues [and passed it around] and uttered with your mouths that of which you had no knowledge. You counted it a trifle, while it was serious in the sight of Allah.
>
> Should you not have said, when you heard of it, "It is not right of us to talk about this. Transcendent are You! This is a grievous calumny."
>
> Allah admonishes you that you never repeat the like of this, if you are [in truth] believers.

And those who had slandered Aisha were flogged but later forgiven.

The Story of Zaynab bint Jash

There is no other account in the Qur'an that, to me as a Christian reader of the Qur'an, the *hadith,* and the *tafsir* literature, is more indicative of the fundamental problem with Muhammad's claimed prophethood than that of his relationship with Zaynab bint Jash. When one takes into consideration not only the situation itself but also its results in the lives of countless millions down through the centuries, the importance of following the biblical pattern for the recognition of prophethood is readily seen.[12]

Zaynab bint Jash was by all accounts a strikingly beautiful woman. She also was a married woman, to a young man named Zayd bin Muhammad, the Prophet's own adopted son, a freed former slave. He was an early convert to the Islamic faith, and the two men were close. Up to that time, the Arab tribes, like the Jews, Romans, and so many others, had practiced—and honored—the concept of adoption. For a man to marry the divorced wife of his adopted son was a fundamental violation of morality and custom, tantamount to incest. The relationships that arose through adoption were held to be truly valid.

With this background in mind, consider these texts from *Surah Al-Ahzab*:

> Allah has not made for any man two hearts within him, nor has he made your wives whom you declare to be like your mothers your mothers, nor has he made those whom you claim to be your sons your sons. This is but what you say with your mouths. And Allah says the truth and He guides to the path.
>
> Attribute them to their fathers. That is more equitable in the sight of Allah. And if you know not their fathers, then they are your brothers in religion and your clients. And there is no sin for you in the mistakes that you make unintentionally but what your hearts purpose [that will be a sin for you]. Allah is Forgiving, Compassionate. (33:4–5)

And when you said to him on whom Allah has conferred favor and you have conferred favor: "Keep your wife to yourself and fear Allah." And you hide within yourself that which Allah was to bring to light, and you fear the people whereas Allah had a better right that you should fear Him. So when Zayd had accomplished of her what he would, We gave her to you in marriage so that [henceforth] there may be no sin for believers in respect of wives of their adopted sons, when the latter have accomplished of them what they would. The commandment of Allah must be fulfilled.

There is no reproach for the Prophet in what Allah has made his due. That was Allah's way with those who passed away of old, and the wish of Allah is certain to be fulfilled. (33:37–38)

Now, according to Islamic orthodoxy, these words were inscribed on the heavenly tablet in eternity past. They are as eternal as Allah is. And yet here are two sections that both deal with the same awkward situation that arose in history regarding Muhammad, Zayd, and Zaynab.

The first verses cited give Allah's command relating to adoption. No longer would Zayd be known as Zayd bin Muhammad; now he would be known as Zayd bin Haritha. Adoption as a stabilizing and gracious societal element would be forever damaged due to this change. *Why* do this?[13] As the second verses show, there was a major problem among the people—one highlighted by Allah having commanded Muhammad to marry the divorced wife of his adopted son.

To let the Muslim sources explain,[14] we start with Al-Tabari's massive history, which places the story's backdrop in its all-too-human setting:

The Messenger of God came to the house of Zayd b. Harithah. (Zayd was always called Zayd b. Muhammad.) Perhaps the Messenger of God missed him at that moment, so as to ask, "Where is Zayd?" He came to his residence to look for him but did not find him. Zaynab bt. Jash, Zayd's wife, rose to meet him. Because she was dressed only in a shift, the Messenger of God turned away from her. She said: "He is not here, Messenger of God. Come in, you who are as dear to me as my father and mother!" The Messenger of God refused to enter. Zaynab had dressed in haste when she was told "the Messenger of God is at the door." She jumped up in haste and excited the admiration of the Messenger of God, so that he turned away murmuring something that could scarcely be understood. However, he did say overtly: "Glory be to God the Almighty! Glory be to God, who causes the hearts to turn!"

When Zayd came home, his wife told him that the Messenger of God had come to his house. Zayd said, "Why didn't you ask him to come in?" She replied, "I asked him, but he refused." "Did you hear him say anything?" he asked. She replied, "As he turned away, I heard him say: 'Glory be to God the Almighty! Glory be to God, who causes hearts to turn!'"

So Zayd left, and having come to the Messenger of God, he said: "Messenger of God, I have heard that you came to my house. Why didn't you go in, you who are as dear to me as my father and mother? Messenger of God, perhaps Zaynab has excited your admiration, and so I will separate myself from her." Zayd could find no possible way to [approach] her after that day. He would come to the Messenger of God and tell him so, but the Messenger of God would say to him, "Keep your wife." Zayd separated from her and left her, and she became free.

While the Messenger of God was talking with 'A'ishah, a fainting overcame him. When he was released from it, he smiled and said, "Who will go to Zaynab to tell her the good news, saying that God has married her to me?" Then the Messenger of God recited: "And when you said unto him on whom God has conferred favor and you have conferred favor, 'Keep your wife to yourself.'" and the entire passage.

According to 'A'ishah, who said: "I became very uneasy because of what we heard about her beauty and another thing, the greatest and loftiest of matters—what God had done for her by giving her in marriage. I said she would boast of it over us."[15]

Martin Lings narrates the same story in this way:

It happened one day that he went to speak to his Zayd about something and went to his house. Zayd was out, and Zaynab, not expecting any visitors at that time, was lightly clad. But when she was told that the Prophet had come, she was so eager to greet him that she leapt to her feet and ran to the door, to invite him to stay until Zayd returned. "He is not here, O Messenger of God," she said, "but comes out in, my father and my mother be thy ransom." As she stood in the doorway, a radiant figure of joyous welcome, the prophet was amazed at her beauty. Deeply moved, he turned aside, and murmured something which she could not grasp. All she heard clearly were his words of wonderment as he walked away: "Glory be to God the Infinite! Glory be to Him who disposeth men's hearts!" When Zayd returned she told him of the Prophet's visit and of the glorification she had heard him utter. Zayd immediately went to him and said: "I have been told thou camest unto my house. Why didst not enter, thou who art more to me than my father and my mother? Was it that Zaynab hath found favor with thee? If it be so, I will leave her." "Keep thy wife and fear God," said the Prophet with some insistence. He had said on another occasion: "Of all things licit the most hateful unto God is divorce." And when Zayd came again the next day with the same proposal, again the Prophet insisted that he should keep his wife. But the marriage between Zayd and Zaynab had not been a happy one, and Zayd found it no longer tolerable, so by mutual agreement with Zaynab he divorced her. This did not, however, make Zaynab eligible as a wife for the Prophet, for although the Koran had only specified that men were forbidden to marry the wives of sons sprung from their loins, it was a strong social principle not to make a distinction between sons by birth and sons by adoption. Nor was the Prophet himself eligible, for he had already four wives, the most that the Islamic law allows.

Some months passed and then one day when the Prophet was talking with one of his wives the power of Revelation overwhelmed him; and when he came to himself his first words were: "Who will go unto Zaynab and tell her the good tidings that God hath given her to me in marriage, even from Heaven?" Salma was near at hand . . . and she went in haste to Zaynab's house. When she heard the wonderful tidings, Zaynab magnified God and threw herself down in prostration toward Mecca. Then she took off her anklets and bracelets of silver, and gave them to Salma.[16]

Zayd is one of the few people to be mentioned by name in the Qur'an, and it is in this very context, of Allah rebuking Muhammad for hiding what Allah had revealed, and that in reference to Muhammad marrying Zayd's divorced wife.

To overcome immediate charges of impropriety (even of incest), a revelation comes down to solve the great and vexing problem of the marriage of divorced wives of adopted sons. Except, of course, it is more than hard to believe this was a great and vexing problem. We would expect the great and vexing problem to be divorce, let alone even the consideration of marrying your former daughter-in-law.[17] But Allah commands his Prophet to break the customs of his day and marry his first cousin.

Again, in the process, incalculable damage has been done to millions of children and families. In distancing himself from his adopted son, whether or not for political purposes (so that there would be none to take Muhammad's place, as Zayd would have), the culture-enriching, humanity-raising, love-engendering institution of adoption was mortally wounded in Islamic society. And upon what authority? *That of the Qur'an.*

Is this not a clear example of the problem with the orthodox view of the Qur'an's nature? Muhammad suddenly goes into some kind of faint and, when he recovers, announces that adoption is undone and Zaynab is his wife—*this* was inscribed in eternity past upon a tablet in Arabic? It seems even Aisha, his favorite (but who clearly experienced much jealousy toward his other wives), recognized an issue, for she is recorded to have said, "I feel that your Lord hastens in fulfilling your wishes and desires."[18] Certainly this must give one pause in weighing the claims of the Qur'an to status as a divine revelation.

Modern Islamic orthodoxy identifies Muhammad as the ideal man, the model to which all should seek to conform their behavior and lifestyle. Yet here, plainly the Qur'an displays acute embarrassment and must provide an apologetic, a defense of his actions. Many motives are possible, from the seemingly blatant marriage breakup, and the resultant diminishment of the evil of divorce, to the political tensions that were formative of the early generations of Islam and that led to the formation of its two major branches, Sunni and Shia. Whatever the motivation, the attempt to justify Muhammad's actions and their wide-ranging results is obvious and forceful.

The Conquest of Mecca

One might well say it was inevitable. When the Meccans failed repeatedly to crush the small but growing new movement, their own downfall seemed certain. The Muslims expanded through alliances, as Muhammad consolidated Arab tribes under the banner of Islamic monotheism, while the Meccan leadership dwindled and lost influence.

In 628, he marched on Mecca, not to conquer it but to engage in *hajj* (pilgrimage). While the group was stopped from entering, an agreement known as the Treaty of Hudaybiyyah was worked out that allowed them to return the following year. At the time, certain terms displeased some of Muhammad's followers, yet in hindsight it sealed the fate of the Meccans.

Finally, in 630, Muhammad led a huge force into Mecca, cleansing the Kaaba by removing its idols and establishing himself as Central Arabia's undisputed leader. A relatively small number of people lost their lives, and he actually angered some faithful adherents by treating his former enemies kindly, primarily to advance his cause of bringing together the tribes. All non-Muslims ultimately were driven out of Mecca and Medina, as it is to this day.

Muhammad's Death

Muhammad's remaining days would be short. He continued to build the Islamic nation, setting his sights on expansion northward. The final revelations he received were focused upon obedience to the *sharia* and the propriety of fighting in defense of the *Ummah*, the Muslim people.

The man who often had said he wished to die in jihad died instead on Aisha's lap in her apartment. Sunnis and Shias differ over the cause. One major strand of tradition attributes his death to the lingering effects of poison administered by a woman whose family had been killed by the Muslims. Others reject that Allah's final prophet could die so ignominiously and attribute his passing to stroke or fever. In any case, after a few days of sickness, Muhammad died on Monday, June 8, 632. Tradition says he was sixty-three.

He was buried in Aisha's apartment, a spot over which a green dome stands today. Many Muslims believe the bodies of prophets do not decay and that hence his would look now as it did the day of his death. A few followers known as the Companions of the Prophet are buried nearby, and by tradition, an empty tomb also is there for the burial of Jesus after He returns.

Now that we have a basic outline of the context out of which the Qur'an arose, let us look briefly at what Muslims believe about it and how it came into its present form, and then we will be able to properly, respectfully, truthfully, and accurately analyze what it says about Jesus and the Christian faith.

Notes

1. Recently published works that raise issues concerning the whole Islamic narrative include Tom Holland, *In the Shadow of the Sword* (New York: Doubleday, 2012) and, on a more popular level, Robert Spencer, *Did Muhammad Exist?: An Inquiry into Islam's Obscure Origins* (Wilmington, DE: Intercollegiate Studies Institute, 2012).

2. From a simple historical perspective, the Islamic narrative stands on very thin grounds in its claims. All we know of Abraham comes from the Hebrew Scriptures, which only once mention his coming anywhere near the modern location of Mecca. They record his once going to Egypt, before Ishmael's birth, but he returned to Canaan and died there. There is no evidence that he traveled a thousand miles southeast to a virtually uninhabitable area and built the Kaaba. In fact, that there is almost no evidence even of Mecca's existence prior to the time of Christ is one of the most difficult issues for Islamic apologists to overcome.

3. Martin Lings, *Muhammad: His Life Based on the Earliest Sources* (Rochester, VT: Inner Traditions, 2006), 44–45.

4. *The History of Al-Tabari: Muhammad at Mecca*, Vol. VI, trans. W. Montgomery Watt and M. V. McDonald (Albany: State University of New York Press, 1988), 71.

5. Ibid., 76.

6. *The Life of Muhammad: A Translation of Ibn Ishaq's Sirat Rasul Allah*, with intro and notes by Alfred Guillaume (Karachi: Oxford University Press, 2006), 165–167.

7. *Sahih Al-Bukhari*, 2:177; 6:385–6.

8. Ibid., 5:227.

9. See especially *The Life of Muhammad: Al-Wāqidī's Kitāb al-Maghāzī*, recently published in English for the first time. Ed. Rizwi Faizer, trans. Rizwi Faizer, Amal Ismail, and AbdulKader Tayob (London: Routledge, 2011).

10. Historians may argue as to whether the last was really a battle or rather a comparatively short siege, but for our purposes, we will consider it a battle.

11. This is a major area of Christian/Islamic disagreement. Muslims often assert that the extensive nature of Islamic law (the *sharia*) provides guidance in all of life, and Muhammad's example is an integral part of that law. Christianity holds that personal holiness is not through the law's extensiveness but through applying principles of holiness by the indwelling work of God's Holy Spirit. This is why Christianity can transcend cultural boundaries and does not insist on bringing a particular *kind* of culture, instead making application to every culture, calling all believers to holy living within the parameters of where and when they live.

12. We do not enter here into the oft-repeated *hadith* claim that Muhammad possessed supernatural virility. (One *hadith* says Muhammad would "visit all his wives in a round, during the day and night and they were eleven in number. When asked if such was possible, Anas replied, 'We used to say that the Prophet was given the strength of thirty (men)'" [*Sahih Al-Bukhari*, 1:268].) We might well consider how such can be made conformable to the true evidence of prophethood: godliness, humilty, and consistency with God's revealed truth.

13. There is a strong possibility that another vitally significant issue lurks in this story's background. It is too complex for an introductory work, but the reader drawn toward in-depth discussion should see the fine work of David S. Powers, *Muhammad Is Not the Father of Any of Your Men: The Making of the Last Prophet* (Philadelphia: University of Pennsylvania Press, 2009). Powers examines this text together with fascinating textual variations in the most primitive Qur'anic manuscripts. One of the most plausible contextual reconstructions revolves around leadership succession in the Islamic state, probably the key issue through the first decades of its history and what gave rise to the Sunni/Shia split. One theory examined relates to how prophets were supposed to be related to one another and how Muhammad, to be considered the last of the prophets, simply could not have an adult heir. The removal of the adoptive relationship from Zayd (and his eventual death in battle) is crucial to establishing a non-lineage-based succession in the Caliphate. Combine this with Uthman, the third Caliph, being intimately involved in Qur'anic textual redaction, and one can see how imperative further research into the Qur'anic text and its surrounding history really is.

14. Modern Muslims, especially those more Westernized, are scandalized by this account. Some simply dismiss it as without basis. Zaynab was Muhammad's first cousin, and he had given her in marriage to Zayd in the first place—why would he later be struck by her beauty when he had known her all her life? But this objection seems to ignore the fact that the early sources themselves record Muhammad's being flustered by his encounter with Zaynab.

15. *The History of Al-Tabari: The Victory of Islam,* Vol. VIII, trans. Michael Fishbein (Albany, NY: State University of New York Press, 1997), 2–3.

16. Lings, *Muhammad: His Life Based on the Earliest Sources*, 219–220. In an earlier version of the same work (1983), Lings worded the initial encounter at Zayd's house very differently. Specifically, he included: "Zaynab opened the door, and as she stood in the doorway telling him that Zayd was out but inviting him none the less to enter, a look passed between the two cousins, which made each one conscious of a deep and lasting bond of love between them. In a moment the Prophet knew that Zaynab loved him and that he loved her and that she knew he loved her." This does seem to go a good bit beyond historical narration of the events, to be sure.

17. From the earliest records we possess, history records Christians pointing to this incident as evidence against Muhammad. In one of the first defenses of the faith against Islam, Abd al-Masih b. Ishaq al-Kindi, a Christian with some connection to the court of Caliph al-Ma'mun, around AD 820, wrote: "And what of that affair between him and Zaynab? I have no wish to dwell on it here. I have too much respect for the paper on which I write to mention it; were it not for a matter which he has himself noticed and which he asserts was told him from above." *The Early Christian-Muslim Dialogue: A Collection of Documents from the First Three Islamic Centuries (AD 632—900) Translations with Commentary*, ed. N. A. Newman (Hatfield, PA: Interdisciplinary Biblical Research Institute, 1993), 432.

18. *Sahih Al-Bukhari*, 6:311. The specific context was in reference to Surah 33:51, which gave Muhammad special privileges regarding his wives.

2

The Qur'an:
A Brief Introduction

The Qur'an is just over half the length of the New Testament[1] and about one-fifth as long as the Hebrew Scriptures (Old Testament).[2] It contains 114 surat,[3] roughly equivalent to the concept of a chapter, divided into *ayat*[4] of varying lengths, roughly equivalent to verses. Normally, the surat are named according to something mentioned in their text: for instance, Surah 2, *Al-Baqarah* ("The Cow"), Surah 9, *Al-Taubah* ("Repentance"), etc.[5] According to the traditional story, it was dictated to Muhammad by the angel Gabriel over the course of twenty-two years (610–632).[6]

The Qur'an's organization is neither chronological nor topical. In fact, its arrangement seems rather pedestrian: It is roughly ordered by the size of the surat. Surah 1, *Al-Fatihah*, is little more than the seven-*ayah* opening prayer (as well known to Muslims as the so-called Lord's Prayer is to Christians), but Surah 2 contains a whopping 286 *ayat,* and Surah 3, the next in line, 200.

This has created a stumbling block to many a Western reader making an initial attempt at understanding the Islamic holy book. If you started "at the beginning" and read on to the end, you would be jumping back and forth between periods of Muhammad's life, and in this way, obtaining a meaningful background and context is next to impossible. Not only were the surat written at different times (with different settings and historical referents), but Islamic sources also seem to indicate that even a single given *surah* may cobble together materials from widely divergent periods into one text.

The non-expert reader often is without help, within the text itself, in determining a subject's background or how one subject may relate to another. So over the centuries, an elaborate system of external commentary developed, known as *tafsir*, that is dependent upon Muhammad's collected sayings and actions, known as the *hadith*.[7] These collections have become the normative lens through which the Qur'an is interpreted.

For the reader who endeavors to read the Qur'an with maximized understanding, the following chart, based upon the work of many others,[8] provides what I can only call a broadly chronological order of the surat. That is, its order *generally* presents the Islamic holy book's content according to linear or historical progress. Combine that with some of the editions of the Qur'an that do provide some historical background and you have perhaps the best possibility for reading it in the fairest and most accurate way.[9]

96	68	73	74	1	111	81	87	92	89
93	94	103	100	108	102	107	109	105	113
114	112	53	80	97	91	85	95	106	101
75	104	77	50	90	86	54	38	7	72
36	25	35	19	20	56	26	27	28	17

10	11	12	15	6	37	31	34	39	40
41	42	43	44	45	46	51	88	18	16
71	14	21	23	32	52	67	69	70	78
79	82	84	30	29	83	2	3	33	60
4	99	57	47	13	55	76	65	98	59
24	22	63	58	49	66	64	61	62	48
5	8	9	110						

The chart is shaded, for comparison's sake, to indicate the two major periods of Muhammad's life: Meccan (610–622) and Medinan (622–632). The number of surat in the earlier period is much larger than in the later, but the actual amount of Qur'anic text is more balanced between them, as the largest surat (2, 3, 4, and 5 alone contain 782 total *ayat*) come in the later period.

The Qur'an often refers to being pure, clear, and Arabic. For example:

> By the Book [that makes things] clear, We have made it an Arabic Qur'an that you may understand. And, it is inscribed in the Mother of the Book, which We possess, sublime and wise. (43:2–4)

> These are the signs [or "the verses"] of the Manifest Book. We have sent it down as an Arabic Qur'an, that you may understand. (12:1–2)[10]

Some non-Muslim scholars have proposed the idea of an original in another language than Arabic, but this has not carried much weight with the majority of scholarship. Most Muslims believe the Arabic Qur'an reflects the "Mother of the Book," the heavenly copy, of which the earthly version is a perfectly accurate rendition. But it is also possible that the Qur'an is an extract, a portion of a larger heavenly book of Allah, and this is suggested by the wording of Surah 18:27:

> And recite [and teach] that which has been revealed unto you
> of the Book of your Lord. No one can change His words. You
> shall find no refuge beside Him.

Surely this sounds as if the recitation given to Muhammad is at
least a *part* of the "Book of your Lord." But is it *all*? Given that
the Qur'an affirms light and guidance in other Scriptures (specifically, the Torah [Law] and the Injil [Gospel]) that were "sent
down" by Allah (a reference to divine revelation), the question
then arises: "If no one can change Allah's words, then how is it
Muslims believe that is exactly what happened with the Torah
and the Injil?" We will examine this in chapter 8; it is central to
the discussion between Christians and Muslims.

Sunni Muslim orthodoxy insists that the Qur'an is uncreated.
This concept took time to develop, and at least one Caliph held
that it was created.[11] While there is a great deal of discussion of
this topic in the wide spectrum of Islamic theology, for our purposes, the predominant view, representing the majority of Muslims around the world, should engage our attention. In *Ulum
Al Qur'an: An Introduction to the Sciences of the Qur'an*,[12]
Sheikh Abu Ammar Yasir Qadhi addresses the conservative,
orthodox view.[13] A few quotes will help us to comprehend the
Islamic reverence for the Qur'an:

> One of the more appropriate definitions is as follows: The
> Qur'an is the Arabic speech (*kalaam*) of Allah, which he revealed
> to Muhammad in wording and meaning, and which has been
> preserved in the *mus-hafs*,[14] and has reached us by *mutawaatir*[15]
> transmissions, and is a challenge to mankind to produce some-
> thing similar to it.[16]

Regarding the Qur'an's repeated "challenge . . . to produce
something similar," see note 15 in chapter 8. For now, again, note
Arabic's centrality to the Muslim understanding: The Qur'an

itself exists in no other tongue. Even though the Islamic majority depends on translations, Muslims still would say the Qur'an itself is not translatable, at least in the religious or theological sense. While *Arabic* can be translated into any other language, the *Qur'an's* essence as Allah's very words is tied to the Arabic tongue. That Muslim public prayers also are done in Arabic (Muslims can pray privately to Allah in their own language) speaks to its centrality to Islamic faith and practice.

This definition also emphasizes another idea we will examine (in chapter 11), that being an unquestioned transmission of the text since its revelation to Muhammad. Qur'anic perfection is a major issue in the Christian/Muslim dialogue, hence we will spend a good deal of time on the subject.

When Sheikh Qadhi says the Qur'an is the very speech of Allah, does he mean it is always God speaking? Not necessarily, since others are quoted in it. He is saying none of it comes from any created being, Muhammad included. In conservative, orthodox Muslim thought, one cannot ask, "Does this *surah* represent a stage in Muhammad's growing and developing understanding of Allah and his call as a prophet?" Such questions are out of bounds, as they assume we can determine from the text something about his thinking or insight. In Islamic orthodoxy, *none* of Muhammad appears in the Qur'an. He is the passive human recipient of the angel's dictated words, nothing more.

In Qadhi's terms:

> This part of the definition affirms that the words of the Qur'an are from Allah, and not from Jibreel or even Muhammad, as some of the innovated sects of Islam, such as the *Ash'arees*, allege. According to some scholars, this part of the definition also excludes *hadeeth Qudsee*, since, according to these scholars, *hadeeth Qudsee*[17] is only inspired in meaning, while its wording is from the Prophet.[18]

The words of the Qur'an share the attribute of Allah in that they did not come into existence at a point in time. Surely, the Qur'an as a written document on earth in Arabic has a history and did not exist in that form, say, in the days of Jesus. But for Sunni Islamic orthodoxy, *the Qur'an itself is uncreated.*

> Another characteristic of the *kalaam* of Allah is that it is uncreated. . . . Sufyaan ibn 'Uyaynah said, "He has lied (who says that the Qur'an is created)!" Allah has stated, "To Him belongs the Creation and the Command," so the creation is the creation of Allah, and His Command is the Qur'an.[19]

> In other words, the very fact that a person seeks refuge in the *kalaam* of Allah proves that it is an uncreated Attribute of Allah, for it is not allowed to seek refuge in a created object.[20]

The arguments used to substantiate this viewpoint are many, and we note that not all Muslims in the earliest generations held to it. But it has become the predominant orthodox view, and in many nations, even to broach the subject is to bring question upon your orthodoxy.

Of course, it is argued that this belief is original and goes back to Muhammad himself. For example, Abdullah Ibn Abbas is said to have asserted, "This means that the Qur'an is not created."[21] And Qadhi notes,

> Imam Malik was asked concerning one who says that the Qur'an is created, what should be done to him? He replied, "He should be forced to repent, and if he refuses, then his head should be cut off!" Imam ash-Shaafi'ee stated, "Whoever states that the Qur'an is created is a disbeliever."[22]

> Imam at-Tahaawee, in his famous *Aqeedah at-Tahaaweeyah*, wrote, "They are certain that it is the actual *kalaam* of Allah, not created, unlike the speech of humans. Whoever hears it and

thinks it is the speech of a man is a disbeliever whom Allah has condemned and threatened with the Fire of Hell. . . ."[23]

The belief system that underlies these strong statements has resulted in a rigid orthodoxy in conservative Muslim circles. It does not allow for open debate on these matters, let alone inquiry into whether these formulations should be continued into the modern period. Such discussions take place most often in Western nations and in institutions of higher learning, but, because of that, they have little impact upon the "Muslim street."

Notes

1. The Arabic Qur'an is 56 percent of the length of the Greek New Testament (*Nestle-Aland 27th Edition* [*NA27*]).

2. The Arabic Qur'an contains 18 percent as many words as the Hebrew text (*Biblia Hebraica Stuttgartensia* [BHS]).

3. *Surat* is the plural of *surah*. Some early sources record disputes over the number of surat in the Qur'an, with some reciters having fewer, and others more, than the 114 included today.

4. *Ayat* is the plural of *ayah*.

5. One important exception is the short Surah 112, *Al-Ikhlas*, "The Sincerity" or "Purity," wherein the term does not appear and the title is instead a description of the *surah*'s creedal confession of monotheism (*tawhid*).

6. Again, by most accounts, the whole Qur'an was revealed in one night (*Laylat al-Qadr*, the Night of Power, at the end of Ramadan) but was delivered to Muhammad over time.

7. Technically, the *hadith* also include the sayings and actions of his Companions.

8. For an excellent summary of the various suggestions made by Islamic scholars through the centuries regarding Qur'anic chronological order, see N. A. Newman, *Muhammad, the Qur'an & Islam* (Hatfield, PA: Interdisciplinary Biblical Research Institute, 1996), 349–356.

9. There is disagreement on certain particulars, and again, some surat may contain material from earlier or later periods.

10. See also 26:195; 41:3; 39:28; 19:97; 20:113; 16:103; 46:12; 42:7.

11. There is strong evidence that Abu Jafar Abdullah al-Mamun ibn Harun (813–833) held the Qur'an to be created, in line with the *Mutazilite* views shared by others known as the Jahmites and even some Shiites. One of the earliest Christian responses to Islam, the work of the aforementioned al-Kindi, was most probably written during al-Mamun's Caliphate, where more freedom would have been granted to differing views.

12. The English spellings in many Islamic books differ in their convention. For example, in earlier editions, the one cited here used *Qur'aan*. In the citations derived from it I will use standard spellings (Qur'an, etc.).

13. Yasir Qadhi is generally identified with the *Salafi* movement, a very conservative Sunni branch. Also often identified as *Wahhabism*, its adherents focus on the *salaf* (first generations of Muslims) as their guide and example since, as the Qur'an states, they were the "best" of mankind (3:110). Salafi Islam is at the heart of today's worldwide Muslim resurgence.

14. i.e., manuscripts

15. Meaning "universally accepted" or "unchallengeable."

16. Yasir Qadhi, *Introduction*, 25.

17. *Hadith Qudsi* are special hadith that contain the words of Allah. Though considered to have special authority above that of normal hadith sayings, since they are outside the Qur'an, they are not considered to have equal authority with it, nor are they considered eternal.

18. Qadhi, *Introduction,* 28.

19. Ibid., 34.

20. Ibid., 35.

21. Qadhi, *Introduction,* 36. Abbas was commenting on Surah 39:28.

22. Ibid.

23. Ibid., 37.

3

Allah: *Tawhid, Shirk,* the *Mithaq* and the *Fitra*

Ask any sincere follower what defines Islam, and they will answer quickly. *Tawhid*, the glorious monotheistic truth, the heart of Islamic faith, is to the Muslim what the Trinity is to the Christian: the touchstone, the nonnegotiable, the definitional. *Tawhid* defines Islamic worship and proclamation. You must embrace it to enter into the faith, for Islam's great confession, the *Shahada*, begins with the words "I profess that there is only one God worthy of worship." The faithful Muslim father whispers those words in the ear of his infant son at birth. These often are the Muslim's last words on earth. Without *tawhid*, you have no Islam.

The Jewish believer of old likewise repeated daily a confession of faith that was central to his experience, the *Shema*: "Hear, O Israel, Yahweh is our God, Yahweh is one!" (Deuteronomy 6:4). Jewish law commanded each father to discuss its meaning and application with the family as they walked, worked, and ate together. The confession of monotheism marked off the people of God from the nations around them and frequently was a source of great conflict, for those nations took offense to Jewish exclusivism.

The Christian Scriptures likewise are filled with statements of absolute monotheism, both in the Hebrew Old Testament and in the Greek New Testament. Christianity does not abandon or deny the former's testimony but instead shows it fulfilled in the incarnation of Jesus, the Son of God, and in the outpouring of God's Holy Spirit. The unchanging truth of monotheism now is accompanied with the realization that the one God has manifested himself to His creation in an unparalleled way: "There is one God, and one mediator also between God and men, the man Christ Jesus" (1 Timothy 2:5). Likewise, the New Testament's Trinitarian context shows forth in the Christian confession, "One Lord, one faith, one baptism, one God and Father of all who is over all and through all and in all" (Ephesians 4:5–6). And the *Shema* appears in fuller form in light of the incarnation: "There is no God but one . . . for us there is but one God, the Father, from whom are all things and we *exist* for Him; and one Lord, Jesus Christ, by whom are all things, and we *exist* through Him" (1 Corinthians 8:4, 6).

The term *the great monotheistic religions,* then, reflects the reality that Judaism, Christianity, and Islam all proclaim there is only one true God, the maker of heaven and earth. As we will see, many Muslims reject the Christian claim due to our belief in the Trinity, and one of the major questions we will examine is whether they derive this argument from the Qur'an itself. But this brings us to a distinction that is vitally important if we are to comprehend accurately the differences between these religions.

Confusing the categories used to describe these beliefs has caused no end of bewilderment for many trying to sort out the issues. *Trinitarianism is not the opposite of monotheism,* of which there are various forms. Monotheism can be unitarian (belief that the being of God is shared or possessed by only one center of consciousness, or "person"), or binitarian, or Trinitarian, etc.[1]

When we speak of *tawhid*, we need to realize we are not only talking about monotheism, but specifically about unitarian monotheism. While a Muslim may not speak in these categories, there seems little question that, in its modern representations at least, the monotheism represented by *tawhid* is distinctly unitarian. As we will see in chapter 4, whether or not the Qur'an's author understood Christian Trinitarianism is a major and crucial question.

Tawhid and Purity of Worship

One of the primary values of *tawhid* in Islamic thought is the purity it brings to worship. By acknowledging Allah, the one true God, a human being puts himself in the position to worship rightly and so acknowledges himself to be Allah's creation. It might even be said that almost any deviation from true worship is due to an improper, faulty understanding of *tawhid*.

In fact, for most Muslims, *tawhid is an important aspect of the concept of salvation*. Allamah Al-Sadi comments,

> There is nothing that produces such good results nor holds such a variety of virtues like *tawhid*, for *tawhid* with its virtues is the best produce in the world and the Hereafter. . . . And among its virtues is that it is the greatest means of removing the sorrows of this world and the Hereafter, and warding off punishment in both worlds. It is because of its virtues that one is forbidden from eternity in the Fire—provided that his heart contains a mustard seed's equivalent amount of it—and if it is complete in his heart, then it will prevent him from ever entering the

Fire at all. . . . Another of its virtues is that it is the exclusive reason for being granted Allah's pleasure and rewards, and the luckiest of people—who are granted Muhammad's intercession—are those who said *La ilaha illa Allah*[2] with sincerity in their hearts. . . . Among its most important virtues is that all deeds and sayings, both inner and outer, are dependent upon *tawhid* for their acceptability, their completeness, and for the rewards given for them. So all of this is empowered only with the presence of *tawhid* and sincerity for Allah, then these matters can be perfect and complete.[3]

The entire purpose for human creation is encapsulated in Surah 51:56: "I created the jinn and humankind only that they might worship Me." All of life, then, is summed up under the all-important concept of *tawhid*. One who knows and worships Allah correctly is functioning as he or she has been designed. By definition, it follows that in historic Islamic orthodoxy, any and all worship not defined by *tawhid* is in opposition to Allah's will.

The *Shahada*

How does one become a Muslim? Basically, by the profession of faith, in Arabic, in the presence of others. The majority of the human family does not speak Arabic, so one repeats the words as recited with "true intent" and faith.[4] "The words" are known as the *Shahada*, the bearing of witness, and they are (in English), "There is only one God worthy of worship, and Muhammad is His messenger." In Arabic, *la ilaha illa l-Lah, wa-Muhammadun rasulu l-Lah*.

There is some discussion of exactly how to translate the first portion, a literal rendering being "there is no god but Allah," and some Shiites adding a statement relating to Ali as God's friend or vice-regent.[5] But the key element of the *Kalima* (another term used for the *Shahada* as a whole) is found in its assertion of Allah's uniqueness, His oneness, that is, *tawhid.*

According to the Qur'an, Allah has sent many prophets in the past. What has united all of them? They all were sent with the same message:

> We sent no messenger before you, but that We revealed to him, that "there is no god but I, so worship Me!" (Surah 21:25)

So the message of (unitarian) monotheism is what binds together all the messengers God has sent over human history. This likewise explains why Muslims believe Abraham, and David, and Jesus, and His apostles, all were Muslims:[6] They worshiped the same God and proclaimed the same message. And this is why each time Jesus speaks in the Qur'an, His message primarily is that of monotheism, *tawhid.*[7]

Orthodox Islamic theology divides the categories of *tawhid* into three: *tawhid ar-rububiyah* (*tawhid* of lordship), *tawhid al-uluhiya* (*tawhid* of worship), and *tawhid al-Asma was-Sifaat* (*tawhid* of Allah's names and attributes). These become important especially in the discussion below of the violation of *tawhid,* the grave sin of idolatry.

One great irony regarding *tawhid* is that the word itself, in that form, does not appear in the Qur'an. The root, *wahad,* appears numerous times, but the very form that has become enshrined in Islamic theology is not in the Arabic text. This is relevant only in light of the frequent apologetic assertion that since *Trinity* does not appear in the Bible, Christians should not believe in it. Of course, the question that should concern fair-minded folks is this: As to the nature of God, does the Qur'an lead one to conclude that *tawhid* is an accurate summation of its teachings, and does the Bible lead one to conclude that the Trinity is an accurate summation of its teachings? Whether or not the specific term appears in the text is secondary to whether the concept it represents is found therein.

There is no question the Qur'an teaches there is one God (*wahid*). Twenty-two times this term teaches it in various contexts.[8] For example:

> [O Prophet], say [to them]: "I am only a human being like you. It is revealed to me that your God is only One God, so be upright before Him and ask Him to forgive you. And woe to those who associate others with Him" (41:6).

However, the strongest, most consistent affirmations of unitarian monotheism come not in positive affirmations, but in the far more common apologetic contexts that mark the entire life and teaching of Muhammad. That is, its affirmation often is bound up in its denunciation of all forms of polytheism. The regular formula is "Do not say this about Allah, for there is only one Allah, worship Him." The Qur'an will note some error people ascribe to God (a departure from *tawhid*) and then correct it with an assertion of monotheism or a related concept.

In the majority of instances, the clearest affirmations of monotheism and *tawhid* come in the context of the Qur'an's denouncing views held by the People of the Book (specifically, Christians). Since the Qur'an comes into history well after Christianity's central affirmations were widely known, it must deal with those assertions as it seeks to call Christians to "speak only about Allah the truth." We will look at these texts in chapter 4, but we introduce a few of them here to demonstrate how closely related the denial of Christian teaching is to the assertion of *tawhid* and to the related subject of Islam's one unforgivable sin, idolatry (known as *shirk*).

> Those who disbelieve and obstruct [others] from the path of Allah, they have surely strayed far away. Those who disbelieve,

and do wrong, Allah will never forgive them, neither will He guide them to a road. Except the road to Hell, to abide therein perpetually. And that is easy for Allah. O mankind! The Messenger has come to you with the truth from your Lord. Therefore believe; [it is] better for you. But if you disbelieve, still, surely to Allah belongs whatsoever is in the heavens and the earth. Allah is Knowing, Wise. O People of the Book! Commit no excess in your religion, nor say anything but the truth about Allah. The Messiah, Jesus son of Mary, was only a Messenger of Allah, and His word which He conveyed to Mary, and a spirit from Him. So believe in Allah and His Messengers, and say not "three." Cease, [it is] better for you! Allah is only One God. Far is it removed from His transcendence that He should have a son, when His is all that the heavens and all that the earth contain. And Allah is sufficient as [their] Custodian. (Surah 4:167–171)

Note the coordination of denouncing the use of the term *three* with the immediate assertion "Allah is only One God." Whatever the People of the Book are claiming about *three,* the Qur'an's response is to say it is in "excess," a violation of the command to speak only truthfully about Allah.

Likewise, in *Surah al-Maidah*:

They have disbelieved who say: "Allah is the Messiah, the son of Mary." The Messiah (himself) said: "O Children of Israel, worship Allah, my Lord and your Lord. Whoever ascribes partners to Allah, for him Allah has forbidden Paradise. His abode is the Fire. For the unjust there will be no helpers." They have disbelieved who say: "Allah is the third of three," when there is no god save One God. If they cease not what they say, a painful torment will fall upon those of them who disbelieve. (5:72–73)

This similar theme specifically says that to assert deity of the Messiah[9] is an act of unbelief as well as of idolatry (*shirk*). And upon seeking to represent Christian belief in the words "Allah is the third of three," the Qur'an immediately asserts (unitarian) monotheism: "There is no god save One God."

One last text will suffice to establish this pattern:

> Or have they taken other gods besides Him? Say: "Bring your proofs! This is the Reminder of those who are with me and [this is] the Reminder of those before me." But most of them do not know the truth, and they turn away. We sent no messenger before you, but that We revealed to him, that "there is no god but I, so worship Me!" They say: "The All-Merciful has taken a son!" Transcendent is Allah! No, but only honored servants. (21:24–26)

The contrast is between the message that unites all the prophets (there is one God) and the claim of some form of polytheism ("The All-Merciful has taken a son!"). Later we will discuss whether we can determine if the Qur'an is addressing Christianity, pagan religions, or a mixture when it speaks of Allah taking a son. But again its corrective is immediate: "Transcendent is Allah!"

The Unforgivable Sin of *Shirk*

In large portions of conservative thought, the discussion often focuses more on violation of *tawhid* than on its positive aspects. And that brings us to *shirk*, the most feared of all sins. In secular Arabic, the root *shirk* simply means "association, to join together," as in a secular corporation. But in religious usage, *shirk* takes on a whole different meaning as the worst possible negation of *tawhid,* associating anyone, or anything, with Allah. Discussion of the many forms *shirk* can take and its grave dangers to the life of the Muslim are found frequently in the writings and preaching of Islamic scholars and leaders.

The Qur'an is clear: *Shirk* is not forgivable.

> Surely, Allah will not forgive those who assign partners to Him. He forgives all but that to whom He pleases. Whosoever ascribes partners to Allah is guilty of a monstrous sin. (4:48)

A person can have committed *shirk* in their lifetime and still find forgiveness (especially by saying the *Shahada* and becoming a Muslim). The concept is that if one dies in this state (as a *mushrik*, an idolator, one who engages in and does not repent of *shirk*), there is no forgiveness. Allah is free to forgive any other sin, and the *hadith* literature says he can forgive even mass murder, but he will not forgive in the next life anyone who dies as a *mushrik*. This is clear:

> "O my son! Associate [nothing] with Allah, for association is a formidable injustice!" (31:13).

> Praise be to Allah, Who has created the heavens and the earth, and has appointed darkness and light. Yet those who disbelieve ascribe rivals to their Lord. (6:1)

But the *hadith* literature goes into much more detail on the subject, giving much insight into how seriously *shirk* is to be taken by believing Muslims. It says believers are not to pray for their relatives who die as *mushrikim*. Even Muhammad is precluded from praying for his mother, who died in that state.[10]
Sheikh Yasir Qadhi defines *shirk* in this way:

> Thus, *shirk* involves believing in a partner along with Allah. Such a "partner" could be a partner in lordship (*rububiyyah*), or in worship (*uluhiyyah*), or in attributes (*asma wa l-sifat*). In other words, the essence of *shirk* involves giving Allah's rights to other than He. Therefore, to claim that a certain object or deity has the power to bless one with one's needs is *shirk*. Likewise, to

prostrate or make *du'a* to other than Allah is also *shirk*. And the claim that any created object knows everything, or can hear any plea directed to it, is *shirk*. Whenever any specific right of Allah's is given to any other object, whether that object be a living being or an inanimate object, real or imagined, *shirk* has occurred.[11]

There are many important and truthful connections between the Christian understanding of idolatry's seriousness and destructiveness and the Islamic condemnation of *shirk*. The similarities must not be ignored or minimized, and they can provide fruitful basis for conversation and understanding. At the same time, the Islamic *application* of the concept—clearly derived from a fair reading of the above cited texts relating to the Christian proclamation of Christ's deity—is one of the three[12] pillars of denial that define the Christianity-vs.-Islam divide. While some Western adherents do not, many Muslims believe that the doctrine of the Trinity and, in particular, the worship of Jesus is an (unforgivable) act of *shirk*. This has led many of them to conclude that Christians, as a group, are bound for hell as *mushrikim*. This view, which is based upon a consistent reading of the Qur'an as well as many passages in the *ahadith*, is the most prevalent in the Islamic world.

The *Mithaq* and the *Fitra*

Closely related to the concepts of *tawhid* and *shirk* is that of the *mithaq* and the *fitra*, from such texts as Surah 7:172–173:

> And [remember] when your Lord brought forth from the Children of Adam, from their loins, their seed, and made them testify of themselves, [He asked]: "Am I not your Lord?" They said: "Yes, we testify!" Lest you should say on the Day of Resurrection: "Of this we were unaware." Or [lest you] say: "[It is] Only

that our fathers ascribed partners to Allah of old, and we were their descendants after them. Will you destroy us on account of that which those who follow falsehood did?"

This is an example of the Qur'an making reference to a story or topic but not (in the immediate context or, really, anywhere else) expanding fully on it. The *hadith* literature gives a fuller understanding. Forgoing a number of longer quotations for the sake of brevity, we will look at one brief commentary:

> Narrated Abdullah ibn Abbas: Allah's Apostle (peace be upon him) said: Allah made covenant (with the whole of mankind) while creating it from Adam's back in Na'man i.e. Arafah and emitting from his loins all his offspring that He created and scattering them before Him like ants. He then spoke to them in their presence and said: "Am I not your Lord?" They answered: "Yes, we do bear witness thereto (of this We remind you) lest you say on the Day of Resurrection: Verily, we were unaware of this. Or lest you say: Verily, these were our forefathers in times gone by, who began to ascribe divinity to other things besides Allah and we were but their late offspring. Wilt Thou then destroy us for doings of those inventors of falsehood?" (7:172–173). Transmitted by Ahmad.[13]

The idea being conveyed is that of the *mithaq*, the covenant between Allah and all the descendants of Adam. Allah establishes his *rububiyyah* (lordship) over them by asking, "Am I not your Lord?" By answering in the affirmative, all of mankind enters into the covenant. This places them in a position of responsibility, for no one is then able to claim ignorance or to engage in *shirk* without blame—they have, in the *mithaq*, confessed the reality of Allah's creatorship and worthiness of sole worship.

The *fitra*, which then flows from this, is the natural, innate inclination and knowledge of Allah's existence and of monotheism. Hence, the central appeal of Islamic *dawa*[14] is to this preexisting awareness. While many Muslims still make appeal to philosophy and related fields of knowledge, more conservative Muslims will eschew such pleas in light of the already existing knowledge the *fitra* provides. Note the wording of this *hadith*:

> Abu Huraira reported Allah's Messenger (may peace be upon him) as saying: No babe is born but upon Fitra. It is his parents who make him a Jew or a Christian or a Polytheist. A person said: Allah's Messenger, what is your opinion if they were to die before that (before reaching the age of adolescence when they can distinguish between right and wrong)? He said: It is Allah alone Who knows what they would be doing.[15]

Christians can readily see a close parallel to the biblical doctrine, found especially in Paul's epistle to the Romans. The Bible teaches that humans are made in the *imago Dei* (a concept that by its nature is precluded in Islam, at least in its fullest sense). God's image is the source of our knowledge of His existence; people, in unrighteousness, then suppress this (see Romans 1:18–21). But one of the striking differences is highlighted just here, for in the Christian view there is strong moral responsibility for active suppression of the knowledge God has provided of His existence both in our own created nature and in the created world around us. In most cases this emphasis is lacking in the Islamic understanding.

Do Muslims and Christians Worship the Same God?

It is probably the most oft-asked question in the public discourse. While entire books have been written on the subject, we will offer a brief but hopefully clear response.

The Qur'an raises this question directly in Surah 29:46:

O Muslims! Do not argue with the People of the Book except in the best of ways, save with such of them who are unjust; and say: "We believe in that which has been sent down to us and that which has been [sent][16] down to you; our God and your God is One, and to Him we surrender."

Aside from the exhortation to argue with the *Ahl al-Kitab* (People of the Book, Jews and Christians) only "in the best of ways," the text makes the bold claim that "our God and your God is One, and to Him we surrender." The last phrase could be rendered "and we are Muslims to Him," the concept of submission being central to the definition of "Muslim."

So it seems beyond question that the Qur'an is saying People of the Book and Muslims do worship the same God. But what of the texts cited above prohibiting the saying of *three* and identifying specifically Christian worship as an act of *kufir* (unbelief)? How can we be worshiping the same God if our worship condemns us? Is the Qur'an contradicting itself?

The answer is to be found in first recognizing its positive claim. The assertion is that since Abraham, the Prophets, and even Jesus actually were Muslims who all confessed "there is no god worthy of worship but Allah," then it follows that we are all talking about the same God (the God of Noah, Abraham, David, and Jesus). However, this must be joined with the negative assertion that Christians in particular have engaged in *excess*, going beyond the bounds in our worship and in our claims about Christ's exalted nature. The Qur'an is saying that though we are all talking about the same God, only the Muslims, enlightened by His final revelation, are worshiping that one God with purity (*tawhid*). The Jews, by rejecting Muhammad, and the Christians, by exalting and worshiping Jesus, have left the straight path of true worship.

So what is the answer to our question? Islam claims that the same God who sent Moses also sent Jesus and also sent Muhammad. On this very general level, the Qur'an's clear answer to "Are Christians, Muslims, and Jews talking about the same God?" is yes, "our God and your God is One."

But this is far too simplistic, and most well-read Muslims recognize it. For Christians, the deity of Jesus, the eternal relationship of the Father and the Son, and the personality and deity of the Spirit are not side issues that can be relegated to the realm of "excesses." These *define* the object of our worship; they *define* our relationship to God. In light of this, while the referent of *God* may be similar, it cannot be seriously maintained that Muslims and Christians worship the same God. The believing and practicing Muslim would never say Allah could possibly be triune, nor would the believing and practicing Christian deny that God has specially, amazingly, and finally revealed Himself in Jesus Christ.

We can agree with both statements in the Qur'an, acknowledging that Muslims make reference to the one God of Abraham, but at the same time insisting that in the incarnation and in the Spirit's coming, the one God of Abraham has revealed Himself in a way that cannot be rolled back. To deny the witness of the incarnation and the resurrection is to deny the entirety of the Christian faith. For this reason we maintain, together with the thoughtful Muslim, that if worship is an act of truth, then Muslims and Christians are not worshiping the same object. We do not worship the same God.

Notes

1. In the same way, a religion can be henotheistic (belief in one main deity without denying the existence of lesser deities that may or may not be known or worshiped in a relative sense) or polytheistic (belief in multiple or many gods). One could well argue that atheism is religious as well, for in many forms (types of

naturalistic materialism, for example) it promotes the natural order as an ultimate reality or authority.

2. That is, many believe that those who say the *Shahada,* the confession of faith in Allah and in Muhammad, will be the objects of Muhammad's special intercession and hence saved from the Fire. Whether they are in the Fire and are brought out, or are kept from entering into it, is a matter of dispute.

3. Allamah Abd Al-Rahman Al-Sadi, *An Explanation of Muhammad Ibn Abd Al-Wahhab's Kitab al-Tawhid,* trans. Abu Khaliyl (Birmingham, UK: Al-Hidaayah, 2003), 34.

4. Traditionally, there are seven conditions for the *Shahada:* knowledge of the confession's meaning, certainty of its truth, sincerity (as opposed to *shirk*), truthfulness, love, submission, and full acceptance. Various schools of thought emphasize certain aspects in different ways.

5. In light of the emphasis on Allah's uniqueness and on absolute, unquestioned (i.e., unitarian) monotheism, that the *Shahada* in its current form includes the affirmation of Muhammad as the messenger of Allah. The conjunctive *"waw"* would seem to add an inappropriate statement to the pure confession of monotheism. In the very popular *Ash-Shifa* of Qadi Iyad Ibn Musa al-Yahsubi (*Muhammad: Messenger of Allah*), we read,

> The fact that mention of the Prophet is directly connected to mention of Allah also shows that obedience to the Prophet is connected to obedience to Allah and his name to Allah's name. Allah says, "Obey Allah and His Messenger" (2:32) and "Believe in Allah and His Messenger." (4:136) Allah joins them together using the conjunction *wa* which is the conjunction of partnership. It is not permitted to use this conjunction in connection with Allah in the case of anyone except the Prophet. (8)

The exaltation of Muhammad in many strands of Islamic thought (together with the veneration of, kissing of, and bowing toward the *Al-Hajaru l-Aswad,* the Kaaba's Black Stone) seem out of harmony with the oft-repeated emphasis upon *tawhid.*

6. The belief "There is only one God worthy of worship" binds together the prophets, but the second half of the confession would change depending on time and location. Thus, the confession of monotheism, along with the divine authority of Moses, would have been the proper confession for the early Jews, for instance. But since, according to Islamic orthodoxy, Muhammad is the final prophet, sent to the entirety of the world, the limitations on the earlier forms of the confession are no longer relevant, and the current *Shahada* is for all humankind.

7. We will look closely at Jesus in the Qur'an in chapter 5.

8. For relevant uses of *wahid,* see Surat 2:133, 163; 4:102, 171; 5:73; 6:19; 9:31; 12:39; 13:16; 14:48, 52; 16:22, 51; 18:110; 21:108; 22:34; 29:46; 37:4; 38:5, 65; 39:4; 40:16; 41:6.

9. As we will note in chapter 4, the real question here is the accuracy of the Qur'an's understanding of the preexisting Christian belief structure it clearly is seeking to refute. Christians would rarely say, "God is the Messiah." They would say "the Messiah was divine," which is just a part of the truth of what the Bible says about Jesus.

10. This is based on the early interpretation (e.g., see *Tafsir Ibn Kathir,* 4:524–525) that connects Surah 9:113 with Muhammad's asking Allah, while sitting at his

mother's grave, "for permission to invoke Him for forgiveness for her, but He did not give me permission." Early sources also connect this text with Muhammad's seeking forgiveness for his uncle, Abu Talib; however, since they also indicate he was granted a form of intercession for Abu Talib, it seems better to connect this to his seeking forgiveness for his mother and being refused.

11. Sheikh Abu Ammaar Yasir Qadhi, *An Explanation of Muhammad ibn Abd al-Wahhab's Kashf al-Shubahat: A Critical Study of Shirk* (Birmingham, UK: Al-Hidaayah, 2003), 15.

12. The other two pillars are the Islamic denial of the crucifixion (see chapter 6) and the accusation of wholesale corruption of the biblical text (both Old and New Testaments—see chapter 8). That is, *tahrif al-nass*, corruption of the actual text itself, over against *tahrif al-mana*, corruption of the text's meaning or interpretation.

13. *Al-Tirmidhi Hadith*, 121.

14. Islam joins evangelism and apologetics into one concept: *dawa*, the call to Islam and to submit to Allah.

15. *Sahih Muslim*, Book 33, Number 6426.

16. I have inserted the verb because it seems the English translation has a typographical error. The Arabic text contains the same verb, twice, "what has been sent down to us and sent down to you." The text clearly parallels the divine nature of what has been sent down to the People of the Book as well as what has been sent down to Muhammad (the Qur'an).

4

"Say Not Three":
The Qur'an and the Trinity

The word *Trinity* does not appear in the Qur'an, despite its appearance in some of the most popular English renderings. This is not to say the Qur'an does not attempt to address the Trinity—it seems clear that it does. But the question that demands the attention of Christians *and* Muslims is this: Does the Qur'an's author show knowledge of the Trinity to where the criticisms offered are accurate and compelling?

The reason for the question is self-evident: If the Qur'an is the very words of Allah without admixture of man's insights or thoughts, then it would follow inevitably that its representations will be perfectly accurate and its arguments compelling. If one should say that the Trinity is difficult to understand and that the author, living in Mecca, might struggle reasonably to represent it accurately, we point out that according to Islamic orthodoxy, such an observation is irrelevant to the Qur'an. Even if Muhammad misunderstood the Trinity, that would not impact the Qur'an, a divine revelation.

Everyone affected would affirm that by the early decades of the seventh century, God Himself would have a perfect knowledge of what the doctrine of the Trinity actually says. And if that doctrine does not accurately represent His own self-revelation, He would be in the perfect position to refute its falsehoods with devastating precision. But is this what we find in the Qur'an?

As we noted, the exact term *Trinity* does not appear in the Qur'an, but the word *three* does, in the specific context of dealing with the "People of the Book," which here refers specifically to the Christian people. Only a few references directly speak of this concept of *three,* and we will look carefully at them, for they are vitally important to the Christian/Muslim dialogue. We examine the specific witness of the Qur'an regarding Jesus (*Isa ibn Mariam*) in chapter 5. The primary texts relevant to this study come from *Surahs An-Nisa* (4) and *Al-Maidah* (5).

I cannot overemphasize for the Christian reader their importance. We now truly enter into the heart of our study, as with the background established we are ready to earnestly consider the Qur'an's teaching on the central issues that separate us from our Muslim friends and neighbors: the doctrine of God (*tawhid* vs. Trinity), the person of Jesus (a prophet or the Incarnate Son of God), and His crucifixion, resurrection, and all the resultant issues of the gospel and salvation.

We will invest great effort to examine the text fairly and honestly. If we do so more closely than might seem necessary, as Christians we must. Just as we ask the Muslim to handle the Bible fairly and listen to it in its own context, so as lovers of truth and consistency we extend the same courtesy.

Surah 4:166–172: "Say Not Three!"

Surah An-Nisa contains a vitally important section comprising *ayat* 166–172. Though its final portion is the most directly relevant, it is important that we see the discernible flow of thought through this section. The possibility of following a context is unusual for major parts of the Qur'an, so when we find such a continuous thought, we must note it.

Can we know the text's background? As with so much of the Qur'an, it is difficult to say. But one recorded encounter at least is directly relevant to Muhammad's final understanding of his message's relationship to that of the Christian faith: his discussion with the deputation of Christians from Najran. In fact, one early Islamic source connects this very text to that event.

We cannot really know what happened in the discussion, for we only have a much later Islamic version of the event. But the later retelling of the meeting can provide some understanding of how Muslims then "heard" what Christians were saying.

Muslims today insist this is irrelevant for interpreting the Qur'an, since the understanding of Muhammad or of his earliest followers is not germane to divine revelation. But the critical question we face in this section of our study is this: Does the Qur'an accurately represent Christian belief in these texts where it condemns that belief, identifies it as excess and untruth, and teaches that those who refuse to abandon it will enter into hellfire? The Qur'an came into view long after Christian beliefs were clearly defined, so here we have as important a test as one could have for its purported divine nature. If it is what it claims, it certainly can withstand such critical scrutiny.

One early source, the *Tanwīr al-Miqbās min Tafsīr Ibn 'Abbās*, directly connects the encounter with the Najran Christians with the text of Surah 4:

Allah then revealed about the Nestorian Christians of Najran who claimed that Jesus was the son of Allah and that Jesus and the Lord are partners, saying: (O People of the Scripture! Do not exaggerate) do not be extreme (in your religion) for this is not the right course (nor utter aught concerning Allah save the Truth. The Messiah, Jesus son of Mary, was only a messenger of Allah, and His word which He conveyed unto Mary) and through His word he became a created being, (and a spirit from Him) and through His command, Jesus became a son without a father. (So believe in Allah and His messengers) all the messengers including Jesus, (and say not "Three") a son, father and wife. (Cease!) from making such a claim and repent ((it is) better for you!) than such a claim. (Allah is only One God) without a son or partner. (Far is it removed from His Transcendent Majesty that he should have a son. His is all that is in the heavens and all that is in the earth) are His servants. (And Allah is sufficient as Defender) as Lord of all created beings and He is witness of what He says about Jesus.[1]

This early commentary clearly conveys the early Islamic understanding that when the Qur'an says "say not three," the three in mind has to do (1) with a plurality of gods (i.e., polytheism), for the immediate assertion is made that "Allah is only One God," and (2) the "three" is defined as "son, father, and wife." The nature of "sonship" here—one of father + mother = son—is a frightfully erroneous grasp of the Christian view, both today as well as then.[2]

But is this the view of the Qur'an? Christians do not feel themselves bound to every comment made by early Christian writers who might have had a less-than-full knowledge of the Christian Scriptures. Is this insufficient comprehension merely a fluke of history, or does it represent the Qur'anic understanding? That is what we must focus upon.

166. But Allah [Himself] bears witness concerning that which He has sent down to you; with His knowledge has He sent it down; and the angels also testify. And Allah is sufficient witness.

167. Those who disbelieve and obstruct [others] from the path of Allah, they have surely strayed far away.

168. Those who disbelieve, and do wrong, Allah will never forgive them, neither will He guide them to a road.

169. Except the road to Hell, to abide therein perpetually. And that is easy for Allah.

Like so many others, this section begins with the assertion of the divine nature and origin of the Qur'an. Allah is the one who testifies that what has been sent down to Muhammad is divine, and "Allah is sufficient witness." So clear and compelling is this testimony, we are told, that to reject it is to engage in disbelief. And it is one thing to disbelieve, but to obstruct others from Allah's path is even more grievous. Any such ones will not receive divine guidance except to the path of hell itself.

170. O mankind! The Messenger has come to you with the truth from your Lord. Therefore believe; [it is] better for you. But if you disbelieve, still, surely to Allah belongs whatsoever is in the heavens and the earth. Allah is Knowing, Wise.

The call goes out to all people, including (as we will see) Jews and Christians, to follow Muhammad, the deliverer of "truth from your Lord." Even the disbelief expressed by those who opposed Muhammad is not relevant, for that does not change Allah's ownership (lordship) over all things. This strong assertion of *tawhid ar-rububiyah* forms the foundation of the next exhortation.

171. O People of the Book! Commit no excess in your religion,[3] nor say anything but the truth about Allah. The Messiah, Jesus son of Mary, was only a Messenger of Allah, and His word which He conveyed to Mary, and a spirit from Him. So believe in Allah and His Messengers, and say not "three." Cease, [it is] better for you! Allah is only One God. Far is it removed from

His transcendence that He should have a son, when His is all that the heavens and all that the earth contain. And Allah is sufficient as [their] Custodian.[4]

172. The Messiah will never be too proud to be a slave to Allah, nor will the nearest angels. Those who are too proud to worship Him and are arrogant, all such will He assemble to Him.

Here the Qur'an turns its attention directly to the *Ahl al-Kitab*. In this case we do not have to look hard to realize that the group in focus is the Christian (not the Jewish) community. It immediately identifies Jesus as "Messiah," so plainly the Jews are not in view. The Christians ostensibly are those who were being summoned to Islam through the preaching of Muhammad.

The first command is twofold. Positively, it is to speak only the truth about Allah, and on this, we can all agree to be sure. The negative aspect is, "Commit no excess in your religion." The Arabic root, *taghlu*, refers to exceeding the proper limit, to be excessive, exorbitant. Christians here stand accused of going beyond the bounds of truthfulness in their claims about God. It is not a general accusation—the specific matter follows immediately.

"The Messiah, Jesus son of Mary, was only a Messenger of Allah, and His word which He conveyed to Mary, and a spirit from Him." The accusation is of "excess" and untruthfulness in our view of Jesus. The Qur'an claims he is *only*[5] a messenger of Allah. The implication is that the text seeks to limit the nature of Jesus to avoid the error embraced by Christians.

But the Qur'an does not stop there, and its phraseology here is used of no one else: "and His word which He conveyed to Mary, and a spirit from Him." His word? A spirit from Allah? Many have noted this text as indication that the Qur'an recognizes Jesus cannot be limited to "mere messenger" and acknowledges something much more about Jesus than modern Islamic theology admits. Christian missionaries have used it to point to John 1:1 (Jesus, the "Word") and other texts relating to his supernatural birth. For this very reason, Islamic orthodoxy insists this phrase refers to Allah's command, "Be," which brought Jesus into existence (Islam affirms the virgin birth).

As famed Qur'anic commentator Ibn Kathir put it,

> 'Isa is only one of Allah's servants and one of His creatures. Allah said to him, "Be," and he was, and He sent him as a Messenger. 'Isa was a word from Allah that He bestowed on Maryam, meaning He created him with the word "Be" that He sent with Jibril to Maryam. Jibril blew the life of 'Isa into Maryam by Allah's leave, and 'Isa came to existence as a result. This incident was in place of the normal conception between man and woman that results in children. This is why 'Isa was a word and a Ruh (spirit) created by Allah, as he had no father to conceive him. Rather, he came to existence through the word that Allah uttered, "Be," and he was, through the life that Allah sent with Jibril.[6]

Though we would like to know much more about what the Qur'an means by this phrase, the text itself nowhere expands upon the concept.

Whatever the positive teaching, the negative warning that follows is fairly clear: "So believe in Allah and His Messengers, and say not 'three.'" To believe in Allah and His Messengers (Muhammad in particular) requires one *not* to say "three."[7]

Now, first we must ask whether this makes direct reference to the Trinity. Some translations even render *three* as "Trinity," as in Yusuf Ali's popular translation, "Say not Trinity," and in Muhammad Asad's, "and do not say, '[God is] a trinity.'" But this is not the specific term for the Trinity, though it shares the same root as the ordinal number *three*. And the specific Christian phrase for the Trinity (*Al-Aqanim-Al-Thalatha*) does not appear in the Qur'an. So the central question is "Does the Qur'an understand the Trinity to assert the existence of three divine Persons within the one Being that is God (the correct understanding), or does it assume that the Trinity is teaching three separate and distinct gods, a form of polytheism?" And, if the latter, does it identify these gods? As we will see, the Qur'an's early interpreters believed their holy book answered this question clearly. E. M. Wherry noted, "The commentators Baidhawi, Jalaluddin, and Yahya agree in interpreting the *three* to mean 'God, Jesus, and Mary,' in the relation of Father, Mother, and Son."[8] As we will see, that is but a partial list of commentators to hold this view.[9]

The Qur'an is clear: Christians are to cease saying "three." Why? "Allah is only One God." It seems plain that the meaning is "Do not say three [gods], for Allah is only One God." That the Qur'an repeatedly asserts monotheism as the antidote for the Christian claim of "three" indicates the understanding of its author: Christians are in some fashion polytheists, denying, through their beliefs, true monotheism. If the Qur'anic argument is that the "three" in view are Allah, Mary, and Jesus, it is easy to see how such a triad *would* violate any meaningful concept of monotheism! But if that is the Qur'an's view, we must conclude that its author was exceedingly confused as to true Christian belief.[10]

The sentence "Far is it removed from His transcendence that He should have a son" strikes a recurring Qur'anic theme. Many of the idols in the Kaaba would have borne filial relations to each other, gods married to female gods and having sons and daughters. The famed "Satanic Verses" incident is one illustration, and the Qur'an raises the issue a number of times:

> If Allah had willed to take a son, He could have chosen anyone
> He pleased out of His creation: Transcendent is He! He is Allah,
> the One, the Irresistible. (39:4)

The Originator of the heavens and the earth! How can He have
a child, when there is for Him no consort, when He created all
things and has knowledge of all things? (6:101)

Clearly, in each text, the idea is of Allah as the male deity having
a wife or partner by which he could have a child, or a son. We
join the Qur'an in condemning such polytheism, for the Bible
likewise condemns such things:

> There is none like You, O LORD;
> You are great, and great is Your name in might.
> Who would not fear You, O King of the nations?
> Indeed it is Your due!
> For among all the wise men of the nations
> And in all their kingdoms,
> There is none like You.
> But they are altogether stupid and foolish
> *In their* discipline of delusion—their idol is wood!
> Beaten silver is brought from Tarshish,
> And gold from Uphaz,
> The work of a craftsman and of the hands of a
>   goldsmith;
> Violet and purple are their clothing;
> They are all the work of skilled men.
> But the LORD is the true God;
> He is the living God and the everlasting King.
> At His wrath the earth quakes,
> And the nations cannot endure His indignation.
> Thus you shall say to them, "The gods that did not
>   make the heavens and the earth will perish from the
>   earth and from under the heavens."
> *It is* He who made the earth by His power,
> Who established the world by His wisdom;
> And by His understanding He has stretched out the
>   heavens.
>
> Jeremiah 10:6–12

But the Qur'an connects its condemnation of God having a "consort" and offspring with the Christian belief that Jesus is God's Son. We cannot enter here into the abundant evidence that Christians had long before professed belief that the relationship between the Father and the Son was not marked by a female deity and an offspring. The Son of God, the second person of the Trinity, had *eternally* borne that relationship to the Father. He did not *become* the Son at a point in time. The Father/Son terminology refers to a relationship that has always been. There is no female deity, no multiple gods or celestial pregnancies or anything even remotely like this. And yet, when we turn to some of the most respected and widely consulted commentaries (*tafsir*) of the Qur'an, we repeatedly find these misconceptions relating to the Trinity tied directly to the interpretation of the text. We have seen how *Ibn Kathir* took this view (see note 7). Another is found in the *Tafsir al-Jalalayn*:

> So believe in Allah and His Messengers. Do not say, "Three gods: Allah, Isa and his mother." It is better that you stop saying these things. Affirming the Divine Unity [is] better. Allah is only One God. He is too Glorious to have a son![11]

Note what gloss fills out the meaning of "say not three," that being "three gods: Allah, Isa and his mother." The renowned commentator *Abu al-Qasim Mahmud ibn Umar az-Zamakhshari*, in the twelfth century, understood that the Qur'anic presentation differed from what he knew of Christian belief:

> The (word) three is the predicate to an understood subject. If one accepts the Christian view that God exists in one nature (jauhar) with three divine persons, namely the Father, the Son, and the Holy Spirit, and (if one accepts) the opinion that the person of the Father represents (God's) being (dhat), the person of the Son represents (his) knowledge ('ilm), and the person of the Holy Spirit represents (his) life (hayat), then one must supply

the subject as follows: 'God is three(fold).' Otherwise, one must supply (the subject) thus: 'The gods are three.'

But as a faithful Muslim, he was forced to bow to the ultimate authority of the Qur'an, *even when that meant redefining pre-existing Christian beliefs!*

> According to the evidence of the Qur'an, the Christians maintain that God, Christ, and Mary are three gods, and that Christ is the child of God by Mary, as God says (in the Qur'an): 'O Jesus son of Mary, didst thou say unto men: "Take me and my mother as gods, apart from God"?' (5:116), or: 'The Christians say: "The Messiah is the Son of God"' (9:30). Moreover, it is well known that the Christians maintain that in Jesus are (combined) a divine nature derived from the Father and a human nature derived from his mother. . . . At the same time these words [4:171] exclude (the Christian view) that Jesus had with God the usual relationship between sons and (their) fathers . . . [12]

This following reference is one of the most important we will provide. The earliest biography of Muhammad's life, of Ibn Ishaq, contains a passage that not only demonstrates how primitive is this understanding of the Qur'anic teaching of "three" but also makes an astounding claim.

Referring back to the deputation from Najran, we read,

> They were Christians according to the Byzantine rite, though they differed among themselves in some points, saying He is God; and He is the son of God; and He is the third person of the Trinity, which is the doctrine of Christianity. They argue that he is God because he used to raise the dead, and heal the sick, and declare the unseen; and make clay birds and then breathe into them so that they flew away; and all this was by the command of God Almighty, "We will make him a sign to men." They argue that he is the son of God in that they say he had no known father; and he spoke in the cradle and this is something that no child of Adam

has ever done. They argue that he is the third of three in that God says: We have done, We have commanded, We have created and We have decreed, and they say, If He were one he would have said *I have done,* I have created, and so on, but He is He and Jesus and Mary. Concerning all these assertions the Quran came down.[13]

Ibn Ishaq records that Christians believe the Trinity is "He and Jesus and Mary," as do numerous other sources, but note especially the last statement, "Concerning all these assertions the Quran came down." This stupendous claim connects the very reason the Qur'an was revealed with refuting Christian beliefs about God! What makes it all the more important is that *none of the beliefs* Ibn Ishaq *lists could possibly be described as encompassing an accurate summary of the doctrine of the Trinity.* If we take him at his word, the Qur'an came down to refute assertions that were not being made.[14]

This vital section concludes with "The Messiah will never be too proud to be a slave to Allah, nor will the nearest angels." The Qur'an sees the servanthood of Jesus the Messiah as an argument against belief in Christ's deity. But given the extensive discussions already penned by Christians, reflecting clear New Testament teachings (such as that found in Philippians 2:5–11) relating to the incarnation and Jesus being a perfect Man, this again betrays misunderstanding on the author's part. Christians find nothing in His voluntary and proper submission to the Father that is contrary to our beliefs. In fact, we affirm openly and clearly that Jesus, the Incarnate One, submitted to the Father in all things and worshiped Him. How else could He be our perfect substitute? How could He fulfill God's law if He did not worship?

Surah 4:171–172 enshrines a view of the Trinity that believing Christians find confused and erroneous. We do not believe God the Son is the offspring of God and a wife named Mary. When we say "three," we are saying three Persons, not three gods. So, one might well ask, where could such an idea have been derived?

The Muslim who insists on divorcing the Qur'an from its historical context (as Islamic orthodoxy demands, at least as to its author's knowledge and input) cannot even enter into the inquiry. But a suggestion that seems historically relevant and consistent with the context of Muhammad's life would focus on his own experience as an outsider to the Christian faith. He would have had some exposure to Christianity in his travels via caravan into Syria. Again we ask what would a teenage boy have seen had he ventured to look into a Christian church or listened to conversations among Christians?

Inside a small church in a Syrian village, he would have seen statuary. Possibly God represented as creating all things. The crucifix to be sure. The common artistic representation of the Holy Spirit was a dove, which would not, in and of itself, suggest to a young man from Mecca a divine figure.

But what else? A woman. A woman in various exalted poses, a woman holding the baby Jesus. He would have seen and heard much about Mary, for the slow (and unbiblical) process of Mary's exaltation had begun centuries before Muhammad's birth. So in light of the religious experience that was his in Mecca's polytheistic context, would it not be easy for him to interpret what he saw in the light of Allah, Mary, and their child, Jesus? This is not a possible answer for the believing Muslim, but it surely would explain why the Qur'an seems to impute to Christians a view of God that we have never held.

Surah 5:12–19: "They . . . Have Disbelieved"

Surah 5 contains even more direct discussion of Christian claims, with many themes repeated. As noted above, early Islamic sources connected at least some of these *ayat* with the encounter Muhammad is said to have had with the Christians from Najran. In any case, they give us even more information on which to judge the Qur'an's teaching and the accuracy of its representation.

> 5:12. Allah made a pact of old with the Children of Israel, and We raised among them twelve chieftains, and Allah said: "Surely, I am with you. If you establish the ritual prayer and pay the zakat, and believe in My Messengers and support them, and lend to Allah a goodly loan, surely I shall remit your sins, and surely I shall admit you into gardens beneath which rivers flow. Whosoever among you disbelieves after this has gone astray from a straight path."

The author often traces an argument from Moses through Jesus to the Qur'an. Here the chain begins with a reference to Allah making a "pact of old," more literally, a covenant (*mithaq*) with Israel. The reported revelation is not found in this form in the Hebrew Scriptures, just as the statements the Qur'an attributes to Jesus do not appear in the Christian Scriptures. In both cases the language is cast in Islamic forms. Here, ritual prayer and *zakat* (the religious giving of alms) is placed back into the ancient Jewish context. The point is God established a covenant with the Jewish people that they did not keep.

> 13. And because of their breaking their pact, We have cursed them and made hard their hearts. They change words from their context and forget a part of that wherewith they had been reminded. You will not cease to discover treachery among them, all save a few. But bear with them, and pardon them. Surely, Allah loves those who behave with excellence.

We cannot enter here into the assertions made concerning "changing words from their context."[15] But the accusations are harsh: The claim is that the Jews rejected Allah's purposes, becoming hardhearted and treacherous. From this condemnation of the first people to receive a revelation from Allah, the Qur'an moves to the next, the Christians:

14. And with those who say: "Surely, we are Christians," We made a pact, but they forgot a part of that whereof they were admonished. Therefore, We have stirred up enmity and hatred among them till the day of Resurrection, when Allah will inform them of what they have done.

It is hard to say from the text what part of the covenant made with Christians was forgotten. *Ibn Kathir* understands it as referring to obligation to follow Muhammad and to believe "in every Prophet whom Allah sends to the people of the earth."[16] Christian history records no such covenant, and the New Testament itself (see Hebrews 1:1–2) clearly proclaims Jesus' advent as the end of the coming of prophets, so the Qur'an's reasoning is difficult to follow here. But the rest is much easier to understand, for it refers to dissension between various groups that, to the outsider, all look like "Christians." In that day this would have included the Byzantines, Nestorians, Jacobites, and so on.

15. O people of the Book! Now has Our Messenger come to you, expounding to you much of that which you used to hide in the Book, and forgiving much. Now there has come to you light from Allah, and a clear Book.
16. Whereby Allah guides all who seek His good pleasure to ways of peace [and safety], and leads them out of darkness,[17] by His permission, to light, and guides them to a straight path.

The first reference to "people of the Book" probably brings together both Jews and Christians from the preceding context and calls them all to follow after Muhammad, "Our Messenger." He brings the "clear Book," described as a "light" that when followed, can lead one out of the "darkness" of men's ideas to a "straight path."

This provides preceding context to one of the key exhortations relevant to our study. Though the People of the Book have just been noted, here is a section addressed to a group of disbelievers identified by what they say:

> 17. They indeed have disbelieved who say: "Allah is the Messiah, son of Mary." Say: "Who has the least power against Allah, if He had willed to destroy the Messiah son of Mary, and his mother and everyone on earth?" Allah's is the sovereignty of the heavens and the earth.

Of course, it is highly unusual for Christians to express their faith by saying "God is Christ, son of Mary." In fact, proclaiming Christ's deity is not the same as saying "God is Christ." We do not believe the Son exhausts all that can be said about God. The proper and balanced assertion is "The Messiah is divine and human," and, even more to the point, "The Son of God is eternally divine and became man in the person of Jesus the Messiah." In any case, the Qur'an's terminology naturally leads the Christian to ask, "Why would a divine refutation of Christian faith use terminology Christians themselves find imbalanced and odd?" That matter aside, it seems clear the text is attempting, minimally, to identify the Christian confession of the deity of Christ as an act of *kufir*, unbelief.[18]

But this *ayah* seeks to provide an antidote, a responsive argument, and in so doing gives real insight into its author's understanding. The Qur'an gives the very words that, ostensibly, Muhammad and all who follow after him are to give in response to affirmation of Christ's deity: "Who has the least power against Allah, if He had willed to destroy the Messiah son of Mary, and his mother and everyone on earth?" The contention seems to be that Jesus, as a creature, could have been destroyed by Allah; thus, He could not be divine.

If that is the case, though, why include Mary? It would seem the author has in mind the "three" the early commentators note, yet soon (v. 116) we will have reason to note that the text directly identifies Mary's relationship to his argument. For now the idea is clear: Jesus, Mary, and "everyone on earth" are created beings and so can be destroyed by Allah. Therefore, the Christians must be wrong in their assertions about the deity of Christ. This would be true only if Christians believed in the deity of Mary and only if they believed Jesus was *solely* divine. But Christians believe Jesus is the God-Man, the second person of the Trinity become flesh, so they fully believe Jesus was a human being. Once again, we are left looking for our first evidence of an accurate understanding of and insight into the Christian faith by the Qur'an's author.

> 18. The Jews and the Christians say: "We are the sons of Allah, and His loved ones." Say: "Why then does He chastise you for your sins? Surely, you are but human beings of His creating. He forgives whom He will, and punishes whom He will. Allah's is the sovereignty of the heavens and the earth and all that is between them, and to Him is the journeying."

It is again difficult to ascertain what exact claims the author had encountered, but surely it is a substantial misunderstanding of Christian theology to confuse the Bible's claims concerning the status God grants His followers, whether under the Old Covenant (e.g., David, or Isaiah, or Ezekiel) or the New (where believers are identified as the children of and even "sons of God" [Romans 8:19–23]), with its teaching of the unique sonship of Jesus the Messiah.

Christians do not claim to have eternally existed as persons in the Trinity. The sonship available through faith in Christ—the place of love bestowed on the one who repents and believes in Him for salvation—is one of grace, not of being. We know we always remain creatures who never cease being dependent upon our Maker. It is the Son who will exist eternally as the Son and whose sonship is existential. This distinction, so basic to Christian proclamation, seems lost on the author of the Qur'an.

> 19. O people of the Book! Now has Our Messenger come to you to make things clear [again] after an interval [between] Messengers, lest you should say: "There came not to us a bearer of glad tidings nor a warner." Now has a bearer of glad tidings and a warner come to you. Allah has power over all things, and all that is between them. He creates what He will. And He has power over all things.

This section closes with an exhortation and an emphasis on the divine nature of Muhammad's calling. The People of the Book are informed that Allah has sent them a warner bearing glad tidings, evidently involving the refutation of falsehoods and "darknesses" and the proclamation of *tawhid* and the true path. Christians are well within rights to ask, "If you wish to bring me good tidings and correct my errors, should I not see first that you have a right knowledge of what I believe to confirm that your correction can be accurate and truthful?"

Surah 5:68–77: "Allah Is the Third of Three"?

The next section is most essential to our inquiry into the Qur'an's accuracy, one of the fullest we will examine in its references to the Christian faith and in its arguments against that faith.

> 68. Say: "O People of the book! You have nothing [of true guidance] till you observe the Torah and the Gospel, and that which was sent down to you from your Lord." That which was sent down to you [O Muhammad] from your Lord is certain to

increase the transgression and disbelief of many of them. So grieve not for those who disbelieve.

We can agree with this exhortation, to a point. Never were God's Old Covenant followers more pleasing to Him than when observing His Word rightly, and the Christian believer finds true guidance in the inspired words of Jesus and His apostles.[19] Here the Qur'an affirms, as it often does, the Torah and the Gospel as divine revelations and, if these words had any meaning in Muhammad's day, they still existed and were available to their respective communities. The chain of argument is clear: God sent down the Torah, God sent down the Gospel, now God has sent down the Qur'an via Muhammad (see this very argument in v. 44ff.). But "many" Jews and Christians will disbelieve, and Muhammad is not to grieve over them.

> 69. Those who believe [in the Qur'an], the Jews, the Sabaeans, and the Christians, whoever [accepts Islam,] believes in Allah and the Last Day and does right, no fear shall come upon them, neither shall they grieve.

This translation includes some important additions not found in the original Arabic text. There has been much discussion, even in modern times, as to the meaning of this text, for Westernized Muslims have seen in it a message very different from the one conveyed here. Note Muhammad Asad's translation:

> For, verily, those who have attained faith [in this divine writ], as well as those who follow the Jewish faith, the Sabians, and the Christians—all who believe in God and the Last Day and do righteous deeds—no fear need they have, and neither shall they grieve.

Is this text offering salvation for a wider group than Muslims? Or as some have suggested, is this only relevant to those who were Jews, Sabaeans, and Christians *prior to* Muhammad? The text does not seem to answer with clarity, yet if the thought is continuing on from the preceding *ayah*, the object of "disbelief" (v. 68) could provide a clue. If that is specifically a reference to a rejection of Muhammad, then it would seem the text actually is restricting its promises to Muslims.

> 70. We made the pact with the Children of Israel, and We sent to them Messengers. As often as a Messenger came to them with that which their souls desired not, some [of them] they denied, and some they slew.
> 71. They thought no harm would come of it, so they were willfully blind and deaf, after which Allah relented towards them. Now [even after that] many of them are willfully blind and deaf, and Allah sees what they do.

Ayat 70 through 71 seem parallel in thought and structure to 12 through 13, examined earlier. Once again the text begins with the Jews, laments hardness of heart and unbelief, and then moves quickly to the Christians, focusing on false beliefs and excesses. It should be noted that this is a theme struck in the earliest portion of the Qur'an, where in the prayer repeated daily by every faithful Muslim, they pray to be led in the straight path of those Allah favors, "not of those who have incurred your wrath, nor of those who are astray." There is no question whatsoever that the interpretation offered by Muhammad himself in the *hadith* literature of this final section is that those who have incurred Allah's wrath are the Jews, and those who have gone astray are the Christians.

> 72. They have disbelieved who say: "Allah is the Messiah, the son of Mary." The Messiah (himself) said: "O Children of Israel, worship Allah, my Lord and your Lord. Whoever ascribes partners to Allah, for him Allah has forbidden Paradise. His abode is the Fire. For the unjust there will be no helpers."

Here is repeated the same assertion as in 5:17, again with the terminology that does not clarify but only confuses the issue. Now, though, instead of following this attempted recounting of the Christian belief in Christ's deity, the Qur'an takes a different tack.

As we will see in chapter 6, the Qur'an attributes a series of sayings and statements to Jesus. From a historical perspective, there is no evidence that these go back to the historical Jesus of Nazareth, yet Muslims accept them as divine revelation. Here the words attributed to Jesus provide a counterargument to the Qur'anic understanding of the Christian position and bring Jesus forth as a witness against it.

It is uncertain whether all the rest of *ayah* 72 is attributed to Jesus, as our translation punctuates it, or if only the first portion is to be so understood. The bare assertion, "O Children of Israel, worship Allah, my Lord and your Lord," bears at least slight similarity to statements of Jesus in the sense of directing people to worship God (without the use of the Arabic term), but the rest is far removed from anything that evidentially can be attributed to Him, especially in such a context. It involves the concept of *shirk* and assumes the same meaning presented in the Qur'an. The text literally says Allah makes paradise *haram* to him, another concept with distinct Islamic roots. While Jesus often spoke of *gehenna* (hell), He did not do so in these words or contexts.

We must note that it is very difficult to avoid the conclusion that here the Qur'an is associating what it understands to be the Christian confession of Christ's deity with *shirk*, the forbidding of paradise, destruction in the fire, and the denial of any helpers for such "wrongdoers." This surely is the position of many conservative Muslims, and it seems this is the most straightforward reading of the text itself. But we likewise point out that, so far, the basis of these strong condemnations has been found inaccurate and, at best, representative of only a part of the Christian doctrine. The next *ayah* only increases our concern over the accuracy of the Qur'an's understanding.

> 73. They have disbelieved who say: "Allah is the third of three," when there is no god save One God. If they cease not what they say, a painful torment will fall upon those of them who disbelieve.

Once again, the Qur'an references *kufir* and promises "painful torment" for unbelievers. The sign of this unbelief should be startling to anyone familiar with Christian faith: The statement that "Allah is the third of three." Three *what*? Plainly, the third of three gods, for the very next statement is, "there is no god save One God."

What does this mean? And who says it?[20] Given the preceding *ayah*, that the Qur'an is attributing this to Christians really is without question. But when have Christians, in any context, let alone in dialogue with Muslims, ever said any such thing?

Some have insisted that the Qur'an *literally* is relegating Allah to the third of three, placing the other two gods in the first and second positions of a triad. But this may be going beyond the text, even if it lines up with good Arabic grammar, for as we will see, the Qur'an seems to be making reference to Allah, Mary, and Jesus. This was the view of Ibn Kathir:

> Mujahid and several others said that this *Ayah* was revealed about the Christians in particular. As-Suddi and others said that this *Ayah* was revealed about taking 'Isa and his mother as gods besides Allah, thus making Allah the third in a trinity.[21]

Most Muslims today, as probably in Muhammad's day, make the association of "Allah = the Father" in Christian terminology. But no matter the order of the gods, the key tenet to address is the assertion that Christians believe in three, Allah being one of them, and that this belief will bring a painful punishment. We simply must insist that if its author believed Christians hold to three gods, Allah, Mary, and evidently their offspring, Jesus, then the Qur'an is the result of human effort, is marked by ignorance and error, and so is not what Muslims claim it to be. To this place, at the very heart of the matter in the Christian/Muslim dialogue, we have come not by following traditions or prejudices but by following carefully the Qur'an's own words.

> 74. Will they not instead turn to Allah in repentance and seek His forgiveness? For Allah is Forgiving, Compassionate.
> 75. The Messiah son of Mary was none other than a Messenger, before whom Messengers had passed away. And his mother was a saintly woman. They both used to eat [earthly] food. See how We make the signs clear for them; then see how they follow falsehood.

In calling Christians to repentance for saying Allah is the third of three, the Qur'an, in opposition, proclaims Jesus "none other than" one in the line of "Messengers," before whom others had died. By then calling Mary "saintly" and noting that the two of them ate "[earthly] food," the author argues against Christ's deity by asserting that Mary and Jesus were mere humans. The Messengers all had been *mere* humans. Mary was *merely* human. Anyone who eats food, evidently, must be a *mere* human. So it follows, Jesus was a mere human!

From the Qur'an's very pages, and repeated daily by Muslims around the world, *this argument shows no firsthand familiarity with Christian theology.* Since the New Testament plainly confesses the full humanity of Jesus, such arguments are irrelevant even to the knowledgeable opponent of Christian orthodoxy. While some have tried to say the Qur'an is not addressing Christians here, we can safely set aside those efforts and recognize the truth: The Qur'an is in error in its view of Christian belief. With some irony we note the assurance that this alleged establishment of Christ's *mere* humanity has been made "clear" by God Himself.

> 76. Say: "Do you worship in place of Allah that which possesses for you neither harm nor benefit? Allah it is who is the Hearing, the Knowing."
> 77. Say: "O People of the Book! Exceed not in your religion the bounds, and do not follow the vain desires of people who erred in times gone by and led many astray and strayed from the even road."

Here truly is the Qur'an's understanding, now in full light. Worship of Jesus, a mere creature, is seen as taking place *in place of* the worship of Allah, the only true God. Failing to recognize that Christians are worshiping one God who has been manifest in three Persons, each fully sharing the one being that is God, the Qur'an is limited by perspective to unitarian monotheism and hence to the bald accusation of polytheism. Nothing in the Qur'anic text actually addresses the essence of Christian faith, even though it is painfully clear the author *thought* he was doing so.

This section, a consistent unit of thought and argumentation, concludes with another direct reference to Christians engaging in excess (as in Surah 4:171). The author further asserts that those who have taught them these errors had themselves "erred." Christians are accused of following after worthless traditions that have led them from the clear path.

Surah 5:116: Worshiping Mary and Jesus as Gods

The last of our key texts is the clearest of all we have examined, and yet because we have looked so closely at those that have come before we do not need to dwell upon it at length. We already have established the context that makes plain its message and its error. No other Qur'anic text is as blatant in its misrepresentation of the Trinity.

> 116. And when Allah said: "O Jesus son of Mary! Did you say to mankind: 'Take me and my mother for two gods other than Allah?'" He said: "Transcendent are You! It was not mine to say that of which I had no right. In saying it, then You knew it. You know what is in my self, but I know not what is in Your self. It is You, only You, Who know well all hidden things."
>
> 117. I told them only that which You commanded me, [saying]: "Worship Allah, my Lord and your Lord!" I was a witness over them while I dwelt among them, and when You took me, You were the Watcher over them. You are Witness over all things.

Most commentators project this text to the Day of Judgment, and many translations insert such an indication by inserting "And beware the day" or something similar. Allah then asks Jesus if He taught mankind to take Him *and His mother* as "two gods other than Allah." Jesus denies ever doing so, asserting that He only proclaimed that they were to engage in *tawhid*.

At this juncture, we need not belabor the point that is so plainly stated. The charge is blatant polytheism, and here alone is the "three" so listed (though in *ayah* 75 it is obvious two of the three are Jesus and Mary, with Allah assumed). Nowhere does the Qur'an ever give Father, Son, and Holy Spirit or even Allah, Son, and Spirit (the Holy Spirit in the Qur'an being the angel Gabriel, or Jabril).

The followers of Jesus are accused of taking Jesus and Mary *as gods* in derogation of Allah. For this allegation to be true, Christians would have to be seeking to give worship to other than the one true God, and in this case, to three gods, including Mary. That was self-evidently not the view then, and even today, with more than a thousand years of development in the Roman Catholic communion and its unbiblical exaltation of Mary, Rome denies divinizing Mary or giving her full worship.[22]

But even if that modern error *had* been present in the seventh century, the Qur'an *still* would not accurately reflect the resultant situation. It portrays the Trinity as Allah, Mary, and Jesus and is concerned to repeatedly deny that Allah could have a son. The relationship implied—father, mother, child—is far, far removed from anything that can remotely be identified as Christian.[23]

The Muslim must understand what is at stake. It is not an arguable fact that Christianity is clear in its profession of monotheism. Followers of Christ did not believe God had taken a human wife and by her sired a child named Jesus, and hence He was the "son of God."

The Qur'anic text seems plainly to say otherwise. What does this say concerning the truthfulness of its claims to divine origin and inspiration? Is it not more than possible, even likely, that what we are reading came from Muhammad? It is easy to understand how a person living in Mecca could be confused on the subject. Doesn't dedication to truth require one to consider the possibility that the Qur'an is in error because its author was a human being whose own understanding was likewise in error?

We conclude with one last observation on the above text. The Qur'an puts into the mouth of Jesus words that deny He has a special, unique, personal knowledge of the Father, of God Himself. Its author clearly did not know the Gospels or the text of these words of Jesus, recorded long, long before Muhammad claimed to be a prophet:

> All things have been handed over to me by my Father, and no one knows the Son except the Father, and no one knows the Father except the Son and anyone to whom the Son chooses to reveal him. (Matthew 11:27 ESV)

Oh, that the author of the Qur'an could have known the Jesus who made this amazing claim! What a difference it might have made.

Notes

1. *Tanwīr al-Miqbās min Tafsīr Ibn 'Abbās*, trans. Mokrane Guezzou, (Amman: Royal Aal al-Bayt Institute for Islamic Thought, 2007), 109. All but the inner parentheses here indicate Qur'anic citation and differentiate it from the *tafsir* (commentary) being offered.

2. We could profitably note much more concerning the early Islamic sources and the Najran delegation. Many sources connect that meeting with both major sections relevant to our Qur'an/Trinity study (Surat 4 and 5, as well as the first eighty verses of Surah 3). Traditional dating of the encounter, AD 632, would mean it came very late in Muhammad's life, but all the earliest sources (including Ibn Ishaq and the *tafsir* of Muqatil ibn Sulayman) that refer to it connect it directly to the giving of particular Qur'anic portions, especially 3:60–62 and also our key texts in 4:171 and 5:72–73. The differences between the narrations seem to indicate the story being still in development at this point, and all indicate that it is based not in the actual words of Christians with whom Muhammad debated but from the early Qur'anic community, for they all contain misrepresentations and misunderstandings of the Christian beliefs of that time that draw even into Gnostic tales like the story of the birds Jesus allegedly made alive from clay or His speaking from the cradle, both ahistorical and both included in the Qur'an (see chapters 5–6). This observation's importance for our study is clear: The early Islamic centuries provide us with no external reason to believe the Qur'anic narrative provides an accurate representation of the Trinity, for it created a primitive community soaked in error on the subject. For more insight into this rich source of historical and theological information, see "We Will Make Peace with You: The Christians of Najran in Muqatil's Tafsir" (accessible at www.quranandinjil.org/quranicstudies_files/We_will_make_peace.pdf).

3. Ibn Kathir comments on this phrase,

> Allah forbids the People of the Scriptures from going to extremes in religion, which is a common trait of theirs, especially among the Christians. The Christians exaggerated over 'Isa until they elevated him above the grade that Allah gave him. They elevated him from the rank of prophethood to being a god, whom they worshipped just as they worshipped Allah. They exaggerated even more in the case of those who they claim were his followers, claiming that they were inspired, thus following every word they uttered whether true or false, be it guidance or misguidance, truth or lies. (3:55)

4. Our base translation provides an interesting (and fairly rare) note that will be relevant to our discussion below:

> Many Christians have never accepted pure monotheism as advanced by Judaism and Islam, since their love for their Messenger, Jesus (may peace

be upon him) caused them to deify him, just as the Romans deified their emperors. Although Jesus (may peace be upon him), like all the Prophets, brought the message of absolute Divine Unity, later generations of Christians developed a theory of "trinity." As the Qur'an explains, the error of the Jews was excessive formalism, and the error of the Christians, metaphysical confusion and deification of their Messenger, who never claimed to be God. We ask Allah to preserve us from both extremes.

5. The preventive particle *ma* seems to indicate that this emphasis is warranted, that Jesus was *only* a Messenger, as in opposition to the Christian assertion of His divine sonship.

6. *Tafsir Ibn Kathir* (Riyadh: Darusalam, 2003), 3:56.

7. Ibn Kathir comments, "Believe that Allah is One and Alone and that He does not have a son or wife. Know and be certain that 'Isa is the servant and Messenger of Allah. Then immediately thereafter ("Say not: 'Three!'"), do not elevate 'Isa and his mother to be gods with Allah. Allah is far holier than what they attribute to Him" (3:59).

8. E. M. Wherry, *A Comprehensive Commentary on the Qur'an*, Vol. 2 (London: n.p., 1886) 116–117, as found at http://answering-islam.org/Books/Wherry/Commentary2/ch4.htm. He went on to say,

> This misrepresentation of the Scripture doctrine again stamps the Qur'an as a fabrication, and furnishes the evidence of its being such on the ground of its own claims. The history of the Church, as well as the Bible, proves the statement of the text, as interpreted by authoritative commentators, to be false; for even granting that some obscure Christian sect did hold such a doctrine of the Trinity (of which statement we have yet to learn the truth), yet the spirit of Muhammad's inspiration represents it as the faith of the Christians generally. In almost every case where the Qur'an refers to the Christian faith, it is to inveigh against the idea that God has a son. See chap. ix. 31, xix. 31, xliii. 59.

9. When Nestorian Patriarch Timothy I (780–823) held a dialogue with Abbasid Caliph Mahdi (775–785), the encounter (apparently c. 782) began with these words:

> "O Catholicos, a man like you who possesses all this knowledge and utters sublime words concerning God is not justified in saying about God that He married a woman from whom He begat a son."—And I replied to his Majesty: "And who, O God-loving King, who has ever uttered such a blasphemy concerning God?" . . . —And our victorious King said to me: "What then do you say that Christ is?"—And I replied to his Majesty: "O King, Christ is the Word-God, who appeared in the flesh for the salvation of the world."—And our victorious King questioned me: "Do you not say that Christ is the Son of God?"—And I replied to his Majesty: "O King, Christ is the Son of God, and I confess Him and worship Him as such. This I learned from Christ Himself in the Gospel and from the books of the Torah and of the prophets, which know Him and call Him by the name of 'Son of God,' but not a son in the flesh as children are born in the carnal way, but an admirable and wonderful Son," more sublime and higher than mind and words, as it fits a divine Son to be." (*The Early Christian-Muslim Dialogue*, 175)

10. Al-Kindi addressed this very issue. His words echo down through the centuries and remind us we are dealing with issues that have been discussed for a very long time:

> Of course when you protest that God never took Him a wife, [be]gat a son, or had a peer, you say what is absolutely true. Such candor becomes you; it is worthy of you. You protest solemnly, and indeed you speak truly and argue logically when you affirm that he who imposes on God the necessity for friend or fellow, blasphemes Him and virtually imposes on Him the necessity of taking a wife, begetting a son and having a peer. But, God bless you, we do not say that God has a wife, or has [be]gotten a son; we do not impute to the Deity such puerilities and vanities, predicating of God what is true of man. . . . Whereas you, who have read the scriptures, know that such things are never named in them. They are not imposed on our reason; nothing of the sort is hinted at. It is in the Qur'an that these profanities are multiplied against us. . . . Certainly we have never said, nor will ever say, that God, ever Blessed and most High, took a wife or [be]gat a son. . . . As to that which touches His essence, we believe that, co-essential and co-eternal with Him are His Word and Spirit, alike transcendent, exalted above all attribute and predicate (ibid., 418–419).

11. *Tafsir al-Jalalayn*, trans. Aisha Bewley (London: Dar Al Taqwa Ltd, 2007), 232.

12. Helmut Gätje, *The Qur'an and Its Exegesis* (Oxford: Oneworld, 2004), 126–127.

13. Ibn Ishaq, *Sirat Rasul Allah*, trans. Alfred Guillaume, (Oxford: University Press, 2006), 271–272.

14. We briefly note the earlier existence of the Collyridians, a group of women who may have worshiped Mary (at least as inferred from secondhand sources). There is no evidence they survived into Muhammad's day, let alone that he encountered anyone with such beliefs or that the "People of the Book" were Collyridians. The Qur'an's representation of the Trinity is plainly in error, so some have tried to say it is rebuking this small sect. The early Islamic sources offer no support, and as far as any evidence suggests, the Collyridians did not believe Mary was married to God so as to have a child named Jesus, etc. The notion of the Qur'an refuting a group that no longer existed seems more than farfetched.

15. See chapter 8, below.

16. *Tafsir Ibn Kathir*, 3:130.

17. This rendering seems awkward but is the literal reading of the Arabic text.

18. As Ibn Kathir comments (3:133), "Allah states that the Christians are disbelievers because of their claim that 'Isa, son of Maryam, one of Allah's servants and creatures, is Allah. Allah is holier than what they attribute to Him."

19. We shall enter more fully into the discussion of how it is possible for Jews and Christians to obey such texts as this in the Qur'an if, as we are often told, the Torah and the Gospel have been lost, at a later point.

20. Al-Kindi likewise expressed amazement at this accusation against Christians:

> I summon you to the worship of the one God in three persons, perfect in His Word and Spirit—one in three; three in one. You must on no account think of Him as if He were the third of three; So indeed your master misrepresents

us as saying: "They are unbelievers who say that God is the third of three; and if they do not cease from what they say, sore punishment will overtake the unbelievers; or will they return to God and seek His pardon? He is merciful and forgiving." . . . So says your master; but, God be gracious to you, I should like to know who they are who teach that God is a third of three. Are they the Christians, or not? You claim some knowledge of the three Christian sects, and indeed they are the most prominent sects. Do you know any who say that God is the third of three? I am sure you do not, unless you mean the sect known as Marcionites, who speak of three substances which they term divine yet distinct, one of which represents justice, the other mercy and the other for an evil principle. But these Marcionites are not Christians, nor are they known by that name. The Christian community, on the other hand, are innocent of this heresy; nay they reject and disown it. They teach the one God in whom is the Word and the Spirit, and that without any distinction (*The Christian-Muslim Dialogue*, 424–425).

21. *Tafsir Ibn Kathir*, 3:236.

22. For a biblical discussion of Rome's veneration of Mary, see James White, *The Roman Catholic Controversy* (Minneapolis: Bethany House, 1996), 197–218.

23. The Church of Jesus Christ of Latter-day Saints, which claims to be Christian, does hold a view very similar to that represented in Surah 5:116. See the extensive documentation in James White, *Is the Mormon My Brother?* (Solid Ground Christian Books, 1997). Of course, Mormonism arose more than a millennium after Muhammad.

5

Jesus in the Qur'an

The title of this chapter really should be "*Isa ibn Mariam* in the Qur'an," since that is how it normally identifies Jesus. But we will forgo the debate that has raged over the centuries regarding why it uses '*Isa* (Arabic Christians refer to Him as *Yeshua*) and instead concentrate on understanding exactly what the Qur'an says about Jesus. In this chapter we will look at every text that addresses Him by name, along with the surrounding context. We want our Muslim friends to know we have honestly and fairly examined its testimony. Then we will look at one important comparison between Jesus and Muhammad in reference to the issue of intercession.

Muslims often say they are part of the second-largest religion that teaches people to love Jesus. Some prefer "believe in" rather than "love." In either case, is this true? Certainly, in Islam one must believe a man named Jesus, a virgin-born, miracle-working prophet sent by Allah, existed at the beginning of the first century in the environs around Jerusalem. But is this truly the same as teaching people to believe in, or even love Jesus as Christians do?

The name *'Isa* appears twenty-five times in the Qur'anic text, almost always in the form *Isa ibn Mariam*, Jesus the son of Mary. Some have speculated that the addition of *ibn Mariam* is an antidote to the Christian proclamation that Jesus is the Son of God, and this definitely would fit with our chapter 4 conclusions. Sometimes *'Isa* is not used directly and only the title *Messiah* is used. Below are all these texts, with context, in the general chronological order we established (in chapter 2) for the surat of the Qur'an.

The Qur'anic Texts

Surah 19 bears as its title the name of Jesus' mother. The author seems to confuse Mary, mother of Jesus, with Miriam, sister of Moses, though Muslim apologists have offered a number of intriguing explanations.[1] This *surah* gives us the story of Jesus' birth, a fascinating rendition of the biblical account:

> 19:27. At length she brought him [the infant] to her people carrying him. They said: "O Mary! Truly a villainous thing you have done!"
>
> 28. "O sister of Aaron! Your father was not a wicked man, nor was your mother unchaste."
>
> 29. She made a sign, pointing to him. They replied: "How can we speak with he who is in the cradle, a babe?"

The context is Mary returning to her people with the baby Jesus. Shocked, they essentially accuse her of adultery, and she points to Him in His cradle.

> 30. [Whereupon] He [the infant] spoke out: "I am indeed a servant of Allah. He has given me the Book and has appointed me a Prophet.
>
> 31. "And He has made me blessed wheresoever I may be and has commanded me to pray and to give charity to the poor as long as I live.

32. "And [He] has made me dutiful to my mother and has not made me oppressive, wicked.

33. "So peace be upon me the day I was born, the day that I die, and the day that I shall be raised up to life [again]."

This is the one time in the whole Qur'an where Jesus speaks in an identifiable physical location. That is, on all other occasions we have no idea from where He speaks. In essence, elsewhere Jesus is a disembodied voice, but in this instance we have some idea where He is—in His cradle!

Later we will discuss this story having originated outside the Qur'an.[2] In its original form, Jesus claims to be the Son of God, but in this Islamic version, He says He is a prophet. The text (v. 33) uses the very same language Surah 19:15 uses of John the Baptist. Why is this relevant? Because Muslims, based on a particular interpretation of Surah 4:157, deny that Jesus died on the cross. In fact, most believe He was taken up to heaven without dying at all. So when Jesus is quoted, speaking of the day of His death in the very same language as John the Baptist, who died (he was beheaded), it is difficult to harmonize the divergent statements.

34. Such was Jesus, the son of Mary; a statement of the truth about which they [vainly] dispute.

35. It is not befitting to [the majesty of] Allah that He should beget a son. Transcendent is He! When He determines a matter, He only says to it: "Be!" and it is.

36. [And Jesus had declared]: "Assuredly Allah is my Lord and your Lord. Therefore serve Him. That is the Straight Path."

37. Then the sects differed among themselves [concerning Jesus] so woe to those who disbelieve when they witness a Formidable Day [the Day of Judgment]. On that day when they will appear before Us, how clearly will they see and hear; but transgressors are this day in manifest deviation.

Just after presenting an ahistorical event of Him speaking from His cradle, the text proclaims the pointlessness of disputing this true claim about Jesus, Son of Mary (rather than of God), and again asserts that Allah is above having a son, a concept related to the idea of his transcendence *and* to the rejection of "offspring" as a possibility for him.

Surah 6:85 lists Jesus along with Zechariah, John, and Elias and notes he was "of the virtuous." But then the Qur'an makes this interesting observation:

> 87. With some of their forefathers and their offspring and brethren; and We chose them and guided them to a straight path.
>
> 88. Such is the guidance of Allah with which He guides whom He will of His servants. But if they had associated anything with Him, [everything] they did would have been vain.

If Jesus or any of the others had engaged in the sin of *shirk*, everything "they did would have been vain." Jesus' status as "mere" messenger is reinforced. A somewhat similar theme is struck in *Surah Ash-Shura* (42:13):

> He has ordained for you the same Way of Religion He had enjoined on Noah, and that We have now revealed to you, and which We had already enjoined on Abraham and Moses and Jesus, saying: "Establish the Religion and be not divided in it." Dreadful for the polytheists is that to which you are calling them. Allah chooses for Himself whom He will, and guides to His way only him who turns to Him in repentance.

Jesus is one of the messengers Allah sent with the singular message of monotheism. He may have been virgin-born, worked miracles, even raised the dead, but the Qur'an's message is that on the level of being, He was a messenger just like Abraham and Moses and the others.

Surah 43 contains an extended and intriguing section with somewhat confusing references to Jesus:

57. And when the son of Mary is given as an example, your people turn away,

58. And say: "Are our gods better or is he?" They say so only in idle argument, they are but argumentative people.

59. He is nothing but a slave whom We made an example for the Children of Israel.

60. Had We so willed, We could have set among you angels to succeed each other in the earth.

61. And [the second coming of Jesus shall be] a sign of the Hour, therefore, do not have any doubt about it, and follow Me. This is a straight path.

62. And let not the Devil turn you away; he is an open enemy for you.

63. And when Jesus came with clear proofs, he said: "I have brought wisdom to you, and have come to clarify to you some of those things in which you differ, so fear Allah and obey me.

64. "Allah is my Lord and your Lord. So worship Him. This is a straight path."

65. But the factions among them differed. So woe to the unjust from the torment of a painful Day.

Many Christians are shocked to learn that Islam has a doctrine of the second coming of Jesus. It most assuredly does—in fact, Islamic eschatological speculation is more popular in many Islamic lands than similar speculation among Christians is in non-Islamic nations. Of course, in certain such systems, Christ's return is part of a larger scheme, never the central aspect as in Christian belief. The Messiah returns as a Muslim and prays with the Muslim armies.[3] His task, according to the *hadith*, is summed up here:

Narrated Abu Huraira: Allah's Apostle said, "By Him in Whose Hands my soul is, son of Mary (Jesus) will shortly descend amongst you people (Muslims) as a just ruler and will break the cross and kill the pig and abolish the Jizya (a tax taken from the non-Muslims who are in the protection of the Muslim government). Then there will be abundance of money and nobody will accept charitable gifts."[4]

A number of other *ahadith* give tantalizing details about what Jesus would do, other than breaking the cross and killing the pig (both items of detestation, the accusation that Christians worship the cross, for example, being a common element of early Muslim polemics), and these have provided fallow ground for a wide variety of speculative theories about what the future holds. But these go well beyond what is found in the Qur'an.

We also have here another quotation of Jesus, and once again it is mainly without a context. Where was Jesus when He said this? To whom was it said? When? We are not told. But note that the range of topics addressed by Jesus in the Qur'an is very, very narrow. We would like to know what wisdom is referred to here that can clarify differences, but that wisdom is not presented.

Another text that seems to transcend the later orthodox Islamic view of Christ is found in Surah 21:91:

And she who guarded her chastity, so We breathed into her of Our spirit, and We made her and her son a sign for all people.

The idea of Jesus and Mary being a "sign" is continued in Surah 23:50:

And We made the son of Mary and his mother as a sign to mankind, and We gave them refuge on a height, where there was a hollow and a spring.

Al-Baqarah, the longest Surah (2), contains a number of assertions about Jesus. Below, note that "the Angel Gabriel" is an insertion. The text actually says Jesus was strengthened with the Holy Spirit, which Muslims today understand as Gabriel:

> 2:87. And We gave Moses the Book [Torah], and after him We sent Messenger after Messenger. We gave Jesus son of Mary the clear signs and strengthened him with the Holy Spirit [the Angel Gabriel]. Is it so, that whenever a Messenger whose message does not suit your desires comes to you, you grow arrogant, denying some of them, and slaying others?

This and the following citation are similar in emphasizing the lineage of prophets from Moses through Jesus, and, very significantly, on through to Muhammad. Do not miss this important thrust of the text.

> 2:135. They say: "Be Jews or Christians, and you will be rightly-guided." Say [O Muhammad]: "Rather the religion of Abraham, the upright, and he was not of the idolaters."
>
> 136. Say [O Muslims]: "We believe in Allah and that which is sent down to us, and in what was sent down to Abraham, Ishmael, Isaac, Jacob, and the Tribes; what was given to Moses and Jesus and what was given to the Prophets by their Lord. We make no distinction between any of them, and to Him we have surrendered ourselves."
>
> 137. If they believe in what you believe, they shall be rightly-guided; yet if they reject it, they shall surely be in discord. Allah will suffice you [for defense] against them. He is the Hearing, the Knowing.

Note again the claim that Muslims believe in "what was given to Moses and Jesus." Muslims are not to make distinction "between any of them" (the aforementioned prophets, we would assume, or the revelations given to them).

> 2:253. These are the Messengers. We have exalted some above others. To some Allah spoke directly; others He raised in degree.

> We gave Jesus son of Mary clear signs, and strengthened him with the Holy Spirit [the archangel Gabriel]. Had Allah so willed, those who succeeded them would not have fought against one another after the clear signs had come to them. But they disagreed among themselves; some believed, and others did not. Yet had Allah willed, they would not have fought against one another; but Allah does what He will.

This text, other than reiterating previous themes, likewise insists that Allah could have united all the followers of Jesus, but evidently chose not to.

Without question, *Surah Al Imran* (3) contains the heart of the Qur'an's discussion of Jesus, His disciples, His mission, etc. As we noted in chapter 4, many early commentators connected this section to the encounter between Muhammad and the Najran Christians (though we cannot be sure of any details, or if it happened).

> 3:45. When the angels said: "O Mary! Allah gives the *glad* tidings of a word from Him, whose name is the Messiah, Jesus, son of Mary, illustrious in this world and the Hereafter, and one of those who shall be brought near [to Allah]. He will speak to mankind in his cradle and in his manhood, and he is of the righteous."

Ironically, the incident of Jesus speaking from His cradle, which, as we will later document,[5] is derived from ahistorical sources from the preceding centuries, is made an incident that was prophesied before its occurrence in this text!

> 47. She said: "My Lord! How can I have a child, when no man has touched me?" He replied: "Such is the will of Allah. He creates what He will. When He decrees a thing He only says: 'Be!' and it is."

This is the key text to understand in relationship to the Islamic understanding of how Jesus is the "word of Allah." The idea is that Allah spoke the word, "Be," and Jesus came into existence without the necessity of a human father.

48. And he will teach him the Book and the wisdom, and the Torah and the Gospel.

49. And will make him a Messenger to the Children of Israel. He will say: "I bring you a sign from your Lord. From clay I will make for you the likeness of a bird; I shall breathe into it and it shall become a [living] bird, by Allah's leave. I shall give sight to the blind, heal the leper, and raise the dead to life, by Allah's leave. I shall tell you what you eat and what you store up in your houses. Surely that will be a sign for you, if you are believers."

The list of miracles Jesus will perform, some found in the New Testament books, some in later sources, is meant to comprise a singular sign to all true believers. But do not pass over the *limitation* of His ministry. Allah "will make him a Messenger to the Children of Israel." Jesus is not called to be savior, or lord, or anything other than a messenger to a specific people, Israel.

50. [I come] To confirm the Torah that has already been revealed, and to make lawful to you some of the things you were forbidden. I bring a sign to you from your Lord. So fear Him, and obey me.

51. Allah is my Lord and your Lord; so worship Him. That is the Straight Path.

Once again, words are attributed to Jesus about which history never speaks. No first-, second-, third-, fourth-, or fifth-century source provides substantiation that any follower or enemy of Jesus ever heard Him speak in this fashion. But the Muslim understanding is that no such historical foundation is needed for lengthy portions of narrative for its words to be true. This is the Qur'an. It has been preserved. For the large majority, that ends the discussion, even when the same believers will then embrace historical criticism to question the value of His words in the Gospels, which were recorded within the lifetimes of the eyewitnesses of His ministry!

> 52. When Jesus became aware of their disbelief he said: "Who will be my helpers toward Allah?" The disciples said: "We are Allah's helpers. We believe in Allah; and bear you witness that we have surrendered [ourselves to Him]!"
>
> 53. "Our Lord! We believe in that which You have revealed, and we follow him whom You have sent. Account us among those who are witnesses."

This text is foundational to the Islamic belief that Jesus' original and true disciples were Muslims, in the sense that they were submitted to Allah.

> 54. And they [the disbelievers] schemed, and Allah schemed; and Allah is the best of schemers.

This text is often cited as evidence of some kind of dishonesty on Allah's part, but the honest reader recognizes that just as God sent a lying spirit into the mouths of false prophets as a means by which He brought just punishment on those who rebelled against Him (1 Kings 22:23), and just as the New Testament warns that those who refuse to love the truth will be caused to love a lie (2 Thessalonians 2:10–11), this text could well be saying that when people scheme against Allah and his ways, they will find Allah is significantly better at that activity than they are.

> 55. [And remember] When Allah said: "O Jesus! I am gathering you and raising you to Me, and cleansing you of those who disbelieve, and setting those who follow you above those who disbelieve until the Day of Resurrection. Then to Me you will all return, and I shall judge between you as to that in which you used to differ."

This is a *very* important text to note. The normative meaning of the Arabic is that the phrase "I am gathering you" should be rendered, "I will cause you to die," and in fact this is the translation of Muhammad Asad. The reason most translations use a strange and oblique wording is due to Surah 4:157 and its denial of the crucifixion, a topic we will take up in chapter 7.

The second item to note is the promise: Allah says he will "cleanse" Jesus of "those who disbelieve," evidently the disbelievers of *ayah* 54. The result? Allah will set "those who follow you above those who disbelieve until the Day of Resurrection." As *ayah* 56 will indicate, the disbelievers are doomed to hell. There are a number of possible interpretations of these words. One suggestion is that this actually refers to the Muslims, while the self-identifying Christians are the actual unbelievers; this leads to the idea that the Muslims will be "above those who disbelieve until the Day of Resurrection." Others say there are honest, believing Christians, and dishonest, unbelieving Christians, and that Jesus will judge between them at His return, an idea that gets some support from Surah 5:82:

> You will find the most vehement of men in enmity to those who believe [to be] the Jews and the idolaters. And you will find the nearest of them in affection to those who believe [to be] those who say: "We are Christians." That is because there are among them priests and monks, and because they are not proud.

However, if there is a consistent context in this portion,[6] and if in fact some kind of encounter between Muhammad and Christians is in view (especially see *ayah* 61, below), it would be hard to interpret this text as teaching that any Christians, at least orthodox ones, would be made superior to disbelievers until the day of judgment.

> 3:59. The likeness of Jesus with Allah is as the likeness of Adam. He created him of dust, then He said to him: "Be!" and he was.

60. This is the truth from your Lord, so do not be of those who waver.

Again, these *ayat* are directly related to the encounter between Muhammad and the Christians of Najran. At the least, they are meant to give a positive Islamic teaching on the issue of Jesus and to deny His exaltation. He is made to be the parallel to Adam, a created being, not the eternal Son taught by the Christians. Of course, rather than arguing for this from the relevant scriptural texts that even the Qur'an says were sent down from Allah, here divine authority is called upon: "This is the truth from your Lord." To question these words is to reject divine revelation itself.

61. And those who dispute with you concerning him [Jesus], after the knowledge which has come to you, say [to them]: "Come! Let us summon our sons and your sons, and our women and your women, and ourselves and yourselves, then beseech [Allah] to send the curse of Allah upon those who lie."

Having announced what the author clearly sees as a final refutation of the Christian position by asserting Jesus (like all men) is a creation of Allah, the Qur'an then calls upon those who would dispute this proclamation to enter into a mutual agreement, calling down the curse of God upon those who lie. This is the content of the dispute:

62. This is indeed the true account [about the mother of Jesus]. There is no deity but Allah, and He is the August, the Wise.

63. And if they turn away, Allah is Aware of the corrupters.

64. Say: "O People of the Book! Come to an agreement between us and you, that we shall worship none but Allah, that we shall assign no partner to Him, and that none of us shall take others for lords beside Allah." If they turn away, then say: "Bear witness that we are those who surrender [to Allah]."

If the Christians dispute the Qur'an's assertion (and in the process become guilty of polytheism, as understood by the author), they are "corrupters," evidently of the truth just revealed. The People of the Book are called to an agreement renouncing *shirk*, which again the Qur'an assumes is involved in the doctrine of the Trinity. If they refuse, they will not be *muslimin*, those who submit to God, Muslims. This very same theme repeats a few *ayat* later:

> 3:83. Are they [the Christians and Jews] seeking a religion other than the religion of Allah when all that is in the heavens and earth submits to Him, willingly or unwillingly, and they will be returned to Him?
>
> 84. Say [O Muhammad]: "We believe in Allah and that which was sent down to us and that which was sent down to Abraham and Ishmael and Isaac and Jacob and the tribes; and that which was given to Moses and Jesus and the Prophets from their Lord. We make no distinction between any of them, and to Him we have surrendered."
>
> 85. He who seeks a religion other than Islam, it will not be accepted from him, and he will be a loser in the Hereafter.

The exclusive nature of Islam's claims is clearly set forth in direct address to Christians. Allah will not accept "a religion other than Islam," for there has been a consistent line of revelation from Moses through Jesus to Muhammad.[7]

A brief mention in Surah 33:7 again places Jesus in the line of prophets: "We took from the prophets their pact, and from you [O Muhammad] and from Noah and Abraham and Moses and Jesus son of Mary."

As we will see in chapter 7, when we examine it closely, the next text in chronological order, Surah 4:156–159, is vitally important. The only *ayah* in the Qur'an denying the death of

Jesus, Surah 4:157, is the source of one of the major conflicts between Christians and Muslims.

Surah 4:163 again lists Jesus with the prophets, and we already have examined 4:171–172 and its command against "excess" in one's religion.

Surah 57 contains an interesting comment regarding the Qur'an's view of Christians:

> 26. And We sent down Noah and Abraham, and bestowed on their offspring prophethood and the Book. Some were rightly-guided, but many were corrupt.
>
> 27. Then We sent Our Messengers to follow in their footsteps; and We made Jesus, son of Mary, to follow, and gave him the Gospel, and placed compassion and mercy in the hearts of those who followed him. But monasticism they invented—We did not ordain it for them—seeking Allah's pleasure, and they observed it not with right observance. So We gave those of them who believed their reward, but many of them were corrupt.

While there is a certain ambivalence in this text, surely there are few other groups for which the Qur'an has such positive words. Allah placed "compassion and mercy" in the hearts of the followers of Jesus. Some of them are called believers who receive their reward; others are called corrupt.

We will look closely at Surah 61:6 in chapter 9, for it is one of the key texts presenting the idea of prophecies about Muhammad in the Bible. For now, the same *surah* contains this very important *ayah*:

> 61:14. O believers! Be Allah's helpers. When Jesus son of Mary said to the disciples: "Who will come with me to the help of Allah?" The disciples said: "We are Allah's helpers." And a party of the Children of Israel believed, while a party disbelieved. Then We strengthened those who believed against their foe, and they became the uppermost.

What does it mean that those "of the Children of Israel" who believed in Jesus "became uppermost" in regard to those who did not? Is this related to Surah 3:55 (above)? Hard to say, but it presents an intriguing promise that some have found inconsistent with other texts relating to the People of the Book.

The next section in chronological order would encompass the materials we examined from Surah 5 (in chapter 4) concerning the exhortations to the People of the Book not to say "three" or engage in excess. Hence, 5:15–19, 72–78, and 116–117 already have been presented and will not be repeated here. Surah 5:44 and following will be examined in chapter 8, so we will not repeat it here. We will examine 5:110 and its use of preexisting materials relating to Jesus and the clay birds in chapter 10. The next section, then, involves the strange story of the table sent down from Allah:

112. When the disciples said: "O Jesus son of Mary! Is your Lord able to send down for us a table-spread [with food] from Heaven?"[8] He said: "Fear Allah, if you are true believers!"

113. They said: "We wish to eat from it, that we may satisfy our hearts and know that you have told us the truth, and that we may be witnesses of it [the miracle]."

114. Jesus son of Mary, said: "O Allah, our Lord! Send down for us a table-spread [with food] from Heaven, that it may be a feast for us, for the first of us and the last of us, and a sign from You. Give us provision, for you are the Best of Providers."

115. Allah said: "I will send it down for you. But if any of you disbelieves afterward, him I will surely punish with a torment such as I have never inflicted on any other creature."

This story of obscure origin has no real connection to the historical Gospels. Some see this as a test by the disciples, others as a mere request, possibly related to other miracle stories related to food and sustenance (such as the feeding of the five thousand, or even the Last Supper). In any case, it precedes the key text, already examined, of 5:116–117.

The last thing said about Jesus (chronologically) may well be the most troubling, at least in the context of our ever more violent world. Found in one of the final *surahs*, its context is one of the Qur'an's most-cited texts:

> 9:28. O you who believe! The polytheists are impure, therefore, let them not approach the Sacred Mosque after this year of theirs [has ended]. If you fear poverty Allah will enrich you through His bounty if He will. Allah is Knowing, Wise.
>
> 9:29. Fight against those from among the People of the Book who do not believe in Allah nor the Last Day; who do not forbid what Allah and His Messenger have forbidden, and who do not adopt the religion of truth; until they pay the tribute out of hand, utterly subdued.
>
> 30. The Jews say Uzayr is the son of Allah, and the Christians say the Messiah is the son of Allah. Such is what they say with their own mouths, imitating those who disbelieved of old. May Allah defeat them! How perverse they are!
>
> 31. They have made their rabbis and their monks and the Messiah the son of Mary into lords besides Allah; though they were only ordered to worship one god. There is no god but He! Transcendent is He above what they associate [with Him].

Everything in this text is troubling. The polytheists are *najas*, literally unclean, detestable,[9] and to this day are excluded from Mecca and its environs. Muslims are to fight (go to war with) those Jews and Christians who do not believe in Allah or the last day and who, evidently, do not follow the rules laid down by Muhammad and refuse to submit to Islam. The end of this fighting is their subjugation, i.e., so that they pay the poll tax (*jizyah*), which shows their *dhimmitude* to the Muslim state. Our translation says they are to be "utterly subdued," but the word also is rendered "brought low," "feel themselves subdued," and "are in a state of subjection."[10]

The term is *Iblis*, used of Satan himself in Surah 7:13, where he is said to be "of the debased." Then the text identifies the Christian claim that Messiah is God's Son as disbelief, perversity, and a reason for their defeat (though we have yet to find any evidence that the Qur'an's author understood what that assertion means). Even if some tiny group of Jews *had* made such a statement about Uzayr, it neither would represent all Jews nor be a sound basis of accusation against them. The final *ayah* makes the direct accusation of *shirk* against both Jews and Christians.

The Vital Issue of Intercession

Before moving on, it is useful for the Christian reader to grasp something of the Islamic view of Muhammad in comparison to what was just reviewed from the Qur'an in reference to Jesus, son of Mary. Though the majority of this material is drawn from outside the Qur'an, it remains relevant to our task. Once you claim your revelation is consistent with what has come before, but then eviscerate the central message of that preceding Scripture (in this case, Christ's coming, Saviorhood, and intercessory work), you've dug out a void that must be filled. After reducing Jesus to mortal messenger, you are still left with a holy God, a holy law, and human sinfulness. Christianity presents a mediator, one who provides the way for a holy God to redeem and then have relationship with sinful people. God's wrath and holiness meet His mercy and grace in the unique person of Jesus the Messiah. But Muhammad did not understand this message, and, in fact, rejected it, so what happens then?

The prophet of Islam is exalted to fill the void left by the diminishment of Jesus. This is true not only of various sects that have gone outside Islamic orthodoxy in exalting Muhammad but also is seen clearly within orthodox Islam as well. One need only peruse a popular book like the *Ash-Shifa* of *Qadi 'Iyad* (*Muhammad: Messenger of Allah*) to see the trend.[11] It seems inevitable, given human nature. But here one finds the foundation for this exaltation in the early generations of the faith. Though the Qur'an seems to deny that Muhammad performed miracles, the Qur'an being the only miracle men needed to affirm his prophethood,[12] the succeeding generations produced an entire host of supposed miracles that found their way into the *hadith*.[13]

This leads us to our focus at this point, that of intercession. The New Testament places much attention on this aspect of Jesus' heavenly ministry.[14] But for Him to appear in the Father's presence in place of His people requires Him to be more than a mere prophet, and the Qur'an has denied Him that status. So we encounter, in primitive Islamic teaching, the concept of the intercession of Muhammad. It is of two forms, a lesser and a greater.

We had reason earlier to note the "lesser," related to Abu Talib, uncle of Muhammad, having died without embracing Islam. Precluded from praying for his parents, who likewise died as *mushrikim*, in the state of *shirk*, but in this one instance Muhammad was granted the privilege of interceding. Abu Talib not only had helped raise him but also greatly protected him during the first period of his prophethood. According to several *ahadith*,[15] as a result of the intercession, Abu Talib has the best spot in the hellfire (the place of least punishment). Details vary: In some versions he stands in shallow fire only up to his ankles; in others he must wear sandals of fire. The consistent element is that the fire is so hot that, even in hell's least torturous spot, "his brains boil."

The far more important "greater" intercession speaks directly to a parallel between the Christian teaching about Christ and a role imputed to Muhammad in Islamic thought. Once again, versions differ in the amount of detail they contain. In fact, this story is found in a *hadith Qudsi*, which, remember, has a special authority due to conveying words spoken by Allah. But it appears in almost all the reliable collections, making it, for all intents and purposes, unquestionable. It is lengthy, yet well worth close attention:

Narrated Abu Huraira: Some (cooked) meat was brought to Allah Apostle and the meat of a forearm was presented to him as he used to like it. He ate a morsel of it and said, "I will be the chief of all the people on the Day of Resurrection. Do you know the reason for it? Allah will gather all the human being of early generations as well as late generation on one plain so that the announcer will be able to make them all-hear his voice and the watcher will be able to see all of them. The sun will come so close to the people that they will suffer such distress and trouble as they will not be able to bear or stand. Then the people will say, 'Don't you see to what state you have reached? Won't you look for someone who can intercede for you with your Lord?' Some people will say to some others, 'Go to Adam.' So they will go to Adam and say to him. 'You are the father of mankind; Allah created you with His Own Hand, and breathed into you of His Spirit (meaning the spirit which he created for you); and ordered the angels to prostrate before you; so (please) intercede for us with your Lord. Don't you see in what state we are? Don't you see what condition we have reached?' Adam will say, 'Today my Lord has become angry as He has never become before, nor will ever become thereafter. He forbade me (to eat of the fruit of) the tree, but I disobeyed Him . . . Myself! Myself! Myself! (has more need for intercession). Go to someone else; go to Noah.' So they will go to Noah and say (to him), 'O Noah! You are the first (of Allah's Messengers) to the people of the earth, and Allah has named you a thankful slave; please intercede for us with your Lord. Don't you see in what state we are?' He will say, 'Today my Lord has become angry as He has never become nor will ever become thereafter. I had (in the world) the right to make one definitely accepted invocation, and I made it against my nation. Myself! Myself! Myself! Go to someone else; go to Abraham.' They will go to Abraham and say, 'O Abraham! You are Allah's Apostle and His Khalil from among the people of the earth; so please intercede for us with your Lord. Don't you see in what state we are?' He will say to them, 'My Lord has today become angry as He has never become before, nor will ever become thereafter. I had told three lies (Abu Haiyan [the sub-narrator] mentioned them in the Hadith). Myself! Myself! Myself! Go to someone else; go to Moses.' The people will then go to Moses and say, 'O Moses! You are Allah's Apostle and Allah gave you superiority above the others with this message and with His direct Talk to you; (please) intercede for us with your Lord. Don't you see in what state we are?' Moses will say, 'My Lord has today become angry as He has never become before, nor will become thereafter, I killed a person whom I had not been ordered to kill. Myself! Myself! Myself! Go to someone else; go to Jesus.' So they will go to Jesus and say, 'O Jesus! You are Allah's Apostle and His Word which He sent to Mary, and a superior soul created by Him, and you talked to the people while still young in the cradle. Please intercede for us with your Lord. Don't you see in what state we are?' Jesus will say. 'My Lord has today become angry as He has never become before nor will ever become thereafter.' Jesus will not mention any sin, but will say, 'Myself! Myself! Myself! Go to someone else; go to Muhammad.' So they will come to me and say, 'O Muhammad! You are Allah's Apostle and the last of the prophets, and Allah forgave your early and late sins. (Please) intercede for us with your Lord. Don't you see in what state we are?'" The Prophet added, "Then I will go beneath Allah's Throne and fall in prostration before my Lord. And then Allah will guide me to such praises and glorification to Him as He has never guided anybody else before me. Then it will be said, 'O Muhammad, Raise your head. Ask, and it will be granted. Intercede. It (your intercession) will be accepted.' So I will raise my head and say, 'My followers, O my Lord! My followers, O my Lord.' It will be said, 'O Muhammad! Let those of your followers who have no accounts, enter through such a gate of the gates of Paradise as lies on the right; and they will share the other gates with the people.'" The Prophet further said, "By Him in Whose Hand my soul is, the distance between every two gate-posts of Paradise is like the distance between Mecca and Busra (in Sham)."[16]

Another version has an important addition at the story's end, beginning with Muhammad's actual act of intercession, and it touches on the results thereof:

Then I shall intercede and He will set me a limit [as to the number of people], so I shall admit them into Paradise. Then I shall return to Him, and when I shall see my Lord [I shall bow down] as before. Then I shall intercede and He will set me a limit [as to the number of people]. So I shall admit them into Paradise. Then I shall return for a third time, then a fourth, and I shall say: There remains in Hell-fire only those whom the Qur'an has confined and who must be there for eternity. There shall come out of Hell-fire he who has said: There is no god but Allah and who has in his heart goodness weighing a barley-corn; then there shall come out of Hell-fire he who has said: There is no god but Allah and who has in his heart goodness weighing a grain of wheat; then there shall come out of Hell-fire he who has said: There is no god but Allah and who has in his heart goodness weighing an atom.[17]

The story is fascinating in many respects. As mankind goes to various figures, seeking an intercessor in the day of God's wrath and judgment, the responses are telling. Adam, Noah, Abraham, and Moses recount sins committed and hence decline the call, saying it is not for them to intercede. But Jesus mentions no sin.

Ironically, in the *hadith Qudsi* version, He says, "Go to Muhammad, a servant to whom Allah has forgiven all his wrongdoing, past and future." No sin on His own behalf, but He does mention Muhammad's, and its forgiveness! Still, in each version, Jesus says it is not for Him to undertake this intercession, in direct contradiction to the biblical teaching.

Muhammad does accept the people's pleas. He goes before Allah and is taught a new way of worship. In the fuller version, he intercedes either three or four times. Each time part of his Ummah, his people, are removed from the hellfire. This, of course, raises the debate, even among Muslims, as to whether all Muslims or only some will enter for a time into hellfire. That issue aside those removed first are those with the most *iman* (faith), and then those with less and less, until the last ones removed have but an atom of goodness. This does seem to raise the possibility that one could confess the *Shahada* and still be left in hellfire if not even an atom of goodness is in his heart. But in any case, they are rescued through Muhammad's special, unique intercession on their behalf. "So I shall admit them into Paradise" are his own words, at least as recorded by the *hadith*. This is vitally important to remember, for the same story records Jesus declining the call of intercession. Instead He is said to direct men to Muhammad, a clear apologetic argument from the earliest Islamic generations.

Notes

1. The simplest reading of the text leads one to conclude the author was confused as to the family relationships of Moses, Miriam, Mary, et al., but one possibility is that the "confusion" actually is purposeful, connected with the concept of a "family" of Messengers, all related to one another. The wide range of concepts is beyond the scope of our study here.

2. See the discussion in chapter 11.

3. See *Sahih Muslim*, 1348.

4. *Sahih Al-Bukhari*, 1:425.

5. See chapter 11.

6. That is, if this entire section was given as a whole, then we must interpret it all as a unit, if possible. But if it was given over a period of time in different contexts, this could explain its choppiness and the difficulty of following a single thread through its entire length.

7. For a fuller discussion of this theme as it appears in Surah 5:44ff. and its relevance to the claims of the Qur'an, see chapter 8.

8. For an interesting modern example of scholarly Islamic commentators acknowledging and struggling with variant readings in the Arabic text, see the commentary on this phrase in Muhammad Asad, *The Message of the Qur'an* (Bristol, England: 2003), 9, 193–194, fn. 137.

9. Some Westernized Muslims who do not believe Christians are *mushrikim* (idolaters) base their conclusions on a related argument. Some say that because Muslim men are allowed to marry Christian women (Surah 5:5), Christian women cannot be *najas* (unclean). But others say this can only apply to Christian women who believe (i.e., in Muhammad, i.e., embrace Islam; due to such as 2:221; 24:62; 60:10). Numerous *ahadith* statements substantiate the early Islamic view as being that Christians are *mushrikim*, e.g., in *Sahih Al-Bukhari* 7:209: "Allah has made it unlawful for the believers to marry ladies who ascribe partners in worship to Allah, and I do not know of a greater thing, as regards to ascribing partners in worship, etc. to Allah, than that a lady should say that Jesus is her Lord although he is just one of Allah's slaves."

10. Pickthall; Ali and Hilali-Khan; and Shakir, respectively.

11. Qadi 'Iyad Ibn Musa al-Yahsubi, *Muhammad: Messenger of Allah, Ash-Shifa of Qadi 'Iyad* trans. Aisha Bewley (Inverness, Scotland: Madinah, 2008). See also Annemarie Schimmel, *And Muhammad Is His Messenger: The Veneration of the Prophet in Islamic Piety* (Chapel Hill: University of North Carolina Press, 1985), which contains an entire chapter on the intercession of Muhammad.

12. See, for example, Surat 2:118, 145; 6:37, 109; 10:20; 11:2; 13:7, 27; 17:59.

13. For an early example, see the list provided by Ali Tabiri in defense of Muhammad against Christian charges on this issue in *The Early Christian-Muslim Dialogue: A Collection of Documents from the First Three Islamic Centuries (AD 632–900)*, 591–596.

14. See Romans 8:32–34; Hebrews 7, 9–10.

15. Such as *Sahih Al-Bukhari*, 5:222, 224–225.

16. *Sahih Al-Bukhari*, 6:236.

17. *Hadith Qudsi 36*, www.iium.edu.my/deed/hadith/other/hadithqudsi.html #hadith36.

6

The Qur'an and the Cross

Television has ruined the historical perspective of most people in the modern age. We do history now with our eyes. We watch events unfold even as they happen and figure that is how it has always been.

But such is not the case. Eyewitness testimony was a rarity in the ancient world. There were no 24/7 news services, no video cameras, no MP3 players.

There also was no Internet, no newspapers, and the few libraries were widely scattered and filled with hand-copied texts that were far too liable to the ravages of time, water, insects, mold, and, most often, fire. When news of a great event did come to a city—say, of a battle only a few hundred miles away—usually it came days, even weeks after the event itself. And even then the news would be spread primarily by word of mouth, with the inevitable alterations that come due to the vagaries of human memory and context.

The vast majority of what we know about ancient history arrives through two primary means: written documents and archaeological evidence. The two working together give us our knowledge of what has taken place in the distant past. Only in relatively recent times has the historian had access to images, widely distributed written materials, and the like to obtain a much more complete picture of events.

What this also means is that the vast majority of human events and happenings have passed from our collective memory. There are no newspaper archives from antiquity. Almost all the humans who have ever lived on this planet are unknown to us today. We know they lived only because we live and had to have had ancestors! Who they were, what they did, we have no idea.

It is a simple fact of history that most of the human race, up to only a few centuries ago, lived and died in obscurity without leaving any documentable proof of their existence. Those who do genealogical research well know that one eventually comes to a point where records cease and there is legendary material, oral traditions, and then eventually, nothing at all. It is not that the ravages of time have erased the records, but that there *were* no records. Unless you happened to sneak into one of the few histories written in the century in which you lived (if one was written that was relevant to *where* you lived) via some daring feat in battle, etc., chances are you would live and die without leaving any discoverable trace. Of nearly all human beings in antiquity, we know they were there but know next to nothing about them *as individuals*.

We must keep these facts in mind when we address the issue of events in ancient history, and now, the specific event of the crucifixion of Jesus the Messiah. Today there are skeptics who even question His very existence, often demanding modern-level documentation of His life and activities. Of course, if consistently applied to all figures of the past, this would mean we cannot affirm the existence of almost anyone in the ancient world. These hyper-skeptics are rightly relegated to the fringes of the scholarly world.

But what of the crucifixion? When we come to this pivotal event in the life and ministry of Jesus, what evidence do we have that it took place? And, one might ask, what does any of this have to do with the Qur'an? It has great relevance, for this historical event is one of the single most useful tests of the Qur'an's accuracy and validity—a test found within its own pages! But before turning to its claims, let us establish the situation as it stood when Muhammad of Mecca first claimed prophethood.

The Crucifixion in History

"That he was crucified is as sure as anything historical can ever be, since both Josephus and Tacitus . . . agree with the Christian accounts on at least that basic fact." So wrote John Dominic Crossan in *Jesus: A Revolutionary Biography*.[1] Crossan, considered the leading "historical Jesus" scholar, takes a radical stance on most of Jesus' life and was co-founder, with atheist Robert Funk (to whom his book was dedicated), of the infamous "Jesus Seminar," a collection of furthest-to-the-left scholars who became famous for voting on the authenticity of Jesus' teachings with colored marbles. Crossan suggests Jesus was crucified, taken down, buried in a shallow grave, and later dug up and eaten by dogs. His is a thoroughly naturalistic stance, as he surely is not approaching the matter from an orthodox, or historical, Christian perspective. And yet despite his skepticism, he is compelled to conclude that the fact of the crucifixion itself "is as sure as anything historical can ever be."

Bart Ehrman, agnostic former Christian, also is clear on the topic. Ehrman has written in defense of the historical existence of a man named Jesus. Though even his defense is a backhanded attack on the orthodox faith,[2] in his course titled "The Historical Jesus" he notes, regarding the crucifixion, "One of the most certain facts of history is that Jesus was crucified on orders of the Roman prefect of Judea, Pontius Pilate."[3]

Why would these opponents of orthodox Christianity, naturalists both in methodology and outlook, come to the conclusion that the crucifixion of a Jewish rabbi in the backwaters of the Roman Empire comprises one of the past's most unassailable facts? The answer is simple: For anyone willing to let the facts speak for themselves, the evidence is overwhelming. Only those with a preconceived position to defend (e.g., radical skeptics and atheists, who deny Jesus' existence, or Muslims who follow the Qur'an's teachings) deny it.

We need to define, briefly, what "overwhelming evidence" means. There are no video recordings of the event. No unbiased journalists filed a report with the Jerusalem bureau of a major news organization. But if we keep in mind how ancient history is done, how it is sourced, we can easily discern why even honest skeptics confess the reality of the crucifixion.

The New Testament Documents Are Strong Evidence

The earliest pages of the New Testament were written within a few years of the events of Jesus' life. Paul's epistles take us back into the first century's fifth decade, less than twenty years after the crucifixion, and there is no question whatsoever that he knew of, and wrote in light of, that historical event. Not only do his letters demonstrate that by the time of writing—from the late AD 40s to possibly the early 60s—the crucifixion had become a central theme in Christian belief,[4] but they also clearly indicate the sources from which even Paul derived his knowledge of it. In writing to the church at Corinth, the apostle said this:

> I passed on to you most importantly what I also had received, namely, that Christ died for our sins in accordance with the Scriptures, and that He was buried, and that He was raised up on the third day in accordance with the Scriptures, and that he was seen by Cephas (Peter) and then the twelve.[5]

If Paul received this witness from others, then not only is he not the source of the teaching about the crucifixion (a common modern Islamic claim), but the source is to be found earlier than Paul. To be earlier is to be an eyewitness, for he is as early as one can be without having been at the foot of the cross itself. And of course that is exactly what conservative Christians claim for the Gospels, which give us the majority of information about the crucifixion.

But even adopting a liberal stance on the dating of the Gospels does not do away with the reality that the source for the New Testament witness to the crucifixion is eyewitness testimony contemporaneous with the event. For those who know ancient history, that is amazing and compelling. Most of ancient history is derived from later and secondary sources. The New Testament's view is tremendously early and hence, tremendously weighty.

Many modern writers dismiss these documents due to their "religious nature," displaying woeful ignorance. *A large portion of ancient writings are religious in nature, and without them we would know very little about the events of antiquity.* Roman historians worshiped multiple gods, yet we do not dismiss their histories on that basis. Likewise, the New Testament writers speak of historical events, including the crucifixion. They tell us where, and when, and even why, with specific names and dates and places, and as such are incredibly valuable as historical records. Anyone who dismisses ancient records because their writers were not secular humanists without professed bias (a glaring example of self-deception in itself) and without a modern (though rarely observed) code of journalistic neutrality, will find they have no sources left from which to draw knowledge.

It Is the Testimony of the Early Generations of Christians

Christians from the very beginning have confessed and lived in light of the event of the crucifixion. The earliest extant non–New Testament writings whose authors claim to be believers unitedly and unanimously speak as followers of a crucified and risen Messiah. One of the first from whom we have substantial material is Ignatius, bishop of Antioch. In his genuine letters he refers frequently to the cross and to Jesus Christ as "our God." Note these words from his letter to the Smyrnaeans:

> I glorify Jesus Christ, the God who made you so wise, for I observed that you are established in an unshakable faith, having been nailed, as it were, to the cross of the Lord Jesus Christ in both body and spirit, and firmly established in love by the blood of Christ, totally convinced with regard to our Lord that he is truly of the family of David with respect to human descent, Son of God with respect to the divine will and power, truly born of a virgin, baptized by John in order that all righteousness might be fulfilled by him, truly nailed in the flesh for us under Pontius Pilate and Herod the tetrarch (from its fruit we derive our existence, that is, from his divinely blessed suffering), in order that he might raise a banner for the ages through his resurrection for his saints and faithful people, whether among Jews or among Gentiles, in the one body of his church.[6]

There is absolutely no question of the crucifixion's historicity for Ignatius, writing less than eighty years after the event (AD 108). Likewise, when Clement of Rome wrote a letter to the church at Corinth (dated as early as AD 95), the reality of the crucifixion was a given to both communities:

There is nothing coarse, nothing arrogant in love. Love knows nothing of schisms, love leads no rebellions, love does everything in harmony. In love all the elect of God were made perfect; without love nothing is pleasing to God. In love the master received us. Because of the love he had for us, Jesus Christ our Lord, in accordance with God's will, gave his blood for us, and his flesh for our flesh, and his life for our lives.[7]

Another early leader, Polycarp, speaks of "our Lord Jesus Christ, who endured for our sins, facing even death, 'whom God raised up, having loosed the pangs of Hades.'"[8] His letter is dated concurrently with Ignatius and Clement.

It Is the Testimony of Non-Christians

The Jewish historian Josephus makes reference to Jesus in *Antiquities XVIII*, 63–64, and it is highly unlikely that the portion about Jesus' death is a later Christian interpolation (even if some wording elsewhere in the section might be). This work dates from around AD 85.

The Roman historian Tacitus, writing around AD 115, makes derogatory reference to the early Christian movement and mentions that its founder had been executed under Pontius Pilate during the reign of Tiberius. Once again, there was no reason for later Christian scribes to insert such a statement given its nature, its style, and the fact that no one was disputing the existence of Jesus or the reality of His death upon a Roman cross.

Again we must keep in mind the realities of ancient historical research. In truth, that the events in the life of an itinerant Jewish rabbi are recorded *anywhere* is unusual; that they are recorded by contemporary witnesses is astounding; that they are confirmed by a varied stream of witnesses, including non-Christians, is phenomenal.

What About the Gnostics?

For the first century afterward, no one found in recorded history denied the crucifixion of Jesus of Nazareth. But starting in the early second century, we can find some evidence of people saying He did not actually die on the cross. These sources do not go back to His followers. Those who denied the crucifixion did so for the sake of a theology utterly foreign to first-century Judaism, the teachings of Christ's original followers, and monotheism itself.

Ironically, modern Muslims frequently cite these Gnostic sources as evidence in attacking the accuracy of the New Testament's portrayal of the crucifixion. The Gnostics did what they did because they believed, in direct opposition to Jews, Christians, and, later, Muslims, that the deity who created the physical universe is evil. Polytheists in the fullest sense, they held that there are many spiritual powers and beings in the heavens. At the top of this hierarchy is an all-spiritual being from which many others emanated, each moving further away from the fully good source. Finally, a being could be found that was far enough removed to be evil but still powerful enough to create the physical universe. This being, a demiurge, made the heavens and earth. Hence, *the Gnostics would have identified Allah as an evil deity.*

But why did they deny the crucifixion? Because they were dualists. They believed matter to be evil, spirit to be good. If Jesus was good, He could not have had a physical (evil) body. So Jesus only *seemed* to have a fleshly body (both the Bible and the Qur'an affirm the physical existence of Jesus).

If Jesus did not have a physical body, He could hardly have suffered a fully physical process of execution. The Gnostics opposed His followers, claimed for themselves His name, and came up with their own stories based on their presuppositions. No matter how popular among modern skeptics who love to inflate their importance, their views were always a tiny minority. More important, they come from a worldview and theology utterly unknown in first-century Judaism, the very context in which the historical Jesus lived and taught, *and that based upon the united testimony of the New Testament and the Qur'an.* Muslims never show themselves less consistent than when they call the Gnostics to their aid in seeking a way to overthrow the biblical testimony to the crucifixion of the Lord Jesus.

The Qur'an's Stand Against History

When it comes to the cross, the Qu'ran stands firmly and inalterably against the mass of historical evidence and the almost universal view of the populace of its day. But it does so in only one *ayah*, one single verse, of forty Arabic words. It provides no explanation, no context, no defense. Here is the text:

4:156. And because of their disbelief and of their speaking against Mary a tremendous calumny.

157. And because of their saying: "We slew the Messiah, Jesus son of Mary, Allah's Messenger." They slew him not, nor crucified him, but it appeared so to them; and those who disagree concerning it are in doubt thereof; they have no knowledge of it except the pursuit of a conjecture; [but] certainly they slew him not.

158. But Allah raised him up to Himself. Allah is August, Wise.

The key *ayah* is 4:157. Here the Qur'an seems to deny that Jesus was crucified or killed. It only "appeared so to them," and those who differ are following mere conjecture. *Ayah* 158 apparently claims that Allah raised Jesus up rather than allowing Him to be harmed. But what does all of this mean?

In most of the Islamic world, this text is understood to teach what often is called the substitution theory. That is, on the "Muslim street" you would be told this verse teaches that someone else was put in Jesus' place on the cross.

Who? The normal suspect is Judas Iscariot, but some have identified Simon the Cyrene as the victim. In any case, someone else was made to look like Jesus, and it was that person, not Him, who suffered crucifixion. This is based on a rather expanded and inventive translation of the Arabic phrase *shubbiha lahum*, which is most literally translated, "so it was made to appear to them." Yet some translations go far beyond this. The very conservative Hilali-Khan has "but the resemblance of 'Iesa (Jesus) was put over another man (and they killed that man)," while Shakir has "but it appeared to them so (like 'Isa)." These would then see the reference in *ayah* 158 to being "raised up," literally to a taking of Jesus from the earth before death. No crucifixion; hence, no burial, no resurrection, no Christian gospel.

That is the understanding of the majority of the world's Muslims to this day. Most, unaware of the historical facts, consider this a fitting view. "How could Allah allow such a beloved Messenger to die in such a dishonorable way?" is their oft-expressed and honest question.

But Westernized Muslims often back away from asserting this meaning for the text. When asked, many will give the standard Islamic response for a question that goes beyond human knowledge: *Allahu alim*, God knows. This is seen, for example, in the comments of Muhammad Asad:

> Thus, the Qur'an categorically denies the story of the crucifixion of Jesus. There exist, among Muslims, many fanciful legends telling us that at the last moment God substituted for Jesus a

person closely resembling him (according to some accounts, that person was Judas), who was subsequently crucified in his place. However, none of these legends finds the slightest support in the Qur'an or in authentic Traditions, and the stories produced in this connection by the classical commentators must be summarily rejected. They represent no more than confused attempts at "harmonizing" the Qur'anic statement that Jesus was not crucified with the graphic description, in the Gospels, of his crucifixion. The story of the crucifixion as such has been succinctly explained in the Qur'anic phrase *wa-lakin shubbiha lahum*, which I render as "but it only appeared to them as if it had been so"—implying that in the course of time, long after the time of Jesus, a legend had somehow grown up (possibly under the then-powerful influence of Mithraistic beliefs) to the effect that he had died on the cross in order to atone for the "original sin" with which mankind is allegedly burdened; and this legend became so firmly established among the latter-day followers of Jesus that even his enemies, the Jews, began to believe it—albeit in a derogatory sense (for crucifixion was, in those times, a heinous form of death-penalty reserved for the lowest of criminals).[9]

Asad then addresses the concept of the taking up of Jesus in physical form:

Cf. 3:55, where God says to Jesus, "Verily, I shall cause thee to die, and shall exalt thee unto Me." The verb *rafa ahu* (lit., "he raised him" or "elevated him") has always, whenever the act of *raf'* ("elevating") of a human being is attributed to God, the meaning of "honouring" or "exalting." Nowhere in the Qur'an is there any warrant for the popular belief that God has "taken up" Jesus bodily, in his lifetime, into heaven. The expression "God exalted him unto Himself" in the above verse denotes the elevation of Jesus to the realm of God's special grace—a blessing in which all prophets partake, as is evident from 19:57, where the verb *rafa nahu* ("We exalted him") is used with regard to the Prophet Idris.[10]

So what really happened? We are not told, besides the crucifixion itself being categorically denied. *Whatever* occurred is not what Christians claim today.

Many things about this passage call for the Muslim's attention. First, the text asserts that the *Christians*, evidently, are following speculation here and have no certain knowledge. In reality, the text is pure conjecture; it is anything but *mubinun*—clear and perspicuous. Even attempts to follow the argument in the original Arabic yield little clarity. The Jews were boasting that they slew Jesus, the Messiah, the messenger of Allah . . . *really*? It is truly a rarity to hear a Jewish person refer to Jesus as Messiah, let alone boast about having killed Him.[11] But let's continue with the text. It says, "They slew him not." Who is the "they"? In context, the Jews. Could the Romans have done so? While that is not how Muslims have interpreted it over the centuries, the grammar surely would allow for that understanding.

Next, why does it say they did not slay Him, or crucify Him? Are these meant to be taken as separate actions? Some groups have taken this to mean the Qur'an is allowing for Jesus to have been crucified but survived the act and managed to recover in the tomb and escape, a variant of the long-ago-refuted "swoon theory." What *shubbiha lahum* means, we simply do not know; the text is not clear enough to say and has been interpreted in a dozen different ways over the centuries. At *ayah*'s end is the strong, clear statement, "but certainly they slew him not." Who is "they"? The text does not say.

Which raises the next fascinating point: When we encounter other unclear and uncertain Qur'anic texts, we often can turn to the *hadith* for at least the interpretation ascribed to the first few generations after Muhammad. But here we run into a stone wall of silence. As far as we can tell, for at least two hundred years after Muhammad, no Muslim could remember anything he ever said or did that was relevant to Surah 4:157. It has no meaningful presence in the *hadith*. On other texts where the Qur'an directly contradicts the Bible, we can find lots of commentary in that literature, but for this key and central *ayah* we find nothing. It is as if this *ayah* appeared out of nowhere and plopped itself down in the middle of this Surah and made itself at home.

There may be more to this idea in light of other Qur'anic texts. If Surah 4:157 were not found therein, there would be no question about the book's view that Jesus *did* die. As Asad noted above, two, translated fairly and accurately and without prejudice, clearly speak of Jesus' death:

> 3:55. [And remember] When Allah said: "O Jesus! I am gathering you and raising you to Me, and cleansing you of those who disbelieve, and setting those who follow you above those who disbelieve until the Day of Resurrection. Then to Me you will all return, and I shall judge between you as to that in which you used to differ."

> 19:33. So peace be upon me the day I was born, the day that I die, and the day that I shall be raised up to life [again].

Again, Surah 3:55 actually speaks of His death, for the phrase here translated as "I am gathering you" is far better rendered "I shall cause thee to die" (as in Asad's). And in Surah 19:33 Jesus again speaks of His death, but in almost the identical words used of John the Baptist in the same Surah!

> 19:15. So peace be upon him on the day he was born, on the day of his death; and the day when he is raised to life.

There is no argument about the fact that John the Baptist died, so the phrase's meaning is not ambiguous. The point is, were it not for Surah 4:157, the Qur'an would make plain reference to Christ's death and, without addressing its means, at least would stand in line with history in acknowledging its reality (if not its intent, and without addressing the resurrection).

So these forty Arabic words stand alone in the Qur'an. They stand alone without commentary in the *hadith* literature as well. They stand against not only the natural reading of other Qur'anic texts but also against the entire weight of the historical record. Forty Arabic words written six hundred years after the events they describe, more than seven hundred fifty miles from Jerusalem. Forty Arabic words that are not clear, not perspicuous, and yet this is the *entirety* of the foundation upon which the Islamic faith bases its denial of the crucifixion, and hence, resurrection of Jesus Christ.

Consider, in closing, what this says about the Qur'an. Nothing in it suggests its author had even the slightest knowledge of the New Testament centrality of God's redeeming act in Christ on the cross. The author knew nothing of Paul's epistle to the Romans or the book of Hebrews and their in-depth case for and teaching about the Messiah's redeeming death. The author seems blissfully unaware of the evidentiary mountain that substantiates the crucifixion. And yet with a few seconds of oral recitation, the Qur'an places itself, and all who would believe in it, in direct opposition not only to the Injil (Gospel) but also everything history itself says on the subject. The question *must* be asked: Who, truly, is following mere conjecture here? Those who were eyewitnesses on the Hill of the Skull outside Jerusalem? Or the author of the Qur'an, more than half a millennium later?

Notes

1. John Dominic Crossan, *Jesus: A Revolutionary Biography* (San Francisco: HarperSanFrancisco, 1994), 145.

2. Bart Ehrman, *Did Jesus Exist? The Historical Argument for Jesus of Nazareth* (New York: HarperOne, 2012). Islamic apologists, enamored with Ehrman and

often citing his works in their attacks (particularly upon the New Testament), do not seem to realize he is a naturalistic scholar whose conclusions would be as destructive to the supernatural claims of Islam as they are with reference to Christianity.

3. Bart Ehrman, *The Historical Jesus* Part 2, Lecture Transcript and Course Guidebook (The Teaching Company, 2000), 162.

4. For example, in writing to the churches of Galatia (6:14) in Asia Minor, Paul says, "May it never be that I would boast, except in the cross of our Lord Jesus Christ, through which the world has been crucified to me, and I to the world."

5. 1 Corinthians 15:3–5, personal translation.

6. In M. W. Holmes, *The Apostolic Fathers: Greek Texts and English Translations* (Grand Rapids, MI: Baker, 1999), 185.

7. Ibid., 85.

8. Ibid., 207.

9. Muhammad Asad, *The Message of the Qur'an* (Bristol, England: The Book Foundation, 2003), 154, n. 171. While Asad's view is more modern than the majority Muslim view, it is likewise untenable on many grounds. The Qur'an shows no understanding of atonement as presented in the Bible (especially in Hebrews), and to attribute that Christian belief to Mithraic influences rather than first-century Jewish categories is utterly without merit. To then suggest that the Jews had begun to believe the same concept also is untenable.

10. Ibid.

11. Some contend that here the term *Messiah* is being used mockingly, but nothing in the text suggests this, and its normative Qur'anic use with Jesus is respectful (e.g., 3:45; 4:171).

7

The Scales:
Salvation in the Qur'an

For many in the Islamic world, the essence of the Qur'an's view of salvation can be summed up in its teaching about the scales:

> 21:47. And We set up a just balance [scales] for the Day of Resurrection. Thus, no soul will be treated unjustly. Even though it be the weight of a mustard seed, We shall bring it forth to be weighed; and Our reckoning will suffice.

The Qur'an is filled with references to the Day of Judgment, a day of great fear and trembling, as we saw earlier in the *hadith* about Muhammad's intercession. It is a day to dread. The scales will be brought forth to weigh the good and the bad, and each person will be treated with absolute justice:

> 23:99–104. Until when death comes to one of them he says: "My Lord, send me back! That I may do the good works I had left undone." It is but a word he speaks. And behind them is a barrier till the day they will be raised. But when the Horn is

blown, there shall be no kinship among them on that day, nor will they ask of one another. Then those whose scales are heavy, they are the successful. And those whose scales are light have lost themselves, they shall abide in hell forever. The fire shall scorch their faces, and they are sullen therein.

The Qur'an likewise joins together faith in Allah, the Book (Qur'an), and the scales (the judgment) as vitally important:

42:16–18. And those who argue concerning Allah after He has been answered, their argument is null with their Lord, and wrath will fall upon them. Theirs is a severe torment. It is Allah Who has sent down the Book with truth and the scales; and how do you know? The hour may be near. Those who do not believe in it seek to hasten it, but those who believe dread it and know that it is the truth. Indeed, those who dispute concerning the Hour have gone far astray.

The concept of scales and hence the metaphor of judgment is central to Surah 101, "The Calamity":

1. The Calamity!
2. What is the Calamity?
3. And how will you know what the Calamity is?
4. A day when people will become like scattered moths,
5. And the mountains will become like carded wool.
6. Then, as for him whose scales are heavy [with good deeds],
7. He will be in a pleasing life.
8. But as for him whose scales are light,
9. The bottomless pit will be his home.
10. How will you know what it is?
11. A raging fire.

Even when the specific metaphor of scales is not present, one thing is certain: The Qur'an foretells a day of judgment:

99:6–8. That day mankind will come forth in scattered groups to be shown their deeds. And he who has done an atom's weight of good will see it, and he who has done an atom's weight of evil will see it.

For many Muslims, this is sufficient. Good works, faith in Allah and the Qur'an—this is the essence of submission and salvation. Seek to make your scales heavy with good deeds and avoid the bottomless pit filled with raging fire. They see no reason to speculate on predestination or free will or any of the myriad other things that can only complicate the situation.

The problem, though, is that the Qur'an says more on the topic. And, unlike the New Testament's extended didactic portions that lay out doctrines such as justification and atonement, the Qur'an's presentation of salvation is scattered and "in passing." Unlike its constant drumbeats of monotheism and the dangers of *shirk*, for instance, when it comes to salvation itself and how a person can live in proper relationship with God, the picture presented is far less coherent.

As a result, the wide range of views that Muslims express are based not so much on intricate discussions of the text itself[1] as on the school of interpretation of the *hadith* one chooses. Thus we will need to look at a number of such stories from the *hadith* for at least some grasp of the spectrum of Islamic perspectives.

We want to ask, "Does the Qur'an present a single, coherent view of salvation?" But perhaps the more incisive question is whether the doctrine of salvation is distinguishable from proper worship, the embracing of *tawhid*, and the rejection of *shirk*— i.e., submission to Allah. It is easy for Christians to transport concepts derived from the biblical text into the Qur'an, but such will inevitably lead to misunderstanding, for while the Qur'anic and biblical worldviews share certain foundational assumptions, they are worlds apart regarding other definitional beliefs. The transcendence of Allah, especially as put in direct opposition to the incarnation of Jesus and the intimacy of the gospel, creates a stark contrast as to the respective meanings of "salvation."

The triune God of the Christian faith reveals Himself with greatest clarity and force in the gospel (the Father decreeing, the Son accomplishing, the Spirit applying) while maintaining the strictest unity (the Son does nothing by himself, the Spirit is sent by the Father and the Son), so it can be said that His self-revelation is accomplished through the uniting of a particular undeserving people in grace to Him through the gospel. Salvation, central to His purpose in creation itself, hence is a focus of the biblical revelation. In contrast, Allah is not engaged in self-revelation or self-glorification in the matter of human salvation, and there is no gospel that gives a singular coherence to the Islamic perspective.

The Qur'an does give evidence of a concept of salvation by God's mercy and grace. Hundreds of times—in nearly every *surah*—we are told that Allah is the oft-forgiving, the merciful One. And Surah 24:21 says,

> O you who believe! Follow not the steps of the Devil, for whosoever will follow the steps of the Devil, surely he will enjoin on him what is indecent and blameworthy. Had it not been for Allah's grace and His mercy to you none of you would have ever been purified. But Allah causes whom He will to be purified. And Allah is Hearer, Knowing.

This seems to indicate that grace and mercy precede any good works, which finds support in the *hadith* literature as well:

> Narrated Abu Huraira: I heard Allah's Apostle saying, "The good deeds of any person will not make him enter Paradise" (i.e., none can enter Paradise through his good deeds). They (the Prophet's companions) said, "Not even you, O Allah's Apostle?"

He said, "Not even myself, unless Allah bestows His favor and mercy on me." So be moderate in your religious deeds and do the deeds that are within your ability: and none of you should wish for death, for if he is a good doer, he may increase his good deeds, and if he is an evil doer, he may repent to Allah.[2]

Narrated Aisha: The Prophet said, "Do good deeds properly, sincerely and moderately, and receive good news because one's good deeds will not make him enter Paradise." They asked, "Even you, O Allah's Apostle?" He said, "Even I, unless and until Allah bestows His pardon and Mercy on me."[3]

Muslims in general will quote particular Qur'anic texts, but will fit them into a traditional position derived primarily from external (often *hadith*) sources. More liberally minded Muslims often cite texts like Surah 2:62:

Those who believe [in the Qur'an], the Jews, the Christians, and the Sabaeans; whoever believes in Allah and the Last Day and does what is right; shall be rewarded by their Lord; no fear shall come upon them, neither shall they grieve.

Some would read this as indicating a general benevolence of Allah toward all who believe (the phrase "in the Qur'an" being supplied by our translation). More conservative Muslims would limit it to those Jews, Christians, etc., who embrace Islam, leaving those who remain faithful to their traditions under Allah's judgment. This would seem to be a more consistent reading, in light of the rest of the Qur'an's teachings.

Note that the Qur'an speaks of the necessity of faith in Allah:

2:186. When My servants question you about Me, [tell them] I am near, answering the prayer of the suppliant when he prays to Me; therefore let them respond to Me and believe in Me, that they may be rightly-guided.

But even here it speaks of believing in Allah so that one may be "rightly guided," not forgiven, redeemed, and adopted into God's family. We must avoid transposing Christian categories into the Qur'anic text *when we have seen no reason to believe the author understood the Bible's message or content.* Being "rightly guided" is key to understanding the goal of life from the Qur'an's view.

Predestination, or Free Will?

One of the major divisions between Muslim theologians and teachers relates to the ideas of predestination and free will. The Islamic concept is called *qadar*, literally "power," in this case, God's power in decreeing what takes place in time. There is a very strong predestinarian strain in the Qur'an. Note:

> 9:51. Say: "Nothing will befall us except what Allah has ordained for us. He is our Protector. In Allah let the believers put their trust."

> 57:21–23. Race one with another for forgiveness from your Lord and for a garden the breadth of which is as that of the heaven and earth, prepared for those who believe in Allah and His messengers. Such is the favor of Allah; He bestows it on whom He will. Allah's favor is immense. No misfortune can befall in the earth, or your own persons, but it is recorded in a book before We bring it into being. That is easy for Allah. So that you grieve not for the good things you miss or be overjoyed at what you gain. Allah does not love those who are proud and boastful.

This *qadar* also extends to whether a person will, or will not, believe:

> 2:6–7. As for the disbelievers, it is the same whether you warn them, or warn them not [of the final punishment]. They will not believe. Allah has set a seal on their hearts and on their

hearing, and on their eyes there is a covering. Theirs will be a formidable torment.

3:73b–74. Say [O Muhammad]: "The bounty is in the hands of Allah. He bestows it on whom He will. Allah is Vast, Knowing." He chooses for His mercy whom He will. Allah is of immense bounty.

5:40–41. Do you not know that to Allah alone belongs the sovereignty of the heavens and the earth? He punishes whom He will, and forgives whom He will. Allah has power over all things. O Messenger! Do not be grieved by those who hasten to disbelief, of such as say with their mouths: "We believe," but their hearts believe not, and of the Jews: listeners for the sake of falsehood, listeners on behalf of other people who come not to you, changing words from their context and saying: "If this be given to you, receive it, but if this be not given to you, then beware!" He whom Allah dooms to sin, you [by your own efforts] will avail him naught against Allah. Those are they for whom the will of Allah is that He cleanse not their hearts. Theirs is humiliation in the world, and in the Hereafter a formidable torment.

6:107. Had Allah willed, they would not have been polytheists. We have not set you as a keeper over them, nor are you responsible for them.

6:149. Say: "Allah's is the final argument. Had He willed He could have guided all of you."

Lest one think this guidance is not necessarily related to final judgment, these texts make the case very clearly:

7:178. He whom Allah guides, he indeed is led aright, while he whom Allah sends astray, they indeed are losers. And We have designated for Hell many of the jinn and humankind, who have hearts with which they understand not; who have eyes with which they see not; and who have ears with which they hear not. They are like cattle; they are even worse! These are the heedless.

32:13. And, if We had so willed, We could have given every soul its guidance, but the word from Me will be fulfilled. I will fill hell with the jinn and mankind together.

It is important to note that three final quotations directly, and in no uncertain terms, address the relationship between the will of man and the will of Allah:

10:99. If it had been your Lord's will, all who are in the earth would have believed. Will you, then, force the people to become believers?

7:29–31. This is a reminder. He who will, let him take a path to his Lord. But you cannot will unless Allah wills; Allah is Knowing, Wise. He will admit to His mercy whom He will, but for the unjust He has prepared a painful torment.

81:28–29. To those among you who wish for rectitude. And you cannot will, unless Allah wills, who is Lord of the Worlds.

Surah 10 plainly teaches that Allah has the ability to make all men believers; Surah 7 says, "You cannot will unless Allah wills"; and Surah 81 repeats this with "you cannot will, unless Allah wills." Surely it seems that the will of Allah preconditions and determines human will.

These texts (and many others that could be cited) seem clear in their teaching. We also will see they have deep and unquestionable support in the *hadith* literature. But there is another aspect to the Qur'anic teaching as well, one which many, especially in the West, find more attractive:

18:29. Say: "Truth is from your Lord." Now whosoever will, may believe, and whosoever will, may disbelieve.

8:53. That is because Allah never changes the blessing He has bestowed on any people until they first change that which is in themselves, and because Allah is Hearing, Knowing.

13:11. For every [such person] there are guardian [angels] before him and behind him. They guard him by the command of Allah. Allah never changes the condition of a people unless they themselves change what is in themselves. If Allah wills a misfortune, there can be no turning it back, nor will they find besides Him any protector.

When believing Christians face what appears to be tension in a Bible text, they turn to the context, language, and the consistent teaching of the entirety of Scripture. They first examine those portions that address the topic at length, and interpret less clear passages in light of the longer, more direct ones. That is how biblical exegesis is done, though often the ideal is missed in everyday practice. But the nature of the Qur'an is so different from Paul's epistle to the Romans, the sixth chapter of John's gospel, or the entirety of the epistle to the Hebrews, that it does not afford this kind of examination. So what functionally takes the place of textual exegesis in Islamic practice and history? The *hadith*.

The problem with looking to the *hadith* literature is obvious, at least to an outsider: This large body of material is anything but self-consistent, let alone self-interpreting. One scholar will elevate one stream of teaching in the *hadith* while another will chart a different path. Tremendous differences exist among those seeking to shed light on the Qur'an from the *hadith*.

But there are some subjects on which it does seem rather clear, if not perfectly consistent. When it comes to Allah's power (*qadar*) and the will of man, several *ahadith* demand our attention. The first is by far the most telling:

Humayd ibn Abdur Rahman al-Himyari and I set out for Pilgrimage or for Umrah and said: Should it so happen that we come into contact with one of the Companions of the Messenger of Allah (peace be upon him) we shall ask him about what is talked about Taqdir (Division Decree). Accidentally we came across

Abdullah ibn Umar ibn al-Khattab, while he was entering the mosque. My companion and I surrounded him. One of us (stood) on his right and the other stood on his left. I expected that my companion would authorize me to speak. I therefore said: Abu Abdur Rahman! There have appeared some people in our land who recite the Holy Qur'an and pursue knowledge. And then after talking about their affairs, added: They (such people) claim that there is no such thing as Divine Decree and events are not predestined. He (Abdullah ibn Umar) said: When you happen to meet such people tell them that I have nothing to do with them and they have nothing to do with me. And verily they are in no way responsible for my (belief). Abdullah ibn Umar swore by Him (the Lord) (and said): If any one of them (who does not believe in the Divine Decree) had with him gold equal to the bulk of (the mountain) Uhud and then, it (in the way of Allah), Allah would not accept it unless he affirmed his faith in Divine Decree.[4]

It is hard to imagine a stronger affirmation of the "Divine Decree" (*qadar*) from one of the Companions! But just how extensive is this decree? Could Umar have been thinking of something less strict, less all-encompassing than what we might be tempted to think? It does not seem so.

> 'A'isha, the mother of the believers, said that Allah's Messenger (may peace be upon him) was called to lead the funeral prayer of a child of the Ansar. I said: Allah's Messenger, there is happiness for this child who is a bird from the birds of Paradise for it committed no sin nor has he reached the age when one can commit sin. He said: 'A'isha, per adventure, it may be otherwise, because God created for Paradise those who are fit for it while they were yet in their father's loins and created for Hell those who are to go to Hell. He created them for Hell while they were yet in their father's loins.[5]

Muhammad's young wife expresses belief in a child's essential goodness and suggests that as he was not old enough to sin, all should be well with him. But the Prophet says God created some for Paradise, some for hell, a choice made "while they were yet in their father's loins." Aisha cannot be certain of the child's destination simply because he died in his youth.

This *hadith* plainly asserts the very personal nature of *qadar*, that is, its application to each human being:

'Abdullah b. Mas'ud reported: Evil one is he who is evil in the womb of his mother and the good one is he who takes a lesson from the (fate of) others. The narrator came to a person from amongst the Companions of Allah's Messenger (may peace be upon him) who was called Hudhaifa b. Usaid Ghifari and said: How can a person be an evil one without (committing an evil) deed? Thereupon the person said to him: You are surprised at this, whereas I have heard Allah's Messenger (may peace be upon him) as saying: When forty nights pass after the semen gets into the womb, Allah sends the angel and gives him shape. Then he creates his sense of hearing, sense of sight, his skin, his flesh, his bones, and then says: My Lord, would he be male or female? And your Lord decides as He desires and the angel then puts down that also and then says: My Lord, what about his age? And your Lord decides as He likes it and the angel puts it down. Then he says: My Lord, what about his livelihood? And then the Lord decides as He likes and the angel writes it down, and then the angel gets out with his scroll of destiny in his hand and nothing is added to it and nothing is subtracted from it.[6]

Little is left out of the decree's extent here, from how long a person will live, to what he will do, etc. From this vantage, the entirety of one's future is fixed in the womb. And that can have incredible consequence, as we read here:

Narrated 'Abdullah: Allah's Apostle, the truthful and truly-inspired, said, "Each one of you collected in the womb of his mother for forty days, and then turns into a clot for an equal period (of forty days) and turns into a piece of flesh for a similar period (of forty days) and then Allah sends an angel and orders him to write four things, i.e., his provision, his age, and whether he will be of the wretched or the blessed (in the Hereafter). Then the soul is breathed into him. And by Allah, a person among you (or a man) may do deeds of the people of the Fire till there is only a cubit or an arm-breadth distance between him and the Fire, but then that writing (which Allah has ordered the angel to write) precedes, and he does the deeds of the people of Paradise and enters it; and a man may do the deeds of the people of Paradise till there is only a cubit or two between him and Paradise, and then that writing precedes and he does the deeds of the people of the Fire and enters it."[7]

Note the practical result of a strict view of *qadar*: Not only are the details of a person's life set out at a particular time in the womb,[8] but this decree will fix either his eternal happiness or suffering *no matter what his life might be*. That is, a person may live like one of the "people of Paradise"—act rightly, give alms, worship God—until "there is only a cubit or two between him and Paradise" (he is about to enter in), and then, right at the end, "that writing precedes," and he does the deeds of the "people of the Fire" and enters into it. And vice-versa: A person may live an evil life, be about to enter into judgment, and yet if the decree demands it, right at the end he will turn and enter Paradise.[9] The disconnection presented between the life of the good or the evil is not only out of harmony with some of the preceding cited texts but also renders Allah's decree utterly capricious and empties it of moral or ethical meaning. If God's decree does not reveal His holy nature, how is it any different from the arbitrary demands of any human despot?

Forgiveness and God's Holy Nature

This brings us to the all-important question of how Allah can be holy and just and yet act arbitrarily, forgiving some sins and retaining others without reference to sacrifice or the fulfillment of his own law. In Islamic belief, Allah can forgive sins while providing no basis in justice or equity. It is not that there is a purpose in forgiving some and not others—no demonstration of power or righteousness or anything else is intended.

One of the most famous stories in the *hadith* is of the mass murderer who had killed ninety-nine persons. I utilized the story as part of my presentations on Islam for a number of years before engaging in a debate with the imam of a large mosque in New York. Prior to our debate, we participated together on a radio program. In explaining the Islamic view of salvation, he repeated this very story without any prompting on my part. There are a number of versions; I will conflate them together into one for our purposes.[10]

Muhammad told of a man from the sons of Israel who had committed ninety-nine murders. Having done so, he set out asking whether his repentance could ever be accepted. He came upon a monk and asked this vital question. The monk said no, and so the man killed the monk as well, for an even one hundred victims. He then approached a scholar and asked the same question. The scholar told him to go to a village, where wise people would instruct him in what he had to do for his repentance to be accepted. And so he set out.

Unfortunately for him, the point of his death came as he was traveling (Islamic belief in the set date and hour of one's death comes into play here). The angels of mercy, from Paradise, and the angels of punishment, from the Fire, came to claim his soul and argued over him. The angels of punishment seemed to have the easier argument: "He killed 100 persons and has no good works!" But the angels of mercy retorted, "He was on his way to learn about repentance!" So Allah decreed that they were to measure the distance the man had traveled from the city where he began and compare it to the distance to the city to which he was traveling; if he was one cubit closer to where he intended to learn about repentance, he would go to Paradise. Then Allah intervened and caused the earth to shrink between the man and the city so that he was found to be one cubit closer, and the angels of mercy took him to Paradise.

This story clearly delineates the issues Christians and Muslims must discuss together. Here Allah not only forgives the man of horrendous sin but also does so without the slightest reference to the fulfillment of the divine law against murder. The key issue is not God's mercy or even God's desire to forgive. The issue is *how* forgiveness can be obtained without violating His holiness and justice. From the perspective of this *hadith*, forgiveness flows not from God's actions in providing a *basis* for salvation, but from His power alone. He acts capriciously—there are many others who have done less moral evil that He does not forgive and who populate hell—and not in reference to any standard derived from His own unchanging nature.

The Muslim claim is that God can forgive without reference to His law's completion and without regard for the demonstration of His righteousness. Christians believe the glory of God's forgiveness is found in its fulfillment of His desire to express His love, mercy, and grace while simultaneously providing an awesome display of His essential justice, righteousness, and holiness. This leads Christians to confess the truth of the incarnation, for only in the God-Man can the full spectrum of God's attributes be displayed. In the cross, where the God-Man voluntarily takes on the sins of His people, the complete fulfillment of God's righteousness, including His wrath against sin and the holiness of His law, meets His overwhelming mercy, grace, and love in this one act of self-giving and redemption. We see in this one reality, then, a place where the divergence between Christianity and Islam is wide, deep, and definitional. In Islam, forgiveness is an impersonal act of arbitrary divine power. In Christianity, forgiveness is a personal act of purposeful and powerful yet completely just divine grace.

The theme of "forgiveness apart from atonement, from justice, from the vindication of God's character and law" is illustrated in another *hadith*:

> Allah's Messenger (peace be upon him) said that on the Day of Resurrection Allah will separate a man belonging to his people in presence of all creatures and spread ninety-nine scrolls over him, each scroll extending as far as the eye could see, then say, "Do you object to anything in this? Have my scribes who keep note wronged you?" He will reply, "No, my Lord." He will ask him if he has any excuse, and when he tells his Lord that he has none, He will say, "On the contrary you have with Us a good deed, and you will not be wronged today." A document will then be brought out containing, "I testify that there is no god but Allah, and that Muhammad is His servant and Messenger," and He will say, "Come to be weighed." He will ask his Lord, "What is this document along with these scrolls?" And He will reply, "You will not be wronged." The scrolls will then be put in one side of the scale and the document in the other, and the scrolls will become light and the document heavy, for nothing could compare in weight with Allah's name.[11]

In other words, a man faces judgment laden with sins, the recording of which takes ninety-nine massive scrolls. He admits to the recording's accuracy and seems resigned to his just fate. But he is informed that he does have one good deed, one tiny scrap, upon which is written the *Shahada*, the confession of faith. It outweighs all ninety-nine scrolls, and he evidently finds forgiveness.

We would be wrong to take this as a normative teaching and so conclude that all Muslims are assured of salvation by mere recitation of the *Shahada*. Some Muslim interpreters have insisted that this story refers only to a single individual who will receive this kind of grace; the majority will not. But our focus here is more on the basis upon which this man is forgiven for a huge sin debt. How is the truth that there is one true God, Allah, confirmed or glorified or proclaimed to the world by the life of a man who says the words but does not live in light of what they mean? No one who collected that mountain of sin was engaging in acts of piety and faith. Yet a singular confession outweighs all the sin? How is Allah's honor and justice vindicated therein?

Atonement and Justice

When Christians and Muslims discuss their respective faiths, they encounter a number of difficult and weighty barriers to their progress. We have seen some of these already, such as the idea of *shirk* and the Islamic rejection of Jesus as the Son of God. We have seen the Qur'an's denial of the historical reality of His crucifixion (resulting in denial of His burial and resurrection) as well. And when we begin to address the gospel, forgiveness of sins, and atonement, we see that the differences are stark. On the one hand, the Qur'an denies that anyone can carry someone else's burden on the day of judgment:

> 53:38–41. That no soul shall bear another's burden. And that each can have nothing save what he strives for, and that his effort will be seen. And afterward he will be repaid for it with fullest payment. . . .

160

However, its message is somewhat conflicted, for in Surah 29:12–13 we read,

> Those who disbelieve say to those who believe: "Follow our path and we shall bear your sins [for you]." They can bear none of their sins. They are but liars. But they will bear their own loads and other loads beside their own, and they will be questioned on the Day of Arising concerning that which they made up.

Muhammad Asad comments on this text,

> cf. the Prophet's saying: Whoever calls [others] unto the right way shall have a reward equal to the [combined] rewards of all who may follow him until Resurrection Day, without anything being lessened of their rewards; and whoever calls unto the way of error will have to bear a sin equal to the [combined] sins of all who may follow him until Resurrection Day, without anything being lessened of their sins" (Bukhari).[12]

While a full discussion of all this concept's ramifications is beyond our scope, we should at least note with some care another aspect in early Islamic belief that relates to the concept of substitution or atonement. There is a stream of tradition, found in *Sahih Muslim*, that conveys a troubling idea:

> Abu Musa' reported that Allah's Messenger (may peace be upon him) said: When it will be the Day of Resurrection Allah would deliver to every Muslim a Jew or a Christian and say: That is your rescue from Hell-Fire.[13]

> Abu Burda reported on the authority of his father that Allah's Apostle (may peace be upon him) said: No Muslim would die but Allah would admit in his stead a Jew or a Christian in Hell-Fire. 'Umar b. Abd al-'Aziz took an oath: By One besides Whom there is no god but He, thrice that his father had narrated that to him from Allah's Messenger (may peace be upon him).[14]

> Abu Burda reported Allah's Messenger (may peace be upon him)
> as saying: There would come people amongst the Muslims on
> the Day of Resurrection with as heavy sins as a mountain, and
> Allah would forgive them and He would place in their stead the
> Jews and the Christians. (As far as I think), Abu Raub said: I
> do not know as to who is in doubt. Abu Burda said: I narrated
> it to 'Umar b. 'Abd al-'Aziz, whereupon he said: Was it your
> father who narrated it to you from Allah's Apostle (may peace
> be upon him)? I said: Yes.[15]

We should resist the temptation to allow emotion or prejudice to overpower the real issue here: How can God's justice be
shown and vindicated by placing anyone *already condemned
to hellfire* in the place of a Muslim or anyone else? For a substitute to be able to bear another's sins, he must not be under
the same condemnation and judgment! This is why Jesus, the
sinless Lamb of God, is able to be the sin bearer for all who are
united to Him by faith.

The idea of placing a Jew or a Christian in the place of a
Muslim is heinous not because of any prejudice or discrimina-
tion, but because of what it says about Allah's justice. Of course,
some Muslims dispute any actual concept of substitution in
these *ahadith*, saying the Jews and Christians are simply taking
their places in hell, places that would have included Muslims
who had not placed their faith in Allah. This does not seem
to be the obvious reading of these texts, but at any rate, one
other *hadith* in a widely read collection appears to make the
concept very clear:

> On the Day of Resurrection, my Ummah (nation) will be gath-
> ered into three groups, one sort will enter Paradise without ren-
> dering an account (of their deeds). Another sort will be reckoned
> an easy account and admitted into Paradise. Yet another sort will
> come bearing on their backs heaps of sins like great mountains.

Allah will ask the angels though He knows best about them: Who are these people? They will reply: They are humble slaves of yours. He will say: Unload the sins from them and put the same over the Jews and Christians; then let the humble slaves get into Paradise by virtue of My Mercy. (This Hadith is sound and mentioned in Mustadrak of Hakim.)[16]

Here it seems inarguable that, minimally, at some point in Islam's early history, a tradition existed that reflected some understanding of transferal of sin, the very concept orthodox Islam denies in reference to Christ's atoning sacrifice. Beyond this, the aforementioned problems with simple justice in this concept are only magnified by identifying such transfer of sin-guilt to *already condemned sinners and idolaters* as an act of "My Mercy" on Allah's part. This travesty of justice does not deal with the "great mountains" of sins in any meaningful fashion. It is utterly unlike the self-giving sacrifice of Christ, God's Son, who voluntarily takes the sins of God's people upon Himself.

Notes

1. A careful and fair comparison of the literature of biblical exegesis produced by believing Christian scholarship with that of believing Islamic scholarship is striking. The intricate, complex studies found among Muslims in the *hadith sciences* is the closest parallel to the in-depth, original-language-based exegesis of the New Testament among Christians. The Muslim battleground of debate on these issues is focused upon Islamic tradition, while for believing Christians it is focused upon the text of Scripture itself.

2. *Sahih Al-Bukhari*, 7:577.

3. Ibid., 8:474.

4. *Sahih Muslim*, 1:1.

5. *Sahih Muslim*, 33:6436, Arabic 47:6939.

6. *Sahih Muslim*, 33:6393, Arabic 47:6896.

7. *Sahih Al-Bukhari*, 8:593.

8. Note too that if Islam in general adopted this viewpoint, there would be no serious basis for objection to early stage abortion, as apparently the soul is not imparted until after 120 days, before which the child is a "clot" or a "piece of flesh." Muslim apologists fondly assert the Qur'an's alleged scientific accuracy,

yet if this *hadith* represents Muhammad's views (and seems to, in light of Surah 86:6–7), he did not have an accurate view of human development (the very thing the Qur'an supposedly gets right as a testimony to its miraculous nature).

9. This is indicative of the primary difference between the biblical and Islamic teachings on God's eternal decree: The Bible affirms in many texts God's absolute sovereignty (e.g., Psalm 135:6; Ephesians 1:11) with words as full and complete as the Qur'an's. But the God of the Bible is not distant from His creation, and His decree includes His personal interaction with His people and events in time (providence). As a result, while His decree of salvation includes the identity of the elect, most important, their salvation is part of the means by which He glorifies Himself. Hence the decree includes their holiness and sanctification (Titus 2:11–14), so that the life His people live is a vital aspect of His plan and intention.

10. The base story is found, for example, in *Sahih Al-Bukhari*, 4:676.

11. *At-Tirmidhi*, 1463.

12. Muhammad Asad, *The Message of the Qur'an* (Bristol, England: The Book Foundation, 2003), 679.

13. *Sahih Muslim* 37:6665, Arabic 51:7186. In some collections, 2767.

14. *Sahih Muslim* 37:6666, Arabic 51:7188. In some collections, 2767R1.

15. *Sahih Muslim* 37:6668, Arabic 51:7190. In some collections, 2767R3. Some Muslims question the standing of these *hadith* because they are *ahad*, that is, they have a singular chain of narration. However, scholars of *hadith sciences* confess that an *ahad hadith* can be *sahih*, sound, and reliable. At the same time, the vast majority of Muslims have never read these *hadith*, and to their credit, most who do are scandalized by them.

16. S. Masood-ul-Hasan, *110 Ahadith Qudsi* (Riyadh: n.d.), 19–20.

8

Did the "People of the Book" Corrupt the Gospel?

Christians are often surprised to learn that the Islamic holy book addresses them directly. It would seem axiomatic that with tensions rising between our communities all around the world, at the very least we would want to know what the Qur'an says to us so we can provide a meaningful response in love to our Muslim neighbors and friends. So we will look at the major texts addressing the "People of the Book" and the "People of the Gospel" before looking at a crucial element of the Qur'an's polemic relating to corruption of the Torah and the Injil.

The People of the Book

The Qur'an's *Ahl al-Kitab*, "People of the Book," can refer to Jews and Christians together, to Jews alone, or to Christians alone, all depending on the context. And sometimes the context does not sufficiently clarify.

That title acknowledges that God has sent down prophets *and* Scripture to preceding peoples. Clearly there is a connection intended in the author's mind between those preceding peoples and the new people formed by the final book, the final revelation to be sent down, the Qur'an.

What *does* it say to Jews and Christians? Let's look at some key texts, again in chronological order. Aside from the first, almost all the relevant texts are Medinan in origin, coming from the latter portion of Muhammad's life.

> 29:46. O Muslims! Do not argue with the People of the Book except in the best of ways, save with such of them who are unjust; and say: "We believe in that which has been sent down to us and that which has been down to you; our God and your God is One, and to Him we surrender."
>
> 47. Thus We have sent down to you the Book, and to whom We gave the Book, they believe in it; and of these there are some who believe in it. And none deny Our signs save the disbelievers.

This limitation on contentions would seem to call Muslims to the highest standards in their *dawa*, their calling to Islam, and their interaction with Jews and Christians. The theme of "connection" between the three communities is present in the assertion that all have received revelation from God, and that the God who sent down the Torah and Injil is the God who sent down the Qur'an. The argument is clear: If you believed the *ayat* (signs) in the former Scriptures, naturally you should believe those same signs found in the Qur'an.

> 3:69. A group of the People of the Book wish to lead you [Muslims] astray; but they lead none astray except themselves, without being aware of it.
>
> 70. O People of the Book! Why do you deny the signs of Allah, when you yourselves bear witness [to their truth]?

71. O People of the Book! Why do you confound the truth with falsehood, and knowingly conceal the truth?

72. And some of the People of the Book say: "Believe in the morning in that which has been sent down to those who believe, and deny it in the evening, so that they may turn away [from their faith].

Here a certain group of the People of the Book, unidentified and unknown to us today, are said to wish to mislead the Muslims. But why would they do so when the signs of Allah are found in the Qur'an and their own scriptures? Whether the limitation of *ayah* 69 remains in *ayat* 70–71, or whether the subsequent statements are general (to all), is hard to say. But *ayah* 71 makes the broad accusation of confounding the truth with falsehood and knowingly concealing the truth, both actions requiring the clear presence of truth (either in the previous Scriptures or in the Qur'an). The final *ayah* refers to hypocrites who change their story quickly, within a single day, so as to act deceptively.

3:84. Say [O Muhammad]: "We believe in Allah and that which was sent down to us and that which was sent down to Abraham and Ishmael and Isaac and Jacob and the tribes; and that which was given to Moses and Jesus and the Prophets from their Lord. We make no distinction between any of them, and to Him we have surrendered."

85. He who seeks a religion other than Islam, it will not be accepted from him, and he will be a loser in the Hereafter.

This passage is oft-cited in Islamic theology, for it again emphasizes the interconnectedness of the great Abrahamic faiths, at least from the Islamic perspective. What does the Qur'an mean when it says, "We make no distinction between any of them"? *Ibn Kathir* puts it blandly:

Therefore, faithful Muslims believe in every Prophet whom Allah has sent and in every Book He revealed, and never disbelieve in any of them. Rather, they believe in what was revealed by Allah, and in every Prophet sent by Allah.[1]

It is hard to say, exactly, how this can harmonize with general, to-the-present-day rejection of the accuracy of the Jewish and Christian Scriptures (discussed below), but the overall thrust is easily discerned: Muhammad, and the Qur'an, stand firmly in the continued line going back through Jesus and Moses.

However, we cannot pass over easily the last *ayah*, one that reminds us of the penalty of apostasy that is part of the Islamic *sharia*. Allah will not accept apostates. As the *hadith* later would express it, "I would have killed them according to the statement of Allah's apostle, 'Whoever changed his Islamic religion, then kill him.'"[2] This tradition has had tragic consequences down through history and remains the ground for the persecution of many Christians throughout the Islamic world for the grave sin of preaching the gospel and so leading Muslims to apostasy. (See this theme's continuation in 3:98–100.)

> 3:113. [However] they are not all alike. Among the People of the Book there is an upright community who recites the revelations of Allah during the night and fall prostrate before Him.
>
> 114. They believe in Allah and the Last Day, enjoin what is right and forbid what is evil, and vie with one another in good works. They are of the righteous.
>
> 115. And whatever good they do, its reward will not be denied them. Allah knows those who fear [Him].

We would love to be able to identify specifically this "upright community." Most assume they are pious monks Muhammad encountered on his travels, and the reference to recitations and nightly prayers seems to bear this out. There is high praise for this group among the People of the Book, higher than one will find for any other community outside Islam. They are said to be "righteous," God-fearers, and they will receive a reward. How does this fit with other texts that clearly identify Christian worship as *shirk*? Once again, the following *ayah* seems to allow for the same interpretation offered before, that such words refer only to those who accept Muhammad and the Qur'an:

> 116. As for the disbelievers, neither their riches nor their progeny will protect them in the least against Allah. They are the dwellers of the Fire, abiding therein perpetually.

This is the view given by *Ibn Kathir*, that the upright community believes in Muhammad and the Qur'an and would, logically, become Muslims. To the reader not standing within the context of Islamic orthodoxy, however, it surely *seems* like the original intent, at least of this section, was otherwise. A similar strain of thought might possibly lie behind these words:

> 3:199. And there are certainly among the People of the Book some who believe in Allah and that which is revealed to you and that which was revealed to them, humbling themselves before Allah. They will not sell the signs of Allah for a miserable gain! Verily their reward is with their Lord; and Allah is swift in reckoning.

Of course, as soon as one ponders this possibility, another text presents itself:

> 98:1–6. Those who disbelieve among the People of the Book and the polytheists will not desist until a clear proof comes to them. A messenger from Allah reading pure pages. Containing worthy inscriptions. Nor did the People of the Book disagree among themselves until the Clear Proof was given them. And they have been ordered no more than this: To worship Allah sincerely, being True [in faith], to establish the prayer, and to give zakat. And that is the worthy religion. Surely those who disbelieve among

the People of the Book and the polytheists will be forever in the fire of hell. They are the worst of created beings.

Unfortunately, such texts are much more easily used by those seeking a reason to shut down all meaningful communication between Christians and Muslims. Language like "the worst of created beings" and "forever in the fire of hell" is strident at best. But even here the text seemingly raises more questions than it answers. It makes a distinction between the People of the Book and polytheists, once denied elsewhere in the Qur'an. Then it says the People of the Book had no intramural disagreement until getting the Clear Proof, which presumably means Muhammad.[3] And obviously this is untrue, as history shows a number of divisions even among orthodox believers prior to Muhammad. When the Qur'an speaks of those among the People of the Book who disbelieve, who are the ones who *do* believe? If you believe as a Christian, do you remain "in that camp," or do you become a Muslim? Discerning clear categories in the author's thought on such matters is difficult.[4] Finally,

> 5:15. O people of the Book! Now has Our Messenger come to you, expounding to you much of that which used to hide in the Book, and forgiving much. Now there has come to you light from Allah, and a clear Book.

Anyone who reads carefully the Hebrew Scriptures, the New Testament, and the Qur'an with an eye to history and context, must question the claim that the Qur'an in some fashion "expounds" much of what the People of the Book are allegedly hiding. How did Muhammad's preaching, which shows no understanding of the content of the very Book under consideration, expound on it? The countercharge would make more sense: Muhammad is hiding the majority of the Bible's message, in particular that of the New Testament.

Another set of texts with which the Christian should be familiar makes reference either to the gospel (Injil) directly or to the People of the Gospel in particular (a phrase that will be central in our examination of Surah 5:42–48 below). With only two exceptions, the term *gospel* is combined with *Torah*.

Surah 3:3–4 says Allah "sent down the Torah and the Gospel," works that serve as "guidance to mankind." This is important, for the question we must ask of Islam is whether we know what the Torah and the Gospel meant when they were given and whether they had been preserved to Muhammad's day.

Did the People of the Book Corrupt the Scriptures?

This may be the most important question we will address in this work. In my experience, this is the topic to which the conversation most often turns; every Christian should be prepared to discuss it, and every Muslim should consider well what they are saying when they accuse the Scriptures—Torah or Injil, Hebrew Old Testament or Greek New Testament—of being "corrupted."

Today it is almost a given of Islamic orthodoxy to hold that the Bible as a whole, both Hebrew and Greek Scriptures, have suffered wholesale corruption to where, in the main, they are utterly unreliable. Muslims around the world are taught that the Jews and the Christians altered their Scriptures, though there is no agreement as to when this took place. If anything unites Islamic apologists, it is the persistent assertion of Qur'anic perfection in contrast to the corrupted nature of the Bible, particularly the New Testament. So pervasive is this teaching that it has penetrated all the way down to the most unlearned Muslim, who repeats the accusation as if it were fact.

Later we will readdress the Bible's transmission, but for our present purposes we will examine as follows:

First, what does *corruption* mean, as to transmission of an ancient document to the present day? What do Muslims mean?

Second, when did this allegedly take place? Does the Qur'an give any indications?

Third, we will briefly (the topic could be vastly expanded) ask, Does the Qur'an itself teach the corruption of the *text* of the Bible (*tahrif al-nass, tahrif al-lafz*) or the corruption of the *meaning* of the Bible (*tahrif al-mana*)?

Finally, we will look more closely at Surah 5:42–48, key to this topic.

It is easy to find scholarly sources that affirm both the Hebrew Scriptures and the Christian Greek Scriptures to have been corrupted. They *have* been. But what does this mean? In scholarly parlance, *corruption* simply means that, over time, errors have been made in the handwritten copying process. At the least, this is true of all documents that began their existence prior to the printing press and, in reality, prior to 1949, when the photocopying process was invented. Hence, by nature, all ancient documents are "corrupt" to one degree or another. The issue is whether or not this corruption precludes our obtaining the original text.

Of course, this means the Qur'an is also "corrupt," in the sense of its having been a handwritten and hand-copied document, and that variations exist among its existing manuscripts from the first centuries of its transmission. We will note a few variants in chapter 11 of this book.

In the vast majority of instances, the variations we find in the many thousands of New Testament manuscripts (and fewer manuscripts of the Hebrew Scriptures) are not intentional changes (the normal idea Muslims have when they hear the word *corruption*) but errors of sight or hearing. The few that are intentional often were due to a desire on the part of the scribe to harmonize the text or to correct what he thought was an earlier mistake. New Testament scholar Bruce Metzger, having discussed such textual variants, concluded by noting,

> Lest the foregoing examples of alterations should give the impression that scribes were altogether willful and capricious in transmitting ancient copies of the New Testament, it ought to be noted that other evidence points to the careful and painstaking work on the part of many faithful copyists. . . . Even in incidental details one observes the faithfulness of scribes.[5]

The level of "corruption" documented in serious, fair, scholarly works on Old and New Testament textual transmission is utterly beneath the range asserted by most Muslims, who generally only concede that a small amount has escaped corruption and so is still in some sense "the word of God." Muslims join hands with the most destructive liberal critics and in many instances go far beyond their assertions.[6] It is easy to understand the motive for applying one set of standards to the Bible (radical skepticism based on humanistic and liberal scholarship) and a completely different set for the Qur'an. But the Qur'an presents such a profoundly different view of what is actually found in the New Testament especially, that the Muslim is faced with a choice: Reject Muhammad as a prophet and the Qur'an as a revelation from God, or accuse the Christians of radically altering their text from what it originally said.

When is this corruption to have taken place? The normal assumption of Muslims is "early on," maybe as early as the apostle Paul, often accused of originating all the errors of Christianity.[7] Some say during the centuries thereafter, on the allegation that the faith was deeply influenced by Greek thought. We will return to this critical question below, but specifics aside, the vast majority assumes that corruption took place prior to Muhammad's time.

Next, the Qur'an boldly claims that the revelation of God cannot be altered by man. Allah protects what he has sent down. Note a few texts:

15:9. We have, indeed, sent down the Remembrance, and We shall preserve it.

6:114–115. Shall I seek other than Allah for a judge, when He it is who has sent down to you [this] Book, fully detailed? Those to whom We gave the Book [previously] know that it is sent down from your Lord in truth. So be not of those who waver! The Word of your Lord has been completed in truth and justice. There is nothing that can change His words. He is the Hearing, the Knowing.

18:27. And recite [and teach] that which has been revealed unto you of the Book of your Lord. No one can change His words. You shall find no refuge beside Him.

10:64. Theirs is the good news in this world and in the Hereafter. No change can there be in the words of Allah. This is the tremendous triumph.

The doctrine of revelation's divine preservation in these words is clear. How far does it extend? Many Muslims today would limit it *solely* to the Qur'an. However, notice the language. In 15:9 and 6:114 the verb is *nazzal*; this is the very same term used of the Torah in 5:44 and of the Injil in 5:47. The Qur'an contains guidance and light (2:2; 4:174); the Torah and Injil contain guidance and light (5:44, 46). If Allah would allow what he has "sent down"—that which contains "guidance and light" in the Torah and Injil—to be corrupted, even allowing utter falsehood and the promulgation of *shirk* to enter in, then what guarantee has the Qur'an against the same fate?[8]

Regarding the supposed corruption, this is an area of dispute *throughout the history of Islamic interpretation itself.* As unified as modern Islam may seem to be on this matter, the fact is that down through the history of the faith, different views have been held by leading Islamic scholars and clerics. Two primary positions go back to the early centuries.

The first view is *tahrif al-mana,* distortion or changing of the *meaning* (not the words) of the text. This is the clear assertion of Surah 3:78: "And there is a party of them who distort the Book with their tongues, that you may think that what they say is from the Book, when it is not from the Book." This accusation is about misrepresenting the text, distorting its meaning, possibly by inserting extraneous materials into one's interpretation (say, from tradition, or other non-inspired books). But the underlying text itself, given by God, sent down to men, is not altered. This view is expressed, for example, by Imam Bukhari in commenting on Surah 85:21–22, referring to Ibn Abbas, one of the Companions, when he said, "No one removes the words of one of the Books of Allah Almighty, but they twist them, interpreting them improperly."[9]

The second view is *tahrif al-nass* or *tahrif al-lafz,* distortion or corruption of the actual *text* of the earlier Scriptures. This is the position most Muslims hold today. But is this the result of in-depth and fair study? Or something else? While we cannot entirely cover the subject here, a few observations are in order before we move back into the text itself.

The Spanish writer Ibn Hazm was the first to systematize the stronger view of textual corruption (*tahrif al-nass*), but clearly Muslims before him had made the accusation, if not as coherently. It seems fair to say the less strident assertion (*tahrif al-mana,* distorting the meaning) was predominant in a line of such notables as Ibn Abbas, al Tabari, al Razi, and Ibn Taymiyya, all major names in Islamic history, theology, and commentary.[10] But apparently when Muslims began to dialogue extensively with Christians in particular, the latter charge would come to the fore. That is, those who looked primarily to the Qur'an were less likely to make the stronger charge, but those who came to possess more knowledge of the New Testament (and hence saw its message's utter incompatibility with that of the Qur'an) were compelled apologetically to raise the charge of textual corruption. In fact, since one can call upon the same witness for *both* views, it seems some would take one view in non-apologetic contexts and the other in apologetic ones. Especially prior to precritical times, when neither Christians nor Muslims had access to critical information about the early stages of the transmission of their own scriptural texts, the specificity level would not have been as high as it can be today on this subject.

That these views existed side by side is well illustrated by the following quotations from the same page of Ibn Kathir's *Tafsir*. On Surah 3:78:

> Al-Bukhari reported that Ibn Abbas said that the *Ayah* means they alter and add although none among Allah's creation can remove the Word of Allah from His books, they alter and distort their apparent meanings. Wahb bin Munabbih said, "The Tawrah and the Injil remain as Allah revealed them, and no letter in them was removed. However, the people misguide others by addition and false interpretation, relying on books that they wrote themselves.
>
> "As for Allah's Books, they are still preserved and cannot be changed." Ibn Abi Hatim recorded this statement. However, if Wahb meant the books that are currently in the hands of the People of the Book, then we should state that there is no doubt that they altered, distorted, added to and deleted from them. For instance, the Arabic versions of these books contain tremendous error, many additions and deletions and enormous misinterpretation. Those who rendered these translations have

incorrect comprehension in most, rather, all of these translations. If Wahb meant the Books of Allah that He has with Him, then indeed, these Books are preserved and were never changed.[11]

Here, centuries into the Islamic era, affirmation of *tahrif al-mana* and then *tahrif al-nass* both can be found. However, note that Ibn Kathir is limited in his comments to Arabic translations of the Bible. How could he judge their accuracy without access to the original languages, which he did not know?

The question for the modern Muslim would seem to be, "Which of these two views represents the Qur'an's view?" Numerous texts could be cited, but after examining a number of scholarly discussions, Gordon Nickel concluded, "Analysis of these 'scholarly lists' shows that the Qur'anic verses most frequently associated with the Islamic doctrine of scriptural corruption are Q 2:75, 5:13 and 5:41."[12]

> 2:75. Now [O Muslims], do you then hope that they [the Jews] will believe in you, when some of them have already heard the word of Allah and knowingly perverted it, after they had understood its meaning?

> 5:13. And because of their breaking their pact, We have cursed them and made hard their hearts. They change words from their context and forget a part of that wherewith they had been reminded. You will not cease to discover treachery among them, all save a few. But bear with them, and pardon them. Surely, Allah loves those who behave with excellence.

> 5:41. O Messenger! Do not be grieved by those who hasten to disbelief, of such as say with their mouths: "We believe," but their hearts believe not, and of the Jews: listeners for the sake of falsehood, listeners on behalf of other people who come not to you, changing words from their context and saying: "If this be given to you, receive it, but if this be not given to you, then

beware!" He whom Allah dooms to sin, you [by your own efforts] will avail him naught against Allah. Those are they for whom the will of Allah is that He cleanse not their hearts. Theirs is humiliation in the world, and in the Hereafter a formidable torment.

Plainly these texts are anything but *mubinun* (clear, perspicuous), which has led to the varying interpretations in the *tafsir* literature. Surah 2:75 does not say the Jews destroyed and replaced Allah's words. Just the opposite—allegedly they heard the word of Allah (how, if it had been destroyed?) and knowingly perverted it. This perversion is in the realm of understanding, "after they had understood its meaning," and the next *ayah* indicates deception and dishonesty among them. All of this could be understood in the sense of *tahrif al-mana* without implying direct textual corruption.

Surah 5:13 also speaks not of destroying, obliterating, or even inserting anything but of changing words "from their context" and "forgetting." You cannot change words from their context *if the context no longer exists*. Hence obviously this text is referring to *tahrif al-mana*, for the words being altered already exist and are simply being mishandled and abused.

The context of Surah 5:41 is of the alleged unbelief and hypocrisy of those who oppose Muhammad. Once again the only assertion is alteration of words out of their context. This is the common problem in almost all interreligious arguments. But saying, "You are taking that out of context" is not the same as "You have removed the real words and written something else in their place and are trying to pass off your alteration as the original."

Nickel went on to say, "Two other verses which appear very frequently in these lists are Q 3:78 and 2:79."[13]

3:78. And there is a party of them who distort the Book with their tongues, that you may think that what they say is from the

Book, when it is not from the Book. And they say: "It is from Allah," when it is not from Allah, and they knowingly speak a lie concerning Allah.

2:79. Woe to those who write the Book with their own hands, and then declare: "This is from Allah," in order to sell it for a paltry price. Woe unto them because of what their hands have written, and woe unto them for what they have gained [from their trade!].

The "party of them who distort the Book with their tongues" cannot refer to *tahrif al-nass*, for if it is by only one party, and only orally, the written text would remain with those outside this particular group. Since this is being done "with their tongues," an assertion of *tahrif al-mana* is much more logical.

Finally, Surah 2:79 is the text most often cited by Muslim apologists in modern times. But if it is an accusation of *tahrif al-nass*, the supposed form is extreme indeed, for the *ayah* does not speak at all of altering what Allah has sent down or given. It refers to wholesale fraudulent creation of works that their authors say come "from Allah" that seemingly they attempt to sell to others. This is not about inserting foreign material or excising other material from the Torah or Injil, but manufacturing counterfeit Scripture for profit.

Further, the immediately preceding *ayah* says, "There are illiterate men among them who are ignorant of the Book [Torah], and depend on nothing but conjecture and guesswork." How could such men actually edit the very text of the book itself? It truly seems this portion is referring neither to *tahrif al-mana* nor to *tahrif al-nass,* but to other texts, possibly Jewish books of tradition, similar to the Korban Rule that Jesus so soundly condemned (Mark 7:9–13).

We have not had to read these texts unfairly or a-contextually to find them commensurate with an accusation of *tahrif al-mana* rather than *tahrif al-nass*. Also, our reading is in harmony with other information. An incident in Muhammad's life, reported in the *hadith*, is quite relevant to our inquiry.

> A group of Jews came and called on the Apostle of Allah (may peace be upon him) to Quff. So he visited them in their school. They said: Abu al-Qasim, a man of us has committed fornication with a woman; so pronounce judgment upon them. They placed a cushion for the Apostle of Allah (may peace be upon him) who sat on it and said: Bring the Torah. It was then brought. He then withdrew the cushion from beneath him and placed the Torah on it saying: I believed in thee and in Him Who revealed thee.[14]

If this *hadith* represents Muhammad's own views, then minimally the idea of extensive corruption of the Hebrew Scriptures would be untenable; we possess entire copies from long before Muhammad that match what we have now.[15] If he had held the views of most Muslims today, this would have been the time to explain it, but history records nothing to support such a conclusion. Joining this incident with our fair and contextual reading of the key *ayat* above, we must conclude that the now predominant claim of the biblical texts themselves, having undergone major alteration and corruption, is a later polemical and theological perspective not required by the Qur'anic text itself. It comes not from the positive teachings of Muhammad but through the unalterable fact of the Qur'anic author's unfamiliarity with the actual biblical text.[16]

A Voice From History

There is something comforting and confirming about looking back into history and realizing we stand shoulder to shoulder with others who have fought the same battles and been committed to the same truths. We are not engaging this issue for the first time. This discussion has taken place ever since Christians began to ask the first Muslims about what they believed. We have referred to one of the earliest such encounters, a dialogue between Abdullah ibn Ishmail al-Hashimi and Abd al-Masih ibn Ishaq al-Kindi, apparently around AD 820.

Al-Kindi's work provides a vital snapshot of the state of affairs after the first century of Islamic expansion (632–732). We will have reason to look more fully at some of his work in chapter 11; for now, note that he too encountered the accusation of corruption. Notice the distinct parallels between how he responded and our own study:

> But now I fancy you retort that these passages have been "cooked (up)." You escape the inference on the plea that the text has been corrupted; so you can apply your favorite argument and shelter behind it. Let me speak frankly for once and remember what I say, and lay it to heart. I do not argue in the spirit of pride nor from a love of criticism, but that I might win you. My religion imposes this duty on me toward everyone, but I have a special solicitude for you, because of the depths of darkness in which I found you. I do not know that I have found an argument more difficult to dislodge, more desperate to disarm than this which you advance as to the corruption of the sacred text. I marvel that you should allow it. You know that the Jews, though they are hostile to the truth as proclaimed by Him who is; the Light of the world and its glory, yet agree with us on this point. Without any collusion between us, the genuineness of these Old Testament scriptures as inspired is established. They are not corrupt, nor have they been added to or taken from. But, without dwelling on that let me apply one test which is fair to both of us. In God's name I ask you, who accuse us of tampering with the text, can you produce a book which has not been tampered with and which witness(es) to the truth as you hold it; a book which can appeal to such signs and wonders as those which

bear witness to the prophets and apostles, from whose hands we have received the writings which we still hold, as the Jews also do? I know that you cannot do this, nor even tell us how it can done. Your own scriptures bear quite conclusive witness on this point. For they say: "If ever you are in doubt as to what we have revealed, ask those who read the earlier scriptures (i.e., the Jews and Christians)." (Qur'an 10:94a). "Say, We have sent down the Law, in it is good guidance and light; we have sent in their steps Jesus (the) son of Mary in confirmation of what they know of the Law, and we have given him the Gospel, with good guidance and light, in confirmation of what they already know." (Qur'an 5:50). "And if the People of the Book believe and fear God, He will forgive their sins and bring them to a paradise of happiness. If they establish the Law and the Gospel and what was sent down to them from their Lord, they shall eat of that which is above and beneath their feet. From them shall come a people doing righteously, but the majority of them, how evil are their deeds." (Qur'an 5:70). "Say, O People of the Book, ye stand on nothing till ye establish the Law and the Gospel which has been sent down to you from your Lord." (Qur'an 5:72). See how your own book bears witness to us that the true reading of any passage is our reading. You are required to ask and receive judgment from us on such points. Now then, can you affirm that we have corrupted the text? What is this but to contradict your own scriptures? The situation is plain enough; you witness to the truth of our text—then again you contradict the witness you bear and allege that we have corrupted it; this is the height of folly.[17]

A Place for Muslims and Christians to Talk

While much of this work has focused upon educating the Christian reader on the Qur'an's background and content, at this point we will move into a portion of polemic argumentation based upon a key Qur'anic text. We include it to encourage the

Christian to present this material in loving hope that God will use it to promote the gospel among the Muslim people and also as a challenge to the Muslim reader. Here Muslim and Christian can sit down and, in light of reason and truth, talk about what the Islamic holy book claims.[18]

We wish to look carefully at Surah 5:42–48, with a less in-depth look at 5:65–68. It says much about the Torah and the Injil, and it is on the basis of its teaching that we seek to present a challenge to our Muslim readers.

> 5:42. They listen to falsehoods and devour what is unlawful. If they come to you, either judge between them or decline to interfere. If you decline, they cannot hurt you in the least. If you judge, judge between them with equity. Surely Allah loves those who judge with equity.

This section has as its background Muhammad's role in judging conflicts in the growing Islamic community in Medina, which in the early days included those who were not professing Muslims. When adjudicating between various groups, he is told to either stay out of their quarrels or judge fairly.

> 43. Why do they come to you for judgement when they have their own law [the Torah] wherein Allah delivered judgement [for them, and]; then, after that, they turn away? These are not believers.

The Qur'an points out that the Jews would have a basis upon which to judge their quarrels if they would but avail themselves of it. In the Torah, Allah "delivered judgment" for them. This reflects the oft-repeated teaching that Allah did send down the Torah.

> 44. We revealed the Torah wherein there was a guidance and a light, by which the Prophets who surrendered [to Allah] judged the Jews, and the Men of Allah and the rabbis [judged] by such

183

of Allah's Book as they were bidden to observe and be its witnesses. So fear not men, but fear Me. And sell not My signs for a miserable price. Whoever judges not by that which Allah has sent down, such are the disbelievers.

The Allah-revealed Torah is "a guidance and a light," all terms of supernatural origin and truthfulness. The Prophets (*plural*) judged the Jews[19] by "Allah's Book." Note the final line, "Whoever judges not by that which Allah has sent down, such are the disbelievers." In this context, the Jews are scolded for not judging by what Allah has sent down *in the Torah*. A major question of interpretation is, judging what? It seems the most logical reading is "judging amongst themselves," related to the quarrels they were asking Muhammad to examine. But some Muslims have read the text to refer to judging the claims of Muhammad (and as a result embracing Islam), which would, at least, be somewhat related to giving Muhammad a role as judge among them.

> 45. And We ordained for them therein: a life for a life, and an eye for an eye, and a nose for a nose, and an ear for an ear, and a tooth for a tooth, and for wounds retaliation. But, if anyone remits the retaliation [in charity], it is an act of atonement for himself. And whoever judges not by what Allah had revealed, such are the unjust.

From this very rare citation of a biblical text, the well-known *lex talionis* (Exodus 21:23–25; Numbers 24:19–20), it does not follow that Muhammad had access to a written copy of the Hebrew Scriptures. Many people today also know this very text by heart but have never read Exodus or Numbers and would not find the text without assistance. And as with how it is known today, the form in which it is found here is likely from oral transmission.

This is the first step in what is clearly an argument. Allah has sent down the Torah, in which is guidance and light, and those who reject it are disbelievers. Next step?

> 46. And in their footsteps We sent Jesus son of Mary, confirming that which was [revealed] before him, and We bestowed on him the Gospel wherein is guidance and a light, confirming that which was [revealed] before it in the Torah—a guidance and an admonition to the God-fearing.

The next link is forged. Allah has sent Jesus, who has come "confirming that which was revealed before him." It is vital to see how the next person in the chain confirms the authority of the one before and then is given a new revelation: "We bestowed on him the Gospel."[20] This too "is guidance and light," and in its very nature it likewise confirms its predecessor in the line.

Every Christian should read and understand the next *ayah*:

> 47. Let the People of the Gospel judge by that which Allah had revealed therein. Whoever judges not by that which Allah has revealed; such are the corrupt.

Here, the *Ahl al-Injil* are addressed directly, given a command right in the text: "judge by that which Allah had revealed therein." *Therein*, in the Arabic, refers to the gospel. There is no other antecedent. We are to judge by what Allah has revealed in the gospel. Now, let us think very carefully here.

First, what are we to judge? Again, either judge among ourselves in light of the Scripture God has given us, or judge Muhammad's claims as God's final messenger. Both are possible, contextually.

Second, in the gospel is divine revelation that is a light and guidance.

185

Third, these words had to have some kind of meaning to the original addressees. That is, Christians in Muhammad's time—who would hear these words recited to them by Muhammad himself or by other Muslim faithful—had to have a way of obeying this text's command.

That means *"the gospel" had to exist in the days of Muhammad.* If it was corrupted and lost before the seventh century, how could the People of the (already lost) Gospel judge by what Allah had revealed (but then had let disappear)? It makes no sense to command Christians to judge by a lost or corrupted document. So the Qur'an's author believed the gospel was still in Christian possession. And that has tremendous meaning for one simple reason.

We know beyond question what the gospel looked like in AD 632. We know because we have entire copies of the New Testament that long predate Muhammad. Whole codices are extant that were written in the early fourth century, and we have fragments of much of the New Testament going back as far as the early second century.[21] We know what the "People" would have had as "the Gospel." And the Qur'an commands the people of Muhammad's day (and we would expect, by extension, to this day) to *judge* by that standard.

That standard is exactly what we possess today as the New Testament. That was the gospel then; that is the gospel now. Each canonical gospel we read today we can document to have existed in that very form three centuries before Muhammad's ministry. *A Christian judging Muhammad's claims by the New Testament and finding that he was ignorant of the teachings of the apostles, ignorant of the cross, the resurrection, and the divine nature of the incarnate Son of God, and ignorant of the intention and meaning of the gospel itself, is simply doing what the Qur'an commands us to do in this text.*

We must ask our Muslim friends, "What will you do with this text?" Its words prove the gospel existed in the days of Muhammad. A person who says otherwise renders the Qur'an meaningless—how then can he go on believing in it? If it is guidance and light, it must have made sense when it was given.

If the Qur'an means what it says, then we must judge by the standard it commands us to use. When we do, Muhammad fails the test of a prophet who stands in the line of revelation found in Moses and fulfilled in Christ and His apostles. Every Muslim must give serious consideration to this dilemma, one that is brought upon him or her by the very text of the Islamic holy book.

Upon giving this command, the Qur'an continues to forge the chain leading to Muhammad:

> 48. And to you We have sent down the Book with the truth, confirming whatever Books were before it and a witness over them. So judge between them by that which Allah has sent down, and follow not their passions away from the truth which has come to you. For each of you We have appointed a [Divine] law and a traced-out way. Had Allah willed He could have made you one community, but, so that He may try you by that which He has given you [He has made you as you are]. So vie with one another in good works. To Allah you will all be returned, and He will then inform you of that wherein you disputed.

See the argument? Moses/Torah leading to Jesus/Injil leading to Muhammad/Qur'an. The chain is complete. Muhammad's authority is placed squarely upon this foundation. If the chain is broken by the considerations we gave above, the claims of Muhammad fall.

Note that the term translated "a witness" (*muhaymin*), is often understood by modern Muslims as "a guard" or "a correction." Many Muslims interpret this as an assertion that the Qur'an acts as a filter, correcting the errors that crept into the preceding texts. And surely that is how it is used by Muslims who read those other texts anachronistically through the Qur'anic lens. But we have not been able to find any contemporary lexical evidence that *muhaymin* means "corrector." It refers to a guardian, and if anything, this would seem to mean it is to act as one protecting, not correcting, these texts. If the Qur'an's author believed his message to be consistent with that of the Torah and Injil *out of ignorance*, he easily could have made such a claim honestly.

In *ayat* 65–68 a few other vital assertions are made about our subject that shed more light upon the above argument. Note what is said:

> 5:65. If only the People of the Book would believe and fear Allah, surely We would bring them into Gardens of Bliss.
>
> 66. If they had observed [practiced] the Torah and the Gospel and that which was sent down to them from their Lord, they would surely have been nourished from above them and from beneath their feet. Among them there are people who are moderate, but many of them are of evil conduct.

Once again, how could the People of the Book, Jew or Gentile, observe or practice the Torah and the Gospel *if both books were corrupted by the time of Muhammad?* These words had to have meaning when they were written, and the unstated assumption that must be seen is that the Torah and the Gospel were right there for all to see, observe, and practice. The fault for the unbelief is placed not on the books of Scripture but at the feet of the people!

> 67. O Messenger! Make known that which has been sent down to you from your Lord, for if you do not, you will not have conveyed His message. Allah will protect you from men [who mean you harm]. Allah guides not those who disbelieve.

> 68. Say: "O People of the Book! You have nothing [of true guidance] till you observe the Torah and the Gospel, and that which was sent down to you from your Lord." That which was sent down to you [O Muhammad] from your Lord is certain to increase the transgression and disbelief of many of them. So grieve not for those who disbelieve.

We can agree with the sentiment of the beginning of *ayah* 68—we do not have true guidance until we observe the Torah and the Gospel, and yes, we affirm with joy and gladness that it was sent down to us from our Lord. And it is just here that the real issue in the Christian/Muslim dialogue must be decided.

Do these words have meaning? If the gospel was sent down by our Lord, and we judge Muhammad by its clear and consistent teaching on so many subjects, we find him wanting. We cannot accept his prophetic claims. He did not know the gospel. The stories he had heard from his few encounters with Christians did not give him a sufficient knowledge of the New Testament. His teachings are directly contrary to many of the specific truths taught by Jesus and His apostles.

So how can we believe *both* the Qur'an's affirmation of the gospel's continued existence and inspiration *and* the claims that Muhammad is the continuation of that line, God's final messenger? The Qur'an itself presents an unsolvable dilemma at this point, one that can be solved only by admitting the truth of what had been written long before Muhammad claimed prophethood:

> God, after He spoke long ago to the fathers in the prophets in many portions and in many ways, in these last days has spoken to us in His Son, whom He appointed heir of all things, through whom also He made the world. And He is the radiance of His glory and the exact representation of His nature, and upholds all things by the word of His power. When He had made purification of sins, He sat down at the right hand of the Majesty on high. (Hebrews 1:1–3)

Notes

1. *Tafsir Ibn Kathir* (Riyadh: Darussalam, 2003), 2:204.

2. *Sahih Al-Bukhari*, 9.57.

3. As indicated in Jalalu'd-Din Al-Mahalli and Jalalu'd-Din As-Suyuti, *Tafsir Al-Jalalayn* (London: Dar Al Taqwa, 2007), 1346.

4. Note the confusion of categories in Surah 3:110, "And if the People of the Book had believed, it would have been better for them. Some of them are believers, but most of them are corrupt." Who, then, are the People of the Book if some have believed and others have not believed?

5. Bruce Manning Metzger, *The Text of the New Testament: Its Transmission, Corruption, and Restoration*, 2nd ed. (New York: Oxford University Press, 1980), 206.

6. Gordon Nickel points out that in the modern period this almost uniform Islamic position in asserting wholesale textual corruption of the Bible can be traced to recent times:

> In the mid-19th century, the Muslim accusation of *tahrif al-nass* took a kind of quantum leap through the controversy between Indian Muslim scholars and European Christian missionaries in the India of the British Raj. . . . Mawlana Rahmat Allah Kayranawi ("al-Hindi," 1818–91) is credited with moving the textual corruption accusation forward through a famous public debate and through a widely published book. Interestingly, the most influential Indian theologian of the modern period, Shah Wali Allah (1703–62), had previously declared that he did not believe in the corruption of the text of the Torah. . . . Rahmat Allah seized upon a strategic plan for publicly confounding European Christian missionaries. . . . For the first time in the history of Muslim polemic, the Indian theologian used works of historical criticism written in Europe to support his claim that Christians themselves knew of the corruption of the Bible. The substance of Rahmat Allah's polemic in the debate . . . appeared in print . . . in the Arabic *Izhar al-haqq*. . . . 20th-century Arabic authors did not add substantially to Rahmat Allah's polemic (*Narratives of Tampering in the Earliest Commentaries on the Qur'an* [Leiden: Brill, 2011], 24–25).

7. It is hard to trace this anti-Pauline bias back to Muhammad, however. Nothing in the Qur'an directs us to identify Paul as a false teacher, an evil seducer, or a denier of Christ's teachings. If Paul were a renowned promoter of *shirk*, as say so many Muslims today, surely the Qur'an, written more than half a millennium later, would warn us about it. Evidence exists, rather, that a stream of early Islamic belief saw Paul as a faithful messenger of Jesus. Regarding the three Messengers of Surah 36:13–14, Ibn Kathir records a tradition (8:178–179; Al-Suyuti does also), which he himself does not follow, that "The names of the first two Messengers were Sham'un and Yuhanna, and the name of the third was Bulus, and the city was Antioch. . . . Qatadah bin Di'amah claimed that they were messengers of the Messiah, peace be upon him, sent to the people of Antioch." Bulus is the Arabic form of Paul's name.

8. Below, when we consider the final portions of Surah 5:42–48, we will look at one possible answer that Muslims have offered.

9. *Sahih Al-Bukhari,* "The Oneness of God," no. 85, found in the footnote between 9.642 and 643. (Aisha Bewley reproduces the same quote [with typographical error *works* for *words*] at bewley.virtualave.net/bukhari52.html.) Ibn Abbas is famed in early Islamic history for his knowledge of the Qur'an and *tafsir.*

10. This view persists within Islamic scholarship. Mahmoud Ayoub wrote, in 1986,

> Contrary to the general Islamic view, the Qur'an does not accuse Jews and Christians of altering the text of their scriptures, but rather of altering the truth which those scriptures contain. The people do this by concealing some of the sacred texts, by misapplying their precepts, or by "altering words from their right position." However, this refers more to interpretation than to actual addition or deletion of words from the sacred books.

W. M. Watt agreed: "The Qur'an does not put forward any general view of the corruption of the text of the Old and New Testaments" (in Nickel, *Narratives of Tampering,* 6–7).

11. *Tafsir Ibn Kathir,* 2:196.

12. Nickel, *Narratives of Tampering,* 29.

13. Ibid.

14. *Sunan Abu Dawud* Book 33, number 4434. While Muhammad affirmed belief in the Torah, the same *hadith* literature also records a troubling account of his reaction to one of his closest followers reading that same text:

> Umar ibn al-Khattab brought to Allah's Messenger (peace be upon him) a copy of the Torah and said: Allah's Messenger, this is a copy of the Torah. He (Allah's Messenger) kept quiet and he (Umar) began to read it. The (colour) of the face of Allah's Messenger (peace be upon him) underwent a change, whereupon Abu Bakr said: Would that your mother mourn you, don't you see the face of Allah's Messenger? Umar saw the face of Allah's Messenger (peace be upon him) and said: I seek refuge with Allah from the wrath of Allah and the wrath of His Messenger. We are well pleased with Allah as Lord, with Islam as religion, and with Muhammad as Prophet. Whereupon Allah's Messenger (peace be upon him) said: By Him in Whose hand is the life of Muhammad, even if Moses were to appear before you and you were to follow him, leaving me aside, you would certainly stray into error; for if (Moses) were alive (now), and he found my prophetical ministry, he would have definitely followed me (*Al-Tirmidhi Hadith,* 69).

15. Another important item to consider here is the oft-repeated Qur'anic challenge to produce "something like it," regarded as strong evidence of its inspiration and uniqueness. One problem with this argument is that at one point the Qur'an makes the same challenge on behalf of the Qur'an *and* the Torah!

> 28:48–49: But when the truth came to them from Us, they said: "Why is he not given the like of what was given unto Moses?" Did they not disbelieve in what was given to Moses before? They said: "Two magics that support each other;" and they said: "In both we disbelieve." Say: "Then bring a Book from Allah that is a better guidance than these two that I may follow, if you are truthful."

The most natural reading of this text in its context is that the "two magics" are the Torah and the Qur'an together. The challenge to "bring a Book from Allah that is better guidance" then refers to the Qur'an and the Torah. How could the Qur'an say this if the Torah actually had been corrupted in the day of Muhammad?

16. Nickel, ending his thorough examination of the *tafsir*, concluded,

> In summary, Muqatil and Tabari did not in the first instance understand from the words of the Qur'an that Jews and Christians had falsified their scriptures. The passages in which they make or transmit accusations of falsification remain isolated and tentative. This raises the question as to how the Muslim understanding changed to the point where the doctrine of corruption of the earlier scriptures became the dominant Islamic position (*Narratives of Tampering*, 228).

Nickel agrees with our thesis when he says, "One reason for the change in approach may be the needs of polemic" (that is, in attacking the veracity of the text of the Bible).

17. Newman, *The Early Christian-Muslim Dialogue*, 498–499.

18. In fact, we highly recommend a comparison of Surah 5 with John 5 as a possible starting point for dialogue and discussion about the teachings and characteristics of the two books and the faiths they represent.

19. This is important, for some modern Muslims assume that *only* the five books of Moses are revealed of God, yet this assumes that the Qur'an's author functioned on the Jewish division of the Hebrew Scriptures into Torah, Neviim, Ketuvim (Law, Prophets, Writings). While the Qur'an does recognize the Psalms of David (Surah 17:55), its author seems to have lacked a full knowledge of the *extent* of the Hebrew canon.

20. Why is *gospel* singular (not "the Gospels")? Muslims often claim "the gospel" was a single book given to Jesus; since we have no such book today, it must have been lost, so what we have now cannot be inspired or authoritative. This assumes the Qur'an's author had access to and sufficient knowledge of the New Testament text to know its layout and form, which thus far we have found no reason to accept. Christians often refer to "the gospel" as a single unit for the overarching message laid out in the four canonical Gospels. Early Christian writers moved easily between the singular and plural without concern for being specific, and clearly Muhammad, drawing from oral traditions, made no distinction. As the *next ayah* refers to the People of the Gospel in the present tense (contemporaneous with Muhammad), the gospel still existed at the time of the Qur'an's writing, or else the words make no sense.

21. See my introduction to the New Testament textual criticism that is part of *The King James Only Controversy* (Minneapolis: Bethany House, 2009) for a discussion of the relevant texts (e.g., Codex Sinaiticus, Codex Vaticanus, and papyri of the second and third centuries).

9

Prophecies of Muhammad
in the Bible

One aspect of the Qur'an's teaching that captures the attention of most Christians is its claim that the Bible makes prophetic reference to Muhammad, and that by name. Given that most evangelicals are not even certain whether Islam came before or after the days of Jesus, it is fully understandable why they would be unaware of how important it is for the Qur'an, and hence for modern Muslims, to find biblical prophecies about Muhammad.

When I have explained this aspect of Qur'anic teaching to Christian audiences, I have often been met with smiles and bemusement. And yet the concept is deeply ingrained not only in the Qur'anic text but also in the Islamic mind. The perception that Christians simply do not know their Scriptures, or are hiding elements of them, is strong in many Muslim minds, especially in Islamic lands, even when this is combined with a general ignorance of the Bible's actual content.

But as to the Qur'an, if in fact it insists that Muhammad is prophesied in the Bible and we discover this is not the case, we have a clear example of, at best, a misunderstanding by the author. Given modern Islamic insistence that the author is God Himself, documentation of a specific error relating to the Scriptures of those who came before Muhammad would be a crucial element of any honest examination of Muhammad's claims and the Islamic faith. No Muslim who seeks *al-Haqq*, the truth, could ignore such a problem in the text.

First we will examine the key Qur'anic texts and then look to the primary biblical texts Muslims say fulfill the Qur'an's claims. Once again, we face the issue of "multiple views," for while many Muslims point to specific texts and insist that many biblical passages refer to Muhammad, others, especially in the West, hesitate to specify. Indeed, some observe that the Qur'an leaves the matter vague and does not provide specific references, and hence they will not firmly identify exact texts. The more conservative the Muslim, the more likely he or she is to believe that at least the texts we will examine here *are* directly related to Muhammad as a prophet.

"The Unlettered Prophet"

The first text is from the Meccan period, in *Surah Al-Araf*, 7:157:

> Those who follow the Messenger, the unlettered Prophet, whom they find described in their Torah and Gospel—he will enjoin on them good and forbid them evil, he will make lawful for them all good things and prohibit for them what is foul, and he will relieve them of their burden and the fetters that were upon them—those that believe in him, honor him, support him, and follow the light which has been sent down with him: they are the successful.

The key line is "whom they find described in their Torah and Gospel." Yet some translations, such as the Saheeh International, depart from the majority of other English translations and show a particular apologetic bias on the matter of the preservation (or lack thereof) of the biblical text (represented by the Torah and the Injil). These will render this phrase "in what they have of the Torah and the Gospel," implying a loss of a portion of the Scriptures. Nothing in either the context or the language indicates a reference to the corruption of the Torah and Injil. But note these renderings:

> whom they will find described in the Torah and the Gospel (which are) with them (Pickthall)

> whom they find mentioned in their own (scriptures),—in the law and the Gospel (Yusuf Ali)

> whom they find written down with them in the Taurat and the Injeel (Shakir)

> whom they find written down with them in the Torah and the Gospel (Arberry)

> whom they find written down with them in the Torah and the Gospel (Bewley)

> whom they shall find described in the Torah that is with them, and [later on] in the Gospel (Asad)

Some of the more imaginative renderings expand upon the phrase:

> whom they find mentioned in their own Law and Gospel. (Deuteronomy18 and John) (Aziz) Follow the Messenger, the Prophet who is a non-Israelite, and who was unlettered before the Revelation (29:48). They find him well described* in the Torah and the Gospel with them. (The note that is added reads, "Deuteronomy

xviii, 15 and 18. Gospel of John 14:16, 15:26, 16:7 PARACLE-TOS = COMFORTER, from original Greek PERICLYTOS = THE PRAISED ONE. In Aramaic, MAWHAMANA = THE PRAISED ONE) (Shabbir Ahmed) whom they find written with them in the Taurat (Torah) (Deut, xviii, 15) and the Injeel (Gospel) (John xiv, 16) (Hilali-Khan)

We will note the specific citation of biblical texts in our discussion below.

There is much discussion of just what "unlettered prophet" means, but we need not be detained by this. Our focus is on what the Qur'an is claiming.

The context includes a discussion about Moses and the people of Israel. Right before this *ayah*, we read, "I shall ordain it for those who fear [Allah] and pay the *zakat*, and those who believe in Our signs" (i.e., the Qur'an). This defines *who* follows "the Messenger, the unlettered prophet," which is confirmed in the *ayah* that follows:

> 7:158. Say [O Muhammad]: "O Mankind! Truly I am the Messenger of Allah to you all; [the Messenger of] Him to whom belongs the sovereignty of the heavens and the earth. There is no god save Him. He gives life and He gives death. So believe in Allah and His Messenger, the unlettered Prophet who believes in Allah and His words, and follow him that you may be rightly guided."

So this section is meant to be a call to follow Muhammad as the "Messenger of Allah to you all" and a promise of good in this life and in the hereafter for those who do so. The phrase in question is part of the argument (one might say the apologetic) for why those who possess the Torah and the Injil should believe in Muhammad: They find a description of this prophet therein, and if they wish to be successful, they will follow the light that has come from him. It might be that the description itself is included in *ayah* 157, "who enjoins upon them what is right and forbids them what is wrong," etc. That is a legitimate, if not necessary conclusion, for the text does not explicitly identify this as what is actually found in the Torah and the Injil.

Significantly, the Qur'an makes reference to both the Torah and the Injil (though in this context only Moses is in view, so the Injil's addition seems somewhat out of place). Given that this section is clearly apologetic in nature (i.e., it had a direct application in the days of Muhammad, seen in *ayah* 158's instruction for him to speak to the people of his day and call them to follow him as Allah's prophet), the claim "they find described" had to be relevant to those who possessed the Torah and the Injil *at the time of Muhammad*. That is, the people to whom he would speak the words of *ayah* 158 would have to be able to confirm his words from the Scriptures they possessed. Again, we know *exactly* what they had at the beginning of the seventh century and possess entire copies of the Bible that were written long before then.

So it seems the Qur'an makes a definite positive claim that the Torah and the Injil, the Law and the Gospel, include in their written text some mention or description of Muhammad as Allah's prophet. As those books were sent down prior to the Qur'an, such references would, by nature, have to be prophetic. This is why Muslims have for centuries looked into both the Old and New Testaments to find texts that could be applied to Muhammad. But this is not the only text that has driven them to this activity.

"Whose Name Is Ahmad"

61:6. And [remember] Jesus, son of Mary, who said: "O Children of Israel; I am the messenger of Allah to you, confirming that which was before me in the Torah and bringing good news of

a messenger who will come after me, whose name is Ahmad."
Yet when he came to them with clear proofs, they said: "This
is manifest magic."

This *ayah* is another example of Muhammad's appeal to the
examples of Moses and Jesus in defense of his own prophethood.
It is in one of the later *surahs* to be revealed, and hence shows
that he continued to emphasize his prophetic calling in the line of
Moses and Jesus throughout the Meccan and Medinan periods.
The preceding *ayah* had called upon the example of Moses:

> 61:5. And [remember] when Moses said to his people: "O my
> people, Why do you seek to harm me, when you know that I
> am Allah's Messenger to you?" So when they swerved Allah let
> their hearts swerve. Allah does not guide the corrupt.

The argument seems to be that the great messengers of the past
experienced doubt, rejection, and difficulty from those they
sought to call to the ways of God, and so Muhammad falls in
their line even when he faces opposition and disbelief. However,
our main concern here is not this particular argument for his
prophethood,[1] but the striking assertion made almost in passing,
placed in the mouth of Jesus. Like Moses, Jesus is made to say
He is the messenger of Allah. As in other texts (e.g., 5:44–47),
Jesus acts as a confirmer of the revelation given before (in this
case, the Torah), just as Muhammad is to be seen as doing the
same as Allah's messenger. Yet then the statement "and bringing
good tidings of a messenger to come after me, whose name is
Ahmad" is surprising on many counts.

First, of course, no historical referent gives the supposed
example any grounds. That is, if Muhammad were to tell the
people to remember when Jesus said this, they would be left
wondering what he was talking about, since no one since the days

of Jesus had ever imagined he had talked of a coming prophet named Ahmad. Later generations of Muslims might creatively attempt to read such an expectation back into the pre-Islamic period, but there is no evidence Jesus ever said anything even remotely like this. If the Qur'an is seeking once again to substantiate Muhammad's claims to prophethood by reference to preceding prophets and their words, this argument would be particularly problematic and incapable of carrying the weight of truth.

Second, the claim made in the words of Jesus here is twofold, indicating a confirmation of what was in the Torah and then also this assertion about a future messenger named Ahmad. Yet the reaction of those who rejected Jesus, and their statement, "This is obvious magic," seems to have no connection to Jesus' statements. One might imagine that what they said is only in reference to the "clear evidences" Jesus gave, but if this *ayah* is parallel to the preceding one, referencing Moses, then the people's guilt had something to do with their rejecting Moses' authority by deviating from the message he brought. There is no evidence that either the enemies or the followers of Jesus were looking for "a messenger to come after" Him. While the allegation was made that Jesus cast out demons by Satan's power (Matthew 12:27), and this may be what the Qur'an is referring to, we are still left wondering how the prophecy about Ahmad is relevant to the rejection by Jesus' enemies.

The summary the Qur'an offers comes in *ayah* 7: "And who is more wicked than the man who invents a falsehood about Allah when called to Islam? Allah does not guide the unjust." Those who rejected Moses and Jesus invented untruths about Allah even when both Moses and Jesus were inviting them to follow the ways of Allah, and anyone who is wise in Muhammad's day will not follow their example.

It is easy to see how the prophecy of a coming messenger functions in the mind of the author, even if the text gives little explanation and no historical foundation upon which to accept its assertions. The uniqueness of the Christian claims about Jesus is undercut by putting into His mouth a prophecy pointing away from Himself to someone who will follow. And by using Ahmad, the same Arabic root from which Muhammad's name derives, the Qur'an is seeking to solidify the bridge, the connection, from Moses (hence the Jews) through Jesus (hence the Christians) to Muhammad.

Ironically, the Qur'an may contain an exhortation to Muhammad himself to go to the People of the Book if he is doubtful about his own calling and the prediction of his coming in the previous Scriptures. Note the words of Surah 10:94 as found in the Hilali-Khan translation:

> So, if you (O Muhammad) are in doubt concerning that which We have revealed unto you, [i.e. that your name is written in the Taurat (Torah) and the Injil (Gospel)], then ask those who are reading the Book [the Taurat (Torah) and the Injil (Gospel)] before you. Verily, the truth has come to you from your Lord. So be not of those who doubt (it).[2]

The Hilali-Khan has become one of the most popular English translations, but clearly has very conservative (Salafi) tendencies. It inserts paraphrastic *ahadith*-based commentary, as here with "i.e., that your name is written in the Torah and the Injil." If this is not the reason for Muhammad's possible doubt, we still are left with a startling text directing the "final prophet" to inquire of Jews and Christians, because they were "reading the Book before you." But this is exactly what Muhammad did not do, if the Qur'an's content and sharp disconnection from the previous Scriptures is any indication. But if Hilali-Khan is correct, then what would Muhammad have found by inquiring of Jews and Christians on this matter? The reality is the New Testament plainly teaches that Jesus is the final revelation from God due to His unique nature as the Son (Hebrews 1:1–3). Clearly, the Qur'an's author was unaware of this teaching. Christians were looking not for the coming of an Arabian prophet; every generation looks for the return of the risen and glorified Messiah, Jesus. To be sure, if Muhammad had inquired of the Christians, he would not have been encouraged to view himself as a predicted prophet.

Testimony Outside the Qur'an

The *hadith* literature does not invest great interest in this particular aspect of Qur'anic teaching. But some sources do give an insight into how this belief functioned in the early community. Ibn Kathir, one of our earliest and fullest sources of Qur'anic commentary, tells an interesting story that he attaches to his commentary on Surah 7:157, seeing it as supporting the assertions therein. We will summarize it here along with portions of the citation:

> This is the description of the Prophet Muhammad in the Books of the Prophets. They delivered the good news of his advent to their nations and commanded them to follow him. His descriptions were still apparent in their Books, as the rabbis and the priests well know.

Islamic writers of this period commonly assert that Jews *and* Christians were awaiting a prophet out of Arabia. They do not provide contemporary evidence from Jewish or Christian sources, only hearsay stories from Islamic sources.

Ibn Kathir goes on to tell of a man who met Muhammad:

So I passed by him while he was walking between Abu Bakr and 'Umar, and I followed them until they went by a Jewish man, who was reading from an open copy of the Tawrah. He was mourning a son of his who was dying and who was one of the most handsome boys. The Messenger of Allah asked him (the father), "I ask you by He Who has sent down the Tawrah, do you not find the description of me and my advent in your Book?" He nodded his head in the negative. His son said, "Rather, yes, by He Who has sent down the Tawrah! We find the description of you and your advent in our Book. I bear witness that there is no deity worthy of worship except Allah and that you are the Messenger of Allah."[3]

At this, Muhammad commands the Companions to care for the boy, and himself leads the funeral prayers for him when he dies (in light of his profession of the *Shahada*). The point, of course, is that while some (the father) refused to acknowledge what was right in front of them, others (the son) were willing to admit that their texts not only prophesied of Muhammad, but in the words above, describe him and his advent!

Does this major claim withstand scrutiny? To this we turn our attention.

Biblical Texts Cited

We will examine carefully the most commonly cited texts in Islamic literature and polemics and ask: Would anyone in Muhammad's time (or today) find in them a description of a coming prophet from Arabia that can find fulfillment only in Muhammad? Could a dying Jewish boy possibly have recognized Muhammad from reading his own Scriptures? If we find Muhammad is not described in the Bible, what impact does this have on our examination of the Qur'an's claims? And if the claim truly finds its basis in Muhammad's self-understanding of his role as a prophet, what does this tell us?

The text most often put forward by Islamic polemicists in support of the above Qur'anic texts is Deuteronomy 18:15–19:

> The LORD your God will raise up for you a prophet like me from among you, from your countrymen, you shall listen to him. This is according to all that you asked of the LORD your God in Horeb on the day of the assembly, saying, "Let me not hear again the voice of the LORD my God, let me not see this great fire anymore, or I will die." The LORD said to me, "They have spoken well. I will raise up a prophet from among their countrymen like you, and I will put My words in his mouth, and he shall speak to them all that I command him. It shall come about that whoever will not listen to My words which he shall speak in My name, I Myself will require *it* of him."

Though the citation of this text goes back to some of the earliest streams of Islamic thought, its prevalence among Muslims today is due primarily to one man: Ahmed Deedat. Millions of Muslims have seen this South African's extended presentation of the text, and while he was not a scholar of any serious training, he was a master speaker and showman. Now millions around the world are convinced that these words from the Law of Moses could not possibly find fulfillment in Jesus but instead must refer to Muhammad.

Deedat's presentation was entertaining and memorable yet anything but an example of sound scholarship or exegesis. Basically, he contrasted Jesus and Moses, insisting that for Jesus to "be like" Moses, He would have needed to be a military leader or governmental leader. He then positively compared Muhammad with Moses in these ways and insisted that as the Arabs are related to the Jews through Abraham, they are "brothers," and so Muhammad can fulfill this prophecy.

In contrast, this text in Deuteronomy considered alone *and* the biblical witness taken fully, completely precludes any possible fulfillment by the seventh-century person of Muhammad. No fair and honest analysis of these ancient words can possibly lead us to view the Muslim prophet as fulfilling their expectation.

First, this text unequivocally limits its fulfillment to a Jewish person. While one might try to say the Hebrew word *brother* (*achi*, translated above as "countryman") could be extended out to mean any nation related to the Jewish people (hence, the Arabs by the claim to descend from Ishmael), words have meaning in the context in which they are used, and this context precludes that interpretation. In Deuteronomy 18:1–2 we read,

> The Levitical priests, the whole tribe of Levi, shall have no portion or inheritance with Israel; they shall eat the LORD's offerings by fire and His portion. They shall have no inheritance among their countrymen; the LORD is their inheritance, as He promised them.

Here the same term is used, translated "countrymen." Clearly only the nation of Israel is in view, as the discussion is about the Levitical priests and their ministry among the Israelites. The tribe of Levi is not given a specific land allotment, as all the tribes are to contribute toward their maintenance by the offerings they are to bring to the tabernacle (and later the temple).

This is further substantiated in verse 5:

> For the LORD your God has chosen him and his sons from all your tribes, to stand and serve in the name of the LORD forever.

So plainly the "countrymen" are "from all your tribes," that is, Israel's twelve tribes. This is the immediate context of the usage in Deuteronomy 18:18.

Also, contextually, the preceding chapter gives the following instruction:

You shall surely set a king over you whom the LORD your God chooses, *one* from among your countrymen you shall set as king over yourselves; you may not put a foreigner over yourselves who is not your countryman. (17:15)

There is no question *countryman* (literally, "brother") means an Israelite—this text specifically contrasts the term with "a foreigner." Muhammad, not of the tribes, would have been considered a foreigner in Israel. He would not be a countryman, and thus Deuteronomy 18:18 cannot be fulfilled in him.

In addition, this reality is not witnessed to only by the Jewish Scriptures. The New Testament likewise sees this text's fulfillment in the person of Jesus, not Muhammad. In the very earliest days of the Christian faith, years before the conversion of the apostle Paul, Peter said,

Moses said, "THE LORD GOD WILL RAISE UP FOR YOU A PROPHET LIKE ME FROM YOUR BRETHREN; TO HIM YOU SHALL GIVE HEED to everything He says to you. And it will be that every soul that does not heed that prophet shall be utterly destroyed from among the people." And likewise, all the prophets who have spoken, from Samuel and *his* successors onward, also announced these days. (Acts 3:22–24)

Peter not only applied Deuteronomy 18 directly to the Messiah, Jesus, he also insisted that all the prophets had announced the days that brought fulfillment in Jesus. This is the most primitive Christian affirmation, and it long precedes the advent of Muhammad.

Note that the prophecy of Deuteronomy 18 finds perfect fulfillment in Jesus, not when we try to find parallels between Jesus and Moses in every aspect of their lives, but in the specific aspect the prophecy indicates: "I [The LORD] will put My words in his mouth, and he shall speak to them all that I command him."

This is exactly what Jesus did, though in a far greater and more intensive way than Moses ever did. Consider these testimonies:

> He who does not love Me does not keep My words; and the word which you hear is not Mine, but the Father's who sent Me. (John 14:24)

> When you lift up the Son of Man, then you will know that I am *He,* and I do nothing on My own initiative, but I speak these things as the Father taught Me. (John 8:28)

Those who, per the Qur'an, would read about this prophet in their Scriptures would not and, in fact, could not find Muhammad here. The most-cited text fails to fulfill the necessary conditions. What about the second-most-cited Scripture text in this regard?

Is Muhammad the "Exalted One" of John 14 Through 16?

The next most oft-cited biblical passage allegedly fulfilling the Qur'an's promise that Muhammad is mentioned therein is the extended section of John 14–16, specifically referring to the Advocate or Helper, traditionally identified by the text itself and by historic Christian belief as the Holy Spirit. Again, due primarily (in modern times) to the popularity of Ahmed Deedat, many Muslims believe this text's original intention was to point us to Muhammad.

Though once more the Qur'an provides no specifics, leaving Muslims free to speculate as to how its promise is to be fulfilled, the most common view is that the Helper should be applied to Muhammad mainly because the term *Ahmed* can mean "exalted one," and popular belief is that the text in John has been altered, hiding the original reading from view. Specifically, many believe that instead of *paracletos* (the Paraclete, Helper, or Advocate), the original had *periklutos*, "the exalted or honored one." As most Muslims have accepted the idea that the biblical text as a whole has been corrupted and changed, it is easy to posit such a theoretical change and therefore "find" Muhammad in the text. Combine this with the argument that Jesus could not be talking about the Holy Spirit because the Holy Spirit had not yet been given, and you have the understanding of most Muslims "on the street."

Christians are often surprised Muslims would make this assertion, as it seems obvious to them that Jesus was talking about the Spirit, not a man in Arabia who would claim prophethood several hundred years later. However, our traditional reading is not evidence in and of itself. We need to be able to demonstrate positively that the text identifies the Helper as the Spirit. In that process, we will see that Muhammad in no way fulfills the description Jesus gave to His disciples of the One who would come, sent from heaven by Him and the Father to be with His disciples forever. Let's look at the relevant texts.

If we allow John's gospel to stand as it is found in all the earliest manuscripts we possess (i.e., we do not assume corruption,[4] for which we have no physical evidence), we find chapters 14–16 provide a consistent story of the final ministry of Jesus to His disciples. This portion is thoroughly Trinitarian, as it speaks of the divine roles of the Father, Son, and Spirit in the divine economy of salvation. Nothing in the context would lead us to think we are about to encounter a prophecy about a coming Arabian prophet.

After referring to prayer to Himself in 14:14,[5] Jesus speaks of "another Helper" or Comforter:

> I will ask the Father, and He will give you another Helper, that He may be with you forever; *that is* the Spirit of truth, whom

the world cannot receive, because it does not see Him or know Him, *but* you know Him because He abides with you and will be in you. (vv. 16–17)

This Helper is personal. Jesus uses the term *allon*, that is, another of the same kind. Just as the Son is, the Spirit is a divine Person—not merely a force or a power but a Person who speaks and acts. Some Muslims have said this means the Helper must be a mere human being, as they insist Jesus was, but that ignores the assertion that the Helper is the Spirit of truth *and* that He will be with the followers of Jesus forever, something a mere human being cannot accomplish. Only a spiritual, divine Person can fulfill this description.

Unlike the Incarnate Son, who must return to the presence of the Father from whence He came, the Spirit's role is to indwell God's people and, encouraging, guiding, and directing, conform them to the image of Christ. This promise is for the immediate disciples to whom Jesus was speaking and to every generation thereafter as well. That raises the first problem for the Muslim interpretation: The "fulfillment," if it referred to Muhammad, was six hundred years in the future! In fact, *everything Jesus says to the disciples would be completely irrelevant to them if He was simply speaking of the coming of Muhammad in the seventh century.*

This Helper is the "Spirit of truth," whom the world cannot receive. Why? Because the Spirit of truth will "abide" with the disciples and be "in" them. Clearly, this is not an incarnation or a prophet or a human being but a divine, spiritual Person. The world does not "see" Him nor "know" Him, yet of course the world saw, and knows to this day, Muhammad. Obviously the historical person Muhammad does not fulfill this text.

And there is much more. A little later (John 14:26), Jesus added,

> But the Helper, the Holy Spirit,[6] whom the Father will send in My name, He will teach you all things, and bring to your remembrance all that I said to you.

Here the Helper is specifically identified as the Holy Spirit, sent in the name of Jesus. Muhammad was not sent in the name of Jesus. Nor did he teach the disciples all things, and surely he did not bring to their remembrance all Jesus said to them. Once again, he was ignorant of the vast majority of the New Testament's teachings (and he was not born for another six centuries).

Forcing Muhammad into a passage about the Holy Spirit turns the text on its head and removes the great comfort and blessing it would have been for the disciples. But even if you were to theorize some kind of "future fulfillment" motif, the fact is, *Muhammad did not give any meaningful insight into the teachings and words of Jesus of Nazareth.* The few words that the Qur'an claims Jesus uttered are far, far removed in their spirit, content, and depth from that of the canonical Gospels and the Jesus of history.

The narrative concerning the Helper continues in John 15 (vv. 26–27), and again it is impossible to find a fulfillment in Muhammad in Jesus' words.

> When the Helper comes, whom I will send to you from the Father, that is the Spirit of truth who proceeds from the Father, He will testify about Me, and you will testify also, because you have been with Me from the beginning.

The Helper is not a prophet among other humans. He is sent by Jesus, first of all. Was Muhammad sent by Jesus? Muslims would deny that Jesus is the one who sent Muhammad. Does Muhammad proceed from the Father? This would make Muhammad divine. Even the use of "the Father" would be offensive to Muslim sensibilities here. But again, the Helper is to testify of Jesus, something Muhammad did not do in any meaningful fashion. And again, the fulfillment *must* be found in the disciples to whom these words were spoken, for their testifying is directly linked to the Spirit's coming.

The last portion of the discussion about the Helper is in John 16:7–14:

> But I tell you the truth, it is to your advantage that I go away; for if I do not go away, the Helper will not come to you; but if I go, I will send Him to you. And He, when He comes, will convict the world concerning sin and righteousness and judgment; concerning sin, because they do not believe in Me; and concerning righteousness, because I go to the Father and you no longer see Me; and concerning judgment, because the ruler of this world has been judged.
>
> I have many more things to say to you, but you cannot bear *them* now. But when He, the Spirit of truth, comes, He will guide you into all the truth; for He will not speak on His own initiative, but whatever He hears, He will speak; and He will disclose to you what is to come. He will glorify Me, for He will take of Mine and will disclose *it* to you.

Note the details Jesus provides about the Helper, the Spirit of truth. He is sent by Jesus. He comes to these specific disciples, not to someone six centuries later; Jesus says He must go away so that the Helper can come (which would be irrelevant if this had to do with Muhammad). The Helper convicts the world concerning sin and righteousness and judgment. Many Muslims would say the Qur'an does this, but note that Jesus makes specific application of what He means. The conviction concerning sin is not because the Qur'an contains laws, but because the world does not believe in Jesus; the conviction concerning righteousness is because Jesus is going to the Father, a concept foreign to Islamic theology, which would deny that Jesus would ever use such terminology, let alone bear such a relationship to God.

The Spirit of truth will guide the disciples into all truth when He comes. Muslims like to connect this to Muhammad's acceptance of the prophetic mantle and obedience to the Qur'an. Again, these words had to have direct meaning to Jesus' disciples, and nothing relevant to Muhammad could impact them.

Further, Jesus did not speak only of a guiding into truth but of a specific type of guidance. The Spirit guides into all truth because "He will not speak on His own initiative, but whatever He hears, He will speak; and He will disclose to you what is to come." Muslims have tried to connect this to Muhammad's prophetic ministry at the expense of "to you" and the fact that this promise is made to a specific group of Jesus' followers—a promise of the Spirit's ongoing ministry among the disciples after Jesus ascends to heaven.

This is proven further by the following statement: "He will glorify Me, for He will take of Mine and will disclose it to you." Again, Muhammad is excluded from any meaningful interpretation of these words, for he did not glorify Jesus. The Spirit, on the other hand, made the teachings of Jesus come alive in the disciples' memories and understandings, resulting in the apostolic ministry of the early church and the production of the New Testament.

We have now looked at the passages most cited by Islamic theologians, commentators, preachers, and apologists and have found that neither text, in any fair or logical reading, can be used to substantiate the Qur'an's claims. Muslims have written entire books[7] finding Muhammad in every possible reference to anything biblically associated with Arabia, and producers of TV series likewise have "found" Muhammad throughout the Bible, even in Isaiah 9:6![8]

But when we look at these passages, we find that they are universally *eisegetical*. They involve reading *into* a text that had one meaning in history—one meaning to its original author and audience—another meaning utterly unknown to the author, audience, and context. Any work of literature can be abused by reading into its words meanings and concepts that its author never intended. But the Qur'an does not say, "You could connect all sorts of things in the Bible to Muhammad as long as you ignore the context." The Qur'an claims the People of the Book read about him in their Scriptures, not that their Scriptures can be twisted to fit someone who would come centuries later.

For example, here are two texts noted in the original sources that were cited in defining the Islamic interpretation of the relevant Qur'anic texts about Muhammad appearing in the Jewish and Christian Scriptures:

> The stone which the builders rejected has become the chief corner *stone*. This is the LORD's doing; it is marvelous in our eyes. (Psalm 118:22–23)

> Jesus said to them, "Did you never read in the Scriptures, 'THE STONE WHICH THE BUILDERS REJECTED, THIS BECAME THE CHIEF CORNER *stone*; THIS CAME ABOUT FROM THE LORD, AND IT IS MARVELOUS IN OUR EYES'? Therefore I say to you, the kingdom of God will be taken away from you and given to a people, producing the fruit of it. And he who falls on this stone will be broken to pieces; but on whomever it falls, it will scatter him like dust" (Matthew 21:42–44).

Here Muslims will see in the stone that the builders rejected a reference to Muhammad, so that God's kingdom will be taken away and given to Muslims rather than Jews and Christians. But it is painfully obvious that Matthew is applying the prophecy to Jesus and has no intention of pointing to anyone else (let alone an Arabian prophet). Asserting a prophetic fulfillment is easy; proving specific indication that the prophecy is fulfilled in a particular person is a completely different matter. The vast majority of texts Muslims point to fall into the category of wishful fulfillment, unlike the specific and compelling fulfillments found in the life and ministry of Jesus.

We will conclude with a text that, while not as popular as Deuteronomy 18 and John 14–16, likely is the third-most-cited text for hoped-for fulfillment in Muhammad. It also illustrates the least compelling arguments Islamic proponents have conjured, and still entire videos circulate online presenting this text as a "startling" and "clear" biblical appearance of Muhammad. Muslims around the world have accepted it uncritically.

I refer to the popular claim (again made by Ahmed Deedat and repeated by many others) that the very name *Muhammad* appears right in the text of the Hebrew Bible. Where? Song of Solomon 5:16:

> His mouth is *full of* sweetness.
> And he is wholly desirable.
> This is my beloved and this is my friend,
> O daughters of Jerusalem.

Let me explain the text's meaning so we can properly examine the Islamic claim. This portion of Scripture is a celebration of the love God has ordained in marriage, drawn from the speech of the bride reflecting on her love for her soon-to-be husband. Some Christian interpreters have seen in these words a prophetic tone relating to Christ and His church, though that would be a fulfillment theme rather than the original author's intent.

In describing her love, the bride says his mouth is *mam'takkim*, "most sweet." Then, in a poetic form, she says he is *machama-ddim*, "altogether desirable." Note the parallel, *mam'takkim* and *machamaddim*. The second term is from *chamad*, which means "desire, desirable thing," "precious object," and "what is pleasing to the eyes." It is used thirteen times in the Hebrew Scriptures. Here, in the plural, it is used intensively, hence, "most desirable," "most pleasing" is being used descriptively of the husband.

What does any of this have to do with Muhammad? Well, logically, linguistically, and historically, nothing at all. But many Muslims believe that here, directly, is his name in the Bible. By ignoring the problems inherent in moving from one language to another, even within the same language family (Hebrew and Arabic are Semitic languages but have differences in grammar and syntactical structures), Muslims have moved from *machama-ddim* to *machamad* (singular) to *muhammad*,[9] finally concluding that here, in the original language, we find Muhammad!

It is hard to take such argumentation seriously, but somehow many do.

First, if every appearance of this term is a reference to Muhammad, does it follow that:

Muhammad is taken away from a house in 1 Kings 20:6?
Muhammad is destroyed by fire in 2 Chronicles 36:19?
Muhammad becomes a ruin in Isaiah 64:10?

If not, why not? Consistency would demand seeing Muhammad in every use of the term, would it not? But of course, such a methodology is horribly flawed and would allow us to "discover" all sorts of things in any foreign-language text with no real basis.

Even beyond this, is there any way for the Qur'an's actual claim to be fulfilled by such a text? Clearly it says the People of the Book see Muhammad in their texts and, as the *ahadith* express it, with sufficient clarity to have recognized him as the promised prophet. Remember the story of the Jewish boy who could recognize Muhammad from reading his Scriptures—is anyone going to seriously suggest that he had been reading Song of Solomon and that by ignoring the context and twisting language he had "seen" Muhammad?

A Major Problem for the Qur'an

We conclude that one of the Qur'an's most central claims about Muhammad is without foundation. The argument is false and cannot be maintained in the light of honest and consistent argumentation. What does this mean for the prophetic claims of Muhammad? We have already noted that the Qur'an does not identify a specific text as the fulfillment of its claim. A full examination of the biblical text yields nothing whatsoever beyond the cited (above) passages that could possibly fulfill the Qur'an's claims. Even the tired accusation of scriptural corruption cannot be called upon here, for obviously *Muhammad believed that the Torah and Injil in the possession of the people of his day pointed to him*, and we know we possess today what they had then.

Among the pressing questions this examination raises, one is "Why did Muhammad feel the need to project himself into the texts of the Jews and the Christians?" And if one of his primary arguments was that he was in the "line of the prophets," a continuation of the divine activity seen in Moses and Jesus, and we discover this is not the case, how can we avoid concluding that the Qur'anic witness itself stands firmly against the prophethood of Muhammad and the truthfulness of Islamic claims?

Notes

1. Note the discussion of this important form of argumentation in the Qur'an in reference to Surah 5:44ff., in chapter 8.

2. Muhammad Muhsin Khan and Muhammad Taqi-ud-Din Al-Hilali, *Interpretation and Meanings of the Noble Qur'an in the English Language*, Part 3 (Houston: Dar-us-Salam, 1999), 68–69.

3. *Tafsir Ibn Kathir*, 4:178.

4. There is a major difference between the scholarly and popular uses of "corruption." In scholarship, *any* written text from antiquity has been "corrupted" in the sense that we have no photocopy or digital means to the original for exact reproduction, and all hand-copying introduces textual variation through human error or even purposeful emendation. Popular, less specific use of "corruption" carries the idea that the original words and meaning have been lost and cannot now be recovered. See the discussion in chapter 11 of the differences in how the Qur'an and the New Testament were transmitted over the centuries.

5. There is a textual variant here, for many later manuscripts do not have the word *Me* in "ask *Me* anything in My name." But the term is found in the earliest manuscripts and in a wide variety of other witnesses, and hence it is strongly attested.

6. Shabir Ally has presented the unique argument that this reading should be questioned based on the observation that one translated manuscript, the Sinaitic Syriac, reads "the Holy" rather than "the Holy Spirit." All Greek manuscripts, all Latin manuscripts—*all* but this one translation—read "Holy Spirit." Muslims would never allow the Qur'an's Arabic text to be challenged based on a later foreign-language translation, yet this is what Shabir Ally does to find a way to insert Muhammad into the Bible. There is another reason to reject his argument: Surah 7:157 plainly states that the People of the Book find Muhammad mentioned in their Scriptures. Are we to think that refers only to one manuscript in a foreign language? Did the Jewish boy of the *hadith* just happen to have that one Syriac manuscript at hand? Surely not.

7. Such as Abdul Ahad Dawud (formerly Reverend David Benjamin Keldani), *Muhammad in World Scriptures*, Volume II, *The Bible* (Kuala Lampur: Islamic Book Trust, 2006).

8. I refer to the lengthy series produced by Dr. Jamal Badawi on Muhammad in the Bible, part of the "Islam in Focus" series, widely available online (e.g., aswatalislam.net).

9. While the triliteral roots are the same, those familiar with Semitic languages know that connection on the root level does *not* guarantee connection on the level of meaning. Contextual and grammatical usage is what determines any word's meaning, and the usage of the root in the poetic form found in Song of Solomon is far removed from anything even slightly relevant to the Arabic name *Muhammad*.

10

The Perfection of the Qur'an?
Parallels and Sources

If the Qur'an is in fact the very Word of God, written on the heavenly tablet, dictated in perfection by Gabriel to Muhammad, and collected and presented to the world without error, then it would follow that we can examine its own claims, its own presentation, upon the most rigorous grounds of truth and consistency. As Christians, we would insist upon "even scales," that is, using the same standards in light of both biblical and Qur'anic claims. We rightly point out that often Muslims examine the Bible with presuppositions they would never bring to the Qur'an, and we likewise exhort Christians to be fair and evenhanded in their examination of the Qur'an.

Far too often Muslims accept Qur'anic claims without examination, while at the same time accepting unfair or imbalanced attacks upon the Bible. Many Islamic websites and books incorporate arguments provided by enemies of the Christian faith, even atheists, without consideration. While Muslims hold that the Bible is fair game for in-depth criticism, the Qur'an, for some reason, is not—the Qur'an is simply to be accepted. We have often heard Muslims claim the Qur'an does not need to be interpreted, just believed. Of course, more widely read Muslims fully recognize the need for its study and interpretation, but among those who are actively seeking to call Christians to follow Islam, it is far more likely to encounter the former mindset than the latter. Christians frequently are accused of "making excuses" when we appeal to context and the text's original languages, while we also are being told that the "clear" and unambiguous Qur'an does not require such study.

One striking example of the need to place the Qur'an on the same "critical examination" playing field is found in its claim that the Egyptians engaged in crucifixion in the days of Joseph. Historians tell us they did *not*; the Qur'an (e.g., Surat 7:124; 12:41; 20:71; 26:49) anachronistically places it in an era where historically it did not exist. Muslims have sought to defend the Qur'an's references to crucifixion with lengthy articles, including suggestions that the Arabic terms might not be referring to the normative understanding of "crucifixion" as it would later appear in history but to some kind of impaling, etc.[1] While we disagree with the conclusions drawn in these defenses, our point here is that *any* ancient text, *any* written document, must be examined in context, in its original languages, and with serious depth. That which is true will be able to withstand consistent examination and analysis.

The Vital Issue of Parallels

Islamic apologists make much of the so-called "Synoptic Problem" in New Testament studies. When you study the Synoptic Gospels (Matthew, Mark, and Luke) in horizontal parallel, you discern differences between them. Which makes sense—what would be the purpose for three carbon-copy gospels? But the nature of these differences is a focus point for negative criticism, and Muslim apologists, seizing upon the least beneficial reviews, say the Synoptic Gospels "contradict" each other. In fact, in my first debate with Shabir Ally, this was his primary focus in attacking the inspiration of the New Testament, centering upon the alleged contradiction between these two accounts:

Matthew 9:18–26	Mark 5:22–43
While He was saying these things to them, a *synagogue* official came and bowed down before Him, and said, "My daughter has just died; but come and lay Your hand on her, and she will live." Jesus got up and *began* to follow him, and *so did* His disciples.	One of the synagogue officials named Jairus came up, and on seeing Him, fell at His feet and implored Him earnestly, saying, "My little daughter is at the point of death; *please* come and lay Your hands on her, so that she will get well and live." And He went off with him; and a large crowd was following Him and pressing in on Him.
And a woman who had been suffering from a hemorrhage for twelve years, came up behind Him and touched the fringe of His cloak; for she was saying to herself, "If I only touch His garment, I will get well." But Jesus turning and seeing her said, "Daughter, take courage; your faith has made you well." At once the woman was made well.	A woman who had had a hemorrhage for twelve years, and had endured much at the hands of many physicians, and had spent all that she had and was not helped at all, but rather had grown worse—after hearing about Jesus, she came up in the crowd behind *Him* and touched His cloak. For she thought, "If I just touch His garments, I will get well." Immediately the flow of her blood was dried up; and she felt in her body that she was healed of her affliction. Immediately Jesus, perceiving in Himself that the power *proceeding* from Him had gone forth, turned around in the crowd and said, "Who touched My garments?" And His disciples said to Him, "You see the crowd pressing in on You, and You say, 'Who touched Me?'" And He looked around to see the woman who had done this. But the woman fearing and trembling, aware of what had happened to her, came and fell down before Him and told Him the whole truth. And He said to her, "Daughter, your faith has made you well; go in peace and be healed of your affliction."

Matthew 9:18–26	Mark 5:22–43
When Jesus came into the official's house, and saw the flute-players and the crowd in noisy disorder, He said, "Leave; for the girl has not died, but is asleep." And they *began* laughing at Him. But when the crowd had been sent out, He entered and took her by the hand, and the girl got up. This news spread throughout all that land.	While He was still speaking, they came from the *house of* the synagogue official, saying, "Your daughter has died; why trouble the Teacher anymore?" But Jesus, overhearing what was being spoken, said to the synagogue official, "Do not be afraid *any longer,* only believe." And He allowed no one to accompany Him, except Peter and James and John the brother of James. They came to the house of the synagogue official; and He saw a commotion, and *people* loudly weeping and wailing. And entering in, He said to them, "Why make a commotion and weep? The child has not died, but is asleep." They *began* laughing at Him. But putting them all out, He took along the child's father and mother and His own companions, and entered *the room* where the child was. Taking the child by the hand, He said to her, "Talitha kum!" (which translated means, "Little girl, I say to you, get up!"). Immediately the girl got up and *began* to walk, for she was twelve years old. And immediately they were completely astounded. And He gave them strict orders that no one should know about this, and He said that *something* should be given her to eat.

Shabir Ally insisted that the differences between these accounts of what is obviously the same incident proves beyond doubt that the New Testament has been corrupted and that only a portion of the divine revelation once given to Jesus is still contained therein. In essence, the basis of his accusation was that there should be no differences between the Gospels in how the story is told.

In response, I pointed out that we must allow each writer to determine his own purposes in recording his account—he must decide who he is addressing, that is, who comprises his primary and secondary audiences. Further, we must permit him to choose the level of detail he includes and hence how long his gospel will be. In ancient times these works would all be hand-copied and would take up significantly more space than they do in printed editions. An author had to determine the degree of detail that would serve his overall goals.

Here, Mark provides more detail about the specific events, while Matthew summarizes, or more technically, telescopes them into a more tightly packed version. He does not include a segment that Mark does, the delegation's coming from Jairus's home with the news that his daughter has died. Matthew simply has Jesus coming to the home with the reality already fixed in everyone's mind that the child is dead, while Mark, giving the longer and fuller version, indicates that at the original encounter, Jairus knew her death was imminent but not that it already had occurred—instead, he came to know this on the way. In both reports, the entire group is aware of the situation as they approach the house filled with mourners. By telescoping, Matthew significantly shortens the narrative while maintaining the story's key elements and its testimony to the Messiah's power over life and death.

We all do this regularly, whenever we narrate events and stories. We may give full chronological versions to those we know will be most interested and may share a passion for what happened. But to others, maybe not as close to us, we telescope, compress, summarize. We are not deceiving anyone; we are not being dishonest; we are telling a story at different depths of entirety.

The biblical record itself (John 21:25) says that no human writing could begin to encompass the entirety of Jesus' teaching and ministry, and thus none of the Gospels should be seen as an exhaustive recording. They are not meant to be journalistic transcripts but living portraits; they are intended to convey a powerful message within the framework of the early church, and realizing this gives us the proper context in which to interpret their unique styles and perspectives. The result is a richer, fuller, deeper portrait, filled with shades and hues of color and texture no single rendition could provide. We are immeasurably richer for having the fourfold Gospels!

We could fill a book with examples of the Synoptic Gospels harmonizing while testifying of the same events, but our interest here is in contrasting this with what we find in the Qur'an. The Qur'an, we are told, has one author, God. Issues that relate to multiple authors with varying emphases and purposes simply cannot arise in examining a dictation from an eternal tablet.

So what *would* account for differences in how the Qur'an tells the same story? If God narrated it perfectly in the first account, why alter it in the second? Surprisingly few Muslims have considered this question, even among those who engage in *dawa* and seek to call Christians to accept and obey the Qur'an. The same Muslims who say differences in the Gospels are evidence of their unreliability rarely if ever consider that the Qur'an contains parallel accounts of the same events that differ in detail, order, and content.

What Did Lot Say to the People of Sodom?

7:80	26:165–166	27:54	29:28–29
Will you commit foulness such as no creature ever did before you? For you come with lust to men instead of women; you are indeed a transgressing people!	What! Of all creatures do you come unto the males? And leave the wives your Lord created for you? No, but you are people who transgress.	Will you commit abomination knowingly? Must you practice lust with men instead of women? No, you are but a people that are ignorant.	You commit obscenity such as no creature did before you. Do you come unto men, and rob on the highway, and practice wickedness in your meetings?

The literary nature of our primary translation, *The Majestic Qur'an*, means that the same Arabic terms sometimes are translated by English synonyms. The nature of the one word *fahishat*, rendered as "foulness," "abomination," and "obscenity," is defined here as "come unto the males," i.e., homosexual behavior. But in Surat 7 and 27 the Qur'an uses an interrogative, "Will you commit?" and in 29 the declarative statement, "You commit." Both 7 and 29 add a reference to the sin's uniqueness, "as no creature did before you," yet one uses the declarative and the other the interrogative.

Surah 27 adds "knowingly" (literally, "while you see"); 29 includes further sins (robbery and wickedness). Surah 7 records the condemnation as "you are a transgressing (*mus'rifuna*) people"; 26 says "you are a people who transgress" using a different term, *aduna*. Surah 27 moves further from both by saying they are ignorant (*tajhaluna*).

With the Gospels, we can see why Matthew or Mark would use different terminology, as they drew from a common oral tradition and sought to reach differing audiences in differing contexts. But how, in the Islamic view, can those three Qur'anic statements be harmonized? Did Lot say this three times?

On a simple literary level, these texts are very similar, yet we are looking at the Qur'an and specifically at the belief that these are the very words of Allah *without human intermediation*. The less conservative Muslim could suggest Muhammad used different terms and cadence and phraseology to produce a pleasing poetic form for his recitations. But Muslim orthodoxy has concluded that none of this can enter into the analysis of these parallel texts.

The heavenly Qur'an has nothing to do with Muhammad's thoughts, knowledge, or even means of expression. So why would Allah recite Lot's words in different ways? Did Lot speak of other sins, as in Surah 29, or not? Did he say "knowingly," as in Surah 27, or not? Islamic orthodoxy's demands as to the nature of the Qur'anic revelation require answers to these questions.

What Did the People of Sodom Say to Lot?

7:82	26:167	27:56	29:29
Drive them out of your city! They are people who keep themselves pure!	If you cease not, O Lot, you will soon be of the outcast.	Expel the household of Lot from your city, for they are people who purify themselves!	Bring Allah's torment upon us if you are truthful!

There is wide variation as to the people of Sodom's response among these four accounts, all narrated, we are told, by Muhammad. It is easier to note the connections than the differences (with Surah 29 being even more "different" than the other three). Surat 7 and 27 refer to Lot and his people as those who "keep themselves pure" or "purify themselves" and include a command to expel or drive them out (with only a slight difference in forms). One could easily assume that each text gives a selection of many shouted-out replies borne of anger against Lot, but this does not mesh with the Islamic belief in the nature of the Qur'anic revelation.

How Did Allah Punish the City of Sodom?

7:84	26:173	27:28	29:31
And We rained a rain upon them. See how was the end of the criminals!	And We rained on them a rain. And dreadful is the rain of those who have been warned.	And We rained a rain upon them. Dreadful is the rain of those who have been warned.	We are about to bring down upon the people of this city punishment from the sky because of their corruption. And We have left a clear sign for people who understand.

In the fifth parallel account, Surah 11, that final judgment is styled, "So when Our commandment came to pass, We overthrew [that city], and rained down on them stones of baked clay, one after another." This provides a parallel with Surat 29, leaving 7, 26, and 27 closely parallel, again with slight differences in wording and phraseology. Surah 7 directs people to "see" how their end came about, while 29 refers to this judgment as a "clear sign for people who understand," and 26 also speaks of it as a sign, yet which did not bring belief.

Note here the precisely identical Arabic text of Surat 26 and 27 in phraseology. Why is this significant? Because it shows the author could provide exact duplicate narration if he wished. In the majority of the parallels we can identify in the text, he does not. Though this raises the question of why, the orthodox Islamic view of inspiration and revelation does not allow us to pursue the matter, for it denies that the author's intentions can be discerned—the author is not Muhammad or a later redactor, but Allah himself.

The Fall of Iblis (Satan)

The next set of parallels we will examine also derives from the Qur'an's retelling of a well-known biblical story.[2] The fall of Iblis, that is, Satan, is narrated in Surat 7 and 38. A comparison of these accounts is very revealing.

What Did Allah Say to the Angels?

7:11	38:71–72
Prostrate yourselves before Adam!	I am creating a human being from clay, so when I have fashioned him and breathed into him of My spirit, then fall down before him prostrate.

There is clearly no effort on the Qur'an's part to project the later view of Islamic orthodoxy by providing identical renderings. Surah 7 gives a brief commandment, Surah 38 a narration of Allah's creative action in making man. Same story, creatively different ways of expressing it, which strikes the reader as consistent with a human author, not a book written on a heavenly tablet.

What Did Iblis Say to Allah When He Refused to Prostrate?

7:12	38:76
I am better than him. You created me of fire while you created him of mud.	I am better than him. You created me of fire while him you created of clay.

Once again, our translation's literary nature might lead us to think there is a difference here when there is not. The Arabic *tinin* is rendered both "clay" and "mud." So again we see that the author is perfectly capable of exact narration and terminology when he wishes, even amid what seem like mainly stylistic alterations in the rest of the narrative.

How Did Allah Respond to Iblis's Refusal?

7:13	38:77
Then go down from it [the Garden]! It is not for you to show arrogance here, so leave! You are of the degraded.	Go out from here! You are accursed![3] And My curse is on you till the Day of Judgment.

This parallel is particularly important, since these are Allah's very words. Allah should quote Allah most accurately, we would think. If Allah introduces stylistic variations in his own recitation of his own speech, this might lead us to think that in fact we are reading Muhammad's words. The two versions communicate the same basic idea but in quite different terms. In one, Iblis is commanded to "go down" (*fa-ih'bit*); this command is not found in the other. Both say "go out" or "leave" (same Arabic term). Surah 7 mentions the impropriety of showing arrogance "here," and 38 has no corresponding element. Surah 7 puts Iblis into a group that it styles "the degraded" or "disgraced ones" (*l-saghirina*),[4] while with different terms 38 says Iblis is accursed and Allah's curse will be upon him until the "Day of Judgment." All of these make perfect sense if a man is providing a poetic recounting of the fall of Iblis, but it is hard to explain such variations given Islamic orthodoxy's conclusions and its apologetic arguments against the New Testament.

What Did Iblis Promise to Do to Allah's Followers?

7:16–17	38:82–83
Now, because You have sent me astray, I shall lurk in ambush for them on Your straight path. Then I shall come upon them from before them and from behind them and from their right and from their left, and You shall not find most of them thankful [for Your mercies].	Then by Your might, I shall beguile them all, save Your sincere servants among them.

Here we note a major expansion on this aspect in Surah 7, in comparison to 38. Either Surah 38 has "telescoped" 7, or 7 is a major embellishment of what was originally found in 38, but in any case, the two versions differ on almost every level. Surah 7 says Allah sent Iblis "astray," and because of this, Iblis will seek to remove people from the straight path of following Allah. Surah 38 includes recognition by Iblis that he will not thus be able to dissuade Allah's sincere servants, yet no such acknowledgment exists in 7.

What Did Allah Say in Response to Iblis's Threat?

7:18	38:84–85
Leave this [Garden], degraded, vanquished. As for those of them who will follow you, I shall fill Hell with you all.	The Truth is, and the Truth I speak, that I shall fill hell with you and with such of them as follow you, all together.

Did Allah command Iblis to go down, "degraded" and "vanquished"? Not if you only read Surah 38. Did Allah say, "The Truth is, and the Truth I speak" when speaking to Iblis? Not if you only read Surah 7. If the Muslim says, "You must consider all that the Qur'an says and harmonize these accounts," the Christian will agree. However, this likewise would undercut the vast majority of arguments used by Islamic apologists against the New Testament's consistency and accuracy and even more so, would bring us back to the modern orthodox conclusion that the Qur'an has no human element.

So the apologist is left attempting to discern why Allah would use different words and phrases to describe the same event in different contexts. These have not merely involved synonyms. At times completely different things are said; at others, entire phrases added or deleted. These are fully understandable in human writing, or when comparing different writers describing the same event, but why are such differences in the Qur'an?

Also, comparison of Surah 20:38–40 shows numerous differences from the parallel account of Moses' early life in 28:7–13. The latter is much fuller, containing many more details. Again, specific statements, allegedly of Allah, are recorded with differing words, requiring the Muslim reader to harmonize and conflate the texts for a final idea of the whole Qur'anic thrust. And a comparison of Surat 2:58–59 and 7:161–162 provides fascinating parallel to the very kind of harmonization necessary in reading the Synoptic Gospels. Surah 2:58 has the specific phrase "enter the city"; the parallel in 7:161 has "dwell in this city." Interestingly, noting the readings, Yusuf Ali commented, "The verbal differences make no difference to the sense."[5]

We could provide numerous other examples. Here are four more parallel passages, all illustrating with clarity that the serious Muslim exegete must face the reality that the Qur'anic text requires exegesis and harmonization:

Surah 20:65–73	Surah 26:41–52	
Surah 20:9–24	Surah 27:7–14	Surah 28:29–33
Surah 11:77–83	Surah 15:61–75	Surah 29:32–34
Surah 26:160–175	Surah 27:54–58	Surah 29:28–30

The believing Muslim should consider well these parallel passages and what they mean both to the accepted Islamic orthodoxy concerning the nature of the Qur'an's inspiration of the Qur'an and to the most popular Islamic arguments used against the validity and accuracy of the Christian Scriptures.

Use of Existing Sources?

There is a strong and consistent theme in the text of the Qur'an:

That when Our signs are recited to him, he says: "Legends of the men of old." We shall brand him on the nose! (68:15–16)

When our signs are recited to him, he says: "These are legends of the ancients." No! Their own deeds have cast a veil over their hearts. No! On that day they will be veiled from their Lord; then they will be exposed to hell. Then it will be said: "This is what you had been denying!" (83:13–17).

When they are asked: "What has your Lord sent down?" They say "[Nothing but the] Legends of the ancients!" That they may bear their burdens in full on the Day of Resurrection and also some of the burdens of those that they lead astray without knowledge. Grievous are the burdens they will bear! (16:24–25)

And those who disbelieve say: "This [Qur'an] is nothing but a lie he has invented, and other people have helped him with it." They have thus committed injustice and falsehood. And they say: "Legends of the ancients that he has put into writing, for they are dictated to him in the early morning and evening." See how they coin examples for you, thus going astray and unable to find their way. (25:4–5, 9)

And when those who disbelieve plot against you [O Muhammad] to fatally wound you, kill you, or drive you out; they plot, but Allah [also] plots; and Allah is the best of plotters. And when

229

Our signs are recited to them they say: "We have heard. Had we wished we could have said the like of this. This is nothing but the legends of the men of old" (8:30–31).

Of them are some who listen to you, but We have placed upon their hearts veils, lest they should understand, and in their ears a deafness. If they saw every sign they would not believe in it; to the point that, when they come to you to argue with you, the disbelievers say: "This is nothing other than the legends of the ancients." And they forbid [others] from it and avoid it, and they ruin only themselves without knowing. If you could see when they are set before the Fire and say, "Would that we be returned! Then we would not deny the signs of our Lord, and would be of the believers!" (6:25–27).

These texts span the length of Muhammad's prophethood (Surah 68 being very early), showing that the accusations of the Qur'an being "legends of the ancients" started at the beginning and continued until he consolidated his control of the state. Many of these citations include dire warnings of eternal punishment upon anyone who would make this allegation against the Qur'an. And yet there seems a tremendous amount of solid, verifiable, and balanced information indicating that at the very least Muhammad showed a familiarity with certain "legends of the ancients" that then appear in the Qur'anic text.

Before we discuss the ramifications of this reality, we must demonstrate it to be so.[6] Let's begin with a lesser-known example, for it illustrates well how Muhammad could have been exposed to various traditions and stories that he believed to be part of the actual revelation given to other peoples.

When Mount Sinai Was Suspended

2:63. [O Children of Israel! Remember] When We made a pact with you, and caused the Mount to tower above you [literally:

"We raised over you"], [saying]: "Hold firmly to what We have given you, and remember that which is therein, that you may be God-fearing."

2:93. And [remember] when We made a pact with you, and raised the Mount above you, [saying]: "Hold fast to what We have given you, and hear [Our commandments]," you said: "We hear and disobey." For their disbelief, they were made to drink into their hearts [the love of] the calf. Say [to them]: "Evil is that which your belief enjoins you to, if you are believers."

4:154. And We caused the Mount [of Sinai] to tower above them [literally: "We raised over them"] at [the taking of] their pact, and We bade them: "Enter the gate prostrate!" and We bade them: "Transgress not the Sabbath!" and We took from them a firm pact.

7:171. And when We raised the Mount above them as if it were a covering and they thought it was going to fall upon them, [We said]: "Take firmly what We have given you, and remember what it contains, that you may fear [Allah]."

Each text refers to the same biblical incident, the giving of the Torah (Law) to the Jews at Sinai. Each indicates that Allah "raised" the mount above them. Surah 7 makes clear this is not simply the mount "towering" above them, but that a miracle is being referred to, for it was raised "as if it were a covering," or more literally, "a canopy," and they thought it might fall upon them.

This seems to be a consistent and early understanding of the text from an Islamic viewpoint as well. In the *Tafsir Ibn Kathir* we read, "Allah states that when He took their pledge from them, He raised the mountain above their heads, so that they affirm the pledge that they gave Allah and abide by it with sincerity and seriousness. . . . And in the *Hadith* about the trials, Ibn

Abbas said, 'When they (the Jews) refused to obey, Allah raised the mountain above their heads so that they would listen.'"[7] In *Tafsir al-Jalalayn*: "Remember *when we made the covenant with you* to act according to what is in the Torah *and lifted up the Mount above your heads:* Mount Sinai was uprooted and held over their heads when they refused to accept."[8] And in *Tafsir al-Qurtubi*:

> It is said that a mountain was removed from its place and raised above the surface of the earth. . . . The Mount was lifted in this way because, when Musa (Moses) brought the Tablets from Allah which contained the Torah to the tribe of Israel, he told them, "Take them and hold fast to them." But they replied, "No! Not unless Allah tells us to do the same as you tell us!" So they were struck dead and then brought back to life. Musa again told them to take them and again they refused. So Allah commanded the angels to uproot one of the mountains of Palestine and it was held over them like a cloud. The sea was behind them and a fire in front of them and they were told to take the covenant otherwise the mountain would fall on top of them. They prostrated in repentance and took the Torah and the covenant.[9]

This fascinating scene would not strike a reader as familiar unless he or she is familiar with Jewish folklore of the first millennium's early centuries. In such literature—in the Babylonian Talmud—we do find in a very similar story the idea that God had in fact suspended Mount Sinai over the people of Israel. As Jacob Neusner translates the relevant sections:

> X. *But how can they present such an argument, since it is written,* "The Lord came from Sinai and rose from Seir to them, he shined forth from Mount Paran" (Dt. 33:2), and further, "God comes from Teman" (Hab. 3:3). *Now what in the world did he want in Seir, and what was he looking for in Paran?* Said R. Yohanan, "This teaches that

the Holy One, blessed be He, made the rounds of each and every nation and language and none accepted it, until he came to Israel, and they accepted it."

Y. *Rather, this is what they say,* "Did we accept it but then not carry it out?"

Z. But to this the rejoinder must be, "Why did you not accept it anyhow!"

AA. Rather, "this is what they say before him, 'Lord of the world, did you hold a mountain over us like a cask and then we refused to accept it as you did to Israel, as it is written, "And they stood beneath the mountain" (Ex. 19:17).'"

BB. And [in connection with the verse, "And they stood beneath the mountain" (Ex. 19:17),] said R. Dimi bar Hama, "This teaches that the Holy One, blessed be He, held the mountain over Israel like a cask and said to them, 'If you accept the Torah, well and good, and if not, then there is where your grave will be.'"[10]

This Jewish reading focuses on trying to explain why God had offered His covenant to many nations, but none accepted it until Israel. Yet God had used a form of force in the sense of lifting up the mountain, hanging it over them, and threatening that if they rejected, then "there is where your grave will be."

The Qur'anic texts seem to be based upon the idea that this story, found in one particular stream of Jewish tradition, either is historical in nature or is a part of the Jewish Scriptures. This would be easily understandable if, in fact, Muhammad was dependent upon oral traditions for his knowledge of the Torah. Without direct access to the text, how could he tell which stories from Jewish narrators were part of the Torah and which were embellishment? As we will see, this question will arise again and again as we identify preexisting sources for elements of the Qur'anic text.

Islamic apologists normally offer two kinds of responses to the existence of preexisting materials that would give rise to the Qur'anic narration of stories. Sometimes they claim the story's origination is post-Islamic, so those other sources are actually depending upon the Qur'an. Sometimes they say the event described is historical and simply is recorded by different sources. This story, found in the Talmud, clearly seems to predate Islam. So in this case, God did in fact hang the mountain over the Jews, and we know this because the Qur'an says so, plus Jewish tradition also records this event. Of course, this assumes the orthodox view of the Qur'an and removes it from the flow of history, a stance Muslims do not allow to Christians or Jews in reference to their Scriptures but which they demand for the Qur'an. But as we multiply the references where preexisting sources can be identified for particular Qur'anic stories, the probability of the Muslim position diminishes proportionately.

But another issue needs to be raised here. The Qur'an's comments make it seem the author assumes his audience would know about or be familiar with this event. This is the same language it uses of stories the author believes are found in the Jewish or the Christian Scriptures. That seems very strange if herein the Qur'an is giving "new" information or revelation. It would make perfect sense, though, if Muhammad assumed (on the basis of having heard the story from a Jewish source) that it was a generally known or accepted concept. The text leads us not to believe this is new revelation but to see that it is drawing upon previously understood and believed concepts, apparently without grasping the difference between what is and is not historically valid as to biblical revelation and Jewish and Christian tradition and mythology.

This is clearly seen in the stories the Qur'an accepts as historical or even biblical that relate to Jesus' life and ministry. Clearly the author had no direct knowledge of or access to the New Testament as a whole or even the Gospels in particular. This again is only a problem for Islamic orthodoxy, for on a historical basis it would be easy to understand such ignorance if we see the Qur'an as the product of Muhammad's teaching and preaching. But Islam closes this door, and surely Allah knew every syllable of the New Testament at the beginning of the seventh century. Let's look at just two instances where the Qur'an elevates to "revelation" what history tells us was nothing more than legend and myth. These are connected together in the Qur'anic text:

3:46. "He will speak to mankind in his cradle and in his manhood, and he is of the righteous."

This refers to Jesus, and the same concept is fully explained in the Surah named after Mary, *Surah Mariam:*

19:27. At length she brought him [the infant] to her people carrying him. They said: "O Mary! Truly a villainous thing you have done!

28. "O sister of Aaron! Your father was not a wicked man, nor was your mother unchaste."

29. She made a sign, pointing to him. They replied: "How can we speak with he who is in the cradle, a babe?"

30. [Whereupon] He [the infant] spoke out: "I am indeed a servant of Allah. He has given me the Book and has appointed me a Prophet.

31. "And He has made me blessed wheresoever I may be and has commanded me to pray and to give charity to the poor as long as I live.

32. "And [He] has made me dutiful to my mother and has not made me oppressive, wicked.

33. "So peace be upon me the day I was born, the day that I die,[11] and the day that I shall be raised up to life [again]."

34. Such was Jesus, the son of Mary; a statement of the truth about which they [vainly] dispute.

This story is unknown to any sources that can meaningfully be traced to the first century and the time of Jesus the Messiah. But it does appear in sources that could have been communicated to Muhammad in his conversations with Christians, especially on caravan excursions up into neighboring Syria. The tale is contained in a source called the *Arabic Infancy Gospel*, normally dated to the fifth or sixth century AD, and itself based upon earlier legendary material like the *Protevangelium of James* and the *Infancy Gospel of Thomas*, both of which bear signs of Gnostic influence. What is significant about this work, outside of its nature as legend and myth without serious connection to the events of Jesus' life, is that with high probability it appeared in Arabic at some point, which would have assisted in the dissemination of its stories among the Arabs. Right at the beginning of its narrative we read,

> He has said that Jesus spoke, and, indeed, when He was lying in His cradle said to Mary His mother: I am Jesus, the Son of God, the Logos, whom thou hast brought forth, as the Angel Gabriel announced to thee; and my Father has sent me for the salvation of the world.[12]

This mythical story's content differs greatly from the *Arabic Infancy Gospel* to the Qur'an, for in the earlier story Jesus says He is God's Son, the Logos (Word), and that He has been sent for the world's salvation, all concepts Muhammad directly denied. But considering the means by which oral stories are passed on, it is not difficult to understand how the general idea of a miraculous event associated with the child Jesus in the cradle could be included in the Qur'an with the specifics of Jesus' words altered to fit the author's overall purposes.

The *Arabic Infancy Gospel* is a rather humorous collection of myths and legends, and the Muslim tempted to consider it a sound source of historical information that might contain a germ of truth should reconsider his position. The book goes on, for example, to tell of how Mary gave to the magi some of Jesus' swaddling clothes. The magi returned to their land with them and during a feast attempted to burn the materials in a fire as part of their religious worship. They would not burn, so they began to treat them as magical amulets, kissing them and putting them on their heads and eyes and saying, "This verily is the truth without doubt."

What should be especially troubling to the Muslim, however, is that the Qur'an fails to make *any* differentiation between what is clearly legendary in character and what is based on the Hebrew or the Christian Scriptures. Stories that developed centuries after the events they pretend to describe are coupled directly with historically based accounts that carry serious weight and truth content. And that it provides no evidence its author has any idea he is combining historical and legendary materials is seen in the second example, the incorporation of the legend of Jesus' youth and the creation of birds from clay, found originally in the Gnostic-tinged *Infancy Gospel of Thomas:*

> This child Jesus, being five years of age, was playing at the ford of a brook. And he gathered together the flowing waters into pools, and he immediately made them pure. He ordered these things with merely a word.
>
> And having made soft clay he made from it twelve sparrows. Now it was the Sabbath when he did these things. And there were many other children playing with him.
>
> Now a certain Jew, seeing what Jesus had done, playing on the Sabbath, went away quickly and reported to his father, Joseph, "Your child is by the brook, and has taken up clay and fashioned twelve sparrows and has profaned the Sabbath!"
>
> And Joseph came to the place and when he saw it he cried out to him saying, "Why are you doing these unlawful things on

the Sabbath?" But Jesus clapped his hands and cried out to the sparrows and said to them, "Depart!" And the sparrows took to flight and went away chirping.

And when the Jews saw this they were amazed and went away and reported to their leaders what they had seen Jesus do.[13]

The various Gnostic "gospels" and writings that arose in the second through fourth centuries show a penchant for "filling in the gaps" left by the canonical Gospels, for man's desire is to inquire into that which God has left behind the veil of His own sovereignty. Since the first-century Gospels written by the followers of Jesus left unanswered (to the minds of some) many questions, especially about His youth, the Gnostics were more than happy to dive in with fertile imagination to fill in "the rest." Tales of Jesus speaking from His cradle or forming and vitalizing clay birds come from this legendary/mythical genre. They have no meaningful connection to the historical Gospels themselves or to their sober accounting of Jesus' life and ministry. They tell absurd stories completely out of line with what we know of Jesus from the very sources the Qur'an seems to recognize as having been Allah-sent. The same *Infancy Gospel*, for example, goes on to say that the child Jesus struck children dead for merely bumping into him, and when their parents complain to Joseph, Jesus strikes them blind! This kind of fantastic legendary material is hardly the kind of source that can be trusted, and yet the Qur'an's author shows not the slightest understanding of its nature and combines them with historical materials. Note how the story of the clay birds gets directly associated with the accounts of Jesus' actual miracles, miracles rooted in a specific historical period and given a meaningful context by the canonical Gospels:

3:49. "And will make him a Messenger to the Children of Israel. He will say: 'I bring you a sign from your Lord. From clay I will make for you the likeness of a bird; I shall breathe into it and it shall become a [living] bird, by Allah's leave. I shall give sight to the blind, heal the leper, and raise the dead to life, by Allah's leave. I shall tell you what you eat and what you store up in your houses. Surely that will be a sign for you, if you are believers.'"

50. "[I come] To confirm the Torah that has already been revealed, and to make lawful to you some of the things you were forbidden. I bring a sign to you from your Lord. So fear Him, and obey me."

5:110. Then Allah will say: "O Jesus son of Mary! Remember My favor upon you and upon your mother; how I strengthened you with the Holy Spirit [the archangel Gabriel] so that you spoke to mankind in the cradle as in maturity; and how I taught you the Book and wisdom and the Torah and the Gospel; and how you shaped of clay the likeness of a bird by My permission, blew upon it, and it was a bird by My permission; and you healed him who was born blind and the leper by My permission; and how you raised the dead by My permission; and how I restrained the Children of Israel from [harming] you when you came to them with clear signs, and those of them who disbelieved exclaimed: 'This is nothing but evident magic!'"

Especially in the last citation, we see how the Qur'an strings together fantastic tales from ahistorical sources with references that can only be to the actual canonical stories from Jesus' own disciples. Again, we would expect this of Muhammad, but Islamic orthodoxy insists this book is eternal and with no human element. Surely Allah knew the difference between historical truth about Jesus and later legendary accretions. Fascinatingly, the Qur'an seems to affirm the canonical story of Jesus healing a man born blind (John 9). Modern Islamic apologists who rely upon liberal scholarship to attack the veracity of the New Testament text should consider well the Qur'an's testimony here.

Further evidence of what seems indeed to be reliance upon the "legends of the ancients" is seen in the narration of Jesus' birth. Scholars have noted many parallels to the common yet mythical stories in circulation among Christians of Muhammad's day. Surah 19:22–26 gives one possible example:

> Thereupon she conceived [the child]; and she went away to a distant place. And the pains of childbirth drove her to the trunk of a palm tree. She said: "Would that I had died before this, and become naught, a thing forgotten!" But [a voice] cried unto her from below her saying: "Do not be sad; your Lord has provided a rivulet at your feet. [As for food] Shake the trunk of the palm tree towards yourself; you will cause ripe dates to fall upon you. So eat and drink, and be consoled; and if you meet any man say: 'I have vowed a fast [of silence] to the All-Merciful, and will not speak with any human being this day.'"

Where did the Qur'an get the idea that Mary was driven to a tree in her birth pangs, and that someone, possibly even Jesus himself (prior to birth, it seems), spoke to her? Or a stream miraculously appearing or a date palm providing nourishment? Once again, an extra-biblical mythological story found in Christian sources contemporaneous with Muhammad contains many of the same elements. From the *Gospel of Pseudo-Matthew*:[14]

> Then, after these things, on the third day after they had started out, Mary was weary from too much sun in the wilderness, and seeing a palm tree she wanted to rest awhile in its shade. Joseph hastened to lead her to the palm and he had her descend from the donkey. When Mary sat down, she looked to the foliage on the palm and saw that it was full of fruit, and she said, "If only I could get some of that fruit from the palm!" Joseph said to her, "I am surprised that you're saying this, when you can see how high the palm is. You are thinking of the fruit of

the palm; but I am thinking about the water that we no longer have in our water skins; we have nowhere to replenish them to quench our thirst."

Then the young child Jesus, sitting in the lap of his mother, the virgin, cried out to the palm tree and said, "Bend down, O tree, and refresh my mother from your fruit." Immediately when he spoke, the palm tree bent its top down to Mary's feet. Everyone gathered the fruit in it and was refreshed. After all its fruit had been gathered, the tree remained bent, expecting that it would rise up at the command of the one who had ordered it to bend over. Then Jesus said to it, "Stand erect, O palm, and be strong, and become a companion of my trees that are in the paradise of my Father. And open up from your roots the hidden springs, that water may flow from them to quench our thirst." Immediately the palm stood erect, and from its roots springs of water began to come forth, clear, cold, and very sweet. When they saw the springs of water flowing, they all rejoiced with a great joy and drank, together with their beasts and companions, giving thanks to God.[15]

The differences between the specifics are intriguing in that they fit so clearly with the kind of oral transmission and transmutation of details so often found when one source seeks to collect into one story portions of previously heard versions. While the Qur'an places the palm tree and the miraculous provision of a stream in the context of Jesus' birth, the Christian legend places it after the birth. This involves knowledge of the New Testament's narration of the events immediately after the Messiah's birth, which Muhammad did not have. The unusual and miraculous elements, the provision of the tree and the stream, have no foundation in the biblical narrative (being part of the later legendary development), yet *this* is the kind of material that draws the attention of the Qur'an's writer and finds its way into the text.

Borrowing From the Tanakh and Jewish Mythology

Compared to what very little knowledge the Qur'an's author had with even the basic stories of the Gospels, let alone anything else in the Christian Scriptures, he shows a significantly greater familiarity with the stories of the Hebrew Scriptures. Numerous stories well known to Jews and Christians appear in the text (at times in oddly edited forms). However, as noted above in reference to Christian sources both historical and legendary, the Qur'an seems to make no differentiation between legendary Jewish tradition and what actually appears in the Hebrew Scriptures. We are struck with the strong contrast between the New Testament's immersion in their actual text and the Qur'an's sharp disconnection from and ignorance of the same (even though, once more, familiar with oral stories and myths drawn from it).

The most oft-cited example of the Qur'an's reliance upon Jewish traditions and myths is Surah 5:30–32:

> 30. The spiteful soul of the other [Cain] led him to the killing of his brother, so he slew him and became one of the losers. Then Allah sent a raven scratching up the ground, to show him how to hide his brother's naked corpse. He said: "Woe is me! Am I not able to be as this raven and so hide my brother's naked corpse?" And he became repentant. For that cause We ordained for the Children of Israel that whosoever kills a human being for other than [the crimes of] manslaughter or corruption in the earth, it shall be as if he had killed all mankind; and whosoever saves the life of one, it shall be as if he had saved the life of all mankind. Our Messengers came to them of old with clear signs, but afterwards many of them became committed to excesses in the earth.

Jews and Christians familiar with Genesis 4 know well what happened when murder entered into the experience of the nascent human family. But where did the bird scratching on the ground come from? God sent a raven to teach a murderer how to hide his victim's corpse? This is a strange addition indeed.

However, the Jews of Muhammad's day would not have been surprised, for once again, in the sources containing the stories that were being told, we find a similar tale. A number of Jewish sources[16] record a tradition, dating to the second to third centuries AD, narrating an event that took place after the murder of Abel. While Adam and Eve sat next to his corpse, a raven came up, scratched in the earth, and buried another bird. Adam and Eve take a lesson from it and bury Abel's body. In the Qur'anic version, Cain does the burying, but in both a raven inspires the human family in the instance of its first death.

How certain are we that this is the Qur'an's source? Surety is increased greatly in that another extra-biblical Jewish tradition is referenced in this same section. The key text on mankind's unity, on the killing of one as the killing of all, is found almost word for word in the Jewish Mishnah, Sanhedrin 4:5:

F In the case of a trial for property cases, a person pays money and achieves atonement for himself. In capital cases [the accused's] blood and the blood of all those who were destined to be born from him [who was wrongfully convicted] are held against him [who testifies falsely] to the end of time.

G For so we find in the case of Cain who slew his brother, as it is said, *The bloods of your brother cry* (Gen. 4:10).

H It does not say, "The *blood* of your brother," but, "The *bloods* of your brother"—his blood and the blood of all those who were destined to be born from him.

I Another matter: The *bloods of your brother*—for his blood was spattered on trees and stones.

J Therefore man was created alone to teach you that whoever destroys a single Israelite soul is deemed by Scripture
as if he had destroyed a whole world.

K And whoever saves a single Israelite soul is deemed by
Scripture as if he had saved a whole world.[17]

So in the matter of only a few sentences, we find the Qur'an
drawing from Jewish traditions that date from the second
through the fifth centuries prior to its writing. The story of
the raven is hardly important. But the second portion, drawn
from traditions found in the Mishnah, is one of the central theological affirmations in Islamic theology. That we can identify a
preexisting source for such a vital section is extremely important.

The next text often pointed to is the story of Abraham in Surah
21. It is lengthy; we will summarize. Abraham refuses to worship
the gods of his people. Upon destroying some of their idols, Abraham testifies that there is only one God. We pick up in *ayah* 68:

> They said: "Burn him and help your gods, if you will!" We said:
> "O fire! Be coolness and peace for Abraham!" They wished to
> snare him, but We made them the Losers.

There is no reference to such an incident, of course, in the Hebrew Scriptures. But *again,* in the Jewish stories and traditions
that existed in the centuries prior to the Qur'an's writing, we
find a reference to Abraham, the destruction of idols, and a
fiery pit. The second-century Midrash Rabbah[18] has a strikingly
similar story: Abraham smashes idols, and then is taken to the
king, who, upon tiring of arguing with him, has him cast into
a fiery furnace, and God saves him from the fire. The same
pattern emerges: An ahistorical Jewish tradition is taken by
the Qur'an's author to be historical and seemingly on the same
level and authority as the actual text of the Hebrew Scriptures.

One last example will suffice for our purposes. Some Muslims dispute the dating of the tradition that appears to lie behind the Qur'anic story of Surah 27:17–44,[19] the incorporation of an odd legendary story into the text follows the pattern we have seen above. As it is fairly long, we will again summarize the information (though extensive comparison shows a remarkable number of details that appear in both stories).

The Qur'an tells of Solomon gathering an army consisting of *jinn*, men, and birds. As they march, he hears an ant speaking and laughs as it warns other ants to hide. He then notes that the hoopoe bird is missing from its place and warns that if it has no excuse it will be punished severely. The bird appears and tells him of the Queen of Sheba and her magnificent throne. Solomon sends a letter to her, and she responds. He invites her to true faith in the one God, Allah. She asks advice of her counselors. As she is traveling to meet him, a *jinn* brings her throne miraculously into the presence of Solomon as a test of her insight. The story ends in *ayah* 44:

> It was said to her: "Enter the hall." And when she saw it she thought it was a pool and bared her legs. [Solomon] said: "It is a hall, made smooth, of glass." She said: "My Lord! I have wronged myself, and I surrender with Solomon to Allah, the Lord of the Worlds."

As for the Jewish fable, according to the 2nd Targum of Esther, Solomon gathered an army of *jinn*, beasts of the land, and birds of the air. A red cock (a bird) was found to be missing, and he ordered it found and threatened it with punishment. But it appeared and told him of the Queen of Sheba. He sent a letter to her via the bird. She asks advice of her nobles on what she should do. When she comes to meet him, Solomon sits on his throne in a palace of glass. When she sees it, she thinks the floor is made of water, and as she crosses, she lifts up her garments, exposing her legs to him.

Obviously the stories are drawn from the same source. The best Muslim apologists can do is try to insist this Jewish story is actually borrowed from the Qur'an, not the other way around. But barring this theory's historical problems, given the number of examples where the Qur'an uncritically incorporates earlier materials where there is no question of their date, what reason have we to assume in this one instance that the Qur'an's story is the original? Besides this, what is more likely: that the author of the Qur'an would incorporate stories he thinks are scriptural and historical among others so as to make a point against polytheism and idolatry (as here), or that the Jews would pick up a story from an as yet utterly unknown book and add it to their own developed traditions and legends? The answer seems obvious.

Notes

1. See example provided at islamic-awareness.org/Quran/Contrad/External/crucify.html.

2. It seems logical to conclude that the variations in the recitations of stories found in written texts (in particular, here, the Hebrew Scriptures) point us to Muhammad having heard them from different sources orally but not having had direct access to the written text (fully fixed in form long before his time). This confirms the Qur'an's tenuous-at-best connection to the preceding revelations, a link that differs fundamentally from the close, intimate, textually based relationship between the Tanakh (Hebrew canon) and the New Testament.

3. The reading of the *Majestic Qur'an* here is "a repudiate," which makes little sense in English and may well be an uncorrected typographical error. I have replaced the reading with a very common rendering of the Arabic term *rajimun*.

4. Note that this term is used elsewhere in the Qur'an and is the very one found in Surah 9:29: "Fight against those from among the People of the Book who do not believe in Allah nor the Last Day; who do not forbid what Allah and His Messenger have forbidden, and who do not adopt the religion of truth; until they pay the tribute out of hand, utterly subdued (*saghiruna*)." The emphasis is on the humbling, subduing, and, it would seem, disgracing of those Christians and Jews who do not submit to Islam.

5. Yusuf Ali, *The Meaning of the Holy Qur'an* (Beltsville, MD: Amana, 2001), 31.

6. There are many discussions in scholarly literature of the possible sources for various stories in the Qur'an. For one summary, see N. A. Newman, *Muhammad, the Qur'an & Islam* (Hatfield, PA: Interdisciplinary Biblical Research Institute, 1996), Appendix D, 363–390.

7. *Tafsir Ibn Kathir*, 1:251–252.

8. *Tafsir al-Jalalayn*, 23.

9. *Tafsir al-Qurtubi, Classical Commentary of the Holy Qur'an*, trans. Aisha Bewley (London: Dar Al Taqwa, 2003), I:268.

10. Jacob Neusner, *The Babylonian Talmud: A Translation and Commentary* (Peabody, MA: Hendrickson, 2011).

11. See our discussion of the Qur'an's teaching on the death of Christ in chapter 6.

12. "The Arabic Gospel of the Infancy of the Saviour" in *The Ante-Nicene Fathers* (Grand Rapids, MI: Eerdmans, 1951), 8:405. Also available online at gnosis. org/library/infarab.htm.

13. Personal translation.

14. Dates differ on this work's actual writing, but scholars are agreed that it draws from the ahistorical *Protoevangelium of James*, written in the second century. The specific story that found its way into the Qur'an is a later addition and development, probably arising around the same time as the story of Jesus speaking from the cradle in the *Arabic Infancy Gospel*.

15. Bart Ehrman and Zlatko Plese, *The Apocryphal Gospels* (Oxford: 2011), 107–109.

16. e.g., The Jewish Encyclopedia (jewishencyclopedia.com/articles/216-abel) mentions Pirke de-R. Eliezer's work (chapter 21); the same story with slight variation is found in the Targum of Jonathan ben Uzziah.

17. Jacob Neusner, *The Mishnah: A New Translation* (New Haven: Yale, 1988), 591.

18. sacred-texts.com/jud/tmm/tmm07.htm.

19. That is, some Islamic apologists have argued that the 2nd Targum of Esther is later than the Qur'an, and hence cannot be the source of its story. However, there is no agreement as to this source's specific dating, with some scholars placing it well before the Qur'an's writing, some as early as the second century, hence nearly five hundred years prior. But the specific date of the literary work's actual composition is not the point; the traditions and myths it incorporates into its text predate its own composition. With such works, often the origin of the legendary material is many decades or even centuries earlier than its written codification. In light of what we have already seen (indiscriminate connection of legendary material with scriptural and historical), there is little reason to doubt that the story found in the 2nd Targum of Esther likewise is one of the "legends of the ancients" that appears in the Qur'anic text.

11

The Perfection of the Qur'an?
Transmission and Text

Wee conclude our examination of what Christians need to know about the Qur'an by looking at the vital question of the accuracy of the transmission of its text over time. The common Islamic claims are strong and clear:

> The Qur'an is the literal word of God, which He revealed to His Prophet Muhammad through the Angel Gabriel. It was memorized by Muhammad, who then dictated it to his Companions. They, in turn, memorized it, wrote it down, and reviewed it with the Prophet Muhammad. Moreover, the Prophet Muhammad reviewed the Qur'an with the Angel Gabriel once each year and twice in the last year of his life. From the time the Qur'an was revealed, until this day, there has always been a huge number of Muslims who have memorized all of the Qur'an, letter by letter. Some of them have even been able to memorize all of the Qur'an by the age of ten. Not one letter of the Qur'an has been changed over the centuries.[1]

This is the view of the vast majority of Muslims in the world. So extensive is the claim that Mazhar Kazi could claim, after quoting Surah 15:9 ("We have, indeed, sent down the Remembrance, and We shall preserve it"),

> Muslims and non-Muslims both agree that no change has ever occurred in the text of the Qur'an. The above prophecy for the eternal preservation and purity of the Qur'an came true not only for the text of the Qur'an, but also for the most minute details of its punctuation marks as well. . . . It is a miracle of the Qur'an that no change has occurred in a single word, a single [letter of the] alphabet, a single punctuation mark, or a single diacritical mark in the text of the Qur'an during the last fourteen centuries.[2]

There are few topics more central to the discussion between Christians and Muslims, as we saw when we looked at the allegation of corruption many Muslims make against the Hebrew and Greek Scriptures of the Bible. We did not then go into the discussion's necessary corollary, the accuracy of the transmission of the Qur'an. It too was written before the advent of printing, prior to modern methods of textual propagation, and so we must ask, "How was it collected, copied, and transmitted?" Can we learn anything by comparing how the New Testament and the Qur'an have been passed down? As this is an area of general ignorance among both Christians and Muslims, we need some background information to address this topic with integrity and understanding.

Two Kinds of Transmission: Controlled and Uncontrolled

An ancient book could be transmitted in a number of ways. Technically, you could inscribe at least a short essay on a rock and that would provide certainty as to the original reading (barring vandalism or weathering), but to get your message out, large rocks generally are not your best means of distribution. If you then use less permanent means of recording, papyri or parchment, you also are working with a perishable medium. So to reach a large audience, you make copies. Depending on length, hand-copying can take a long time.

Most books were not controlled in their distribution. That is, demand and surrounding cultural context determined which books gained wide circulation and which did not. A book might become popular in one area but not another. Or the book's views might mean a particular political leader promotes it and another seeks to have it destroyed. Many factors could influence how many copies were made, and by whom, and all of this would impact the quality of the copying and how many manuscripts survived down to the present.

A controlled book normally would have been copied and distributed by a governmental entity. Someone in power had a vested interest in making sure it gained distribution and did not experience alteration or change. Hence, for instance, a powerful person might create an "official" version and distribute that to key cities while suppressing any other forms of the text.

Throughout the first centuries of its existence, the New Testament experienced not only an uncontrolled, but almost a chaotic distribution. From the middle of the first century until AD 313, Christianity was a *religio illicita* under Roman persecution. At times it was illegal to own or even copy its Scriptures. During relative peace, the church could become established and as part of its ministry copy the Scriptures, but then persecution would rise again, and history records the destruction of literally thousands of these manuscripts.

Still, Christians wanted everyone to know about the Savior, hear about the Lord, so they did not place restrictions upon the copying of their sacred texts. From the earliest days, the individual New Testament books were copied and recopied, even during the original authors' lifetimes, so that their message of life and forgiveness in Christ could be proclaimed to all. Translations into Latin, Coptic, Sahidic, Bohairic, et al., were an early result of this attitude.[3]

This willingness to have the texts copied meant that at no time during the history of their transmission did any one person, any group, any ecclesiastical structure control the books' content, individually or corporately. Despite mythological traditions to the contrary, the early church, as a persecuted minority, was not under the control of a single man or group of men, and the copying of manuscripts was done freely, without centralized control.

The New Testament illustrates the concept of multi-focality: multiple authors, writing at multiple times to multiple audiences, produced a text that from the start, by definition, could never be under any institution or single group's control. They were so scattered that once the epistles of Paul, Peter, and John and the Gospels began to circulate, it would have been impossible to gather them all up and make changes. There is simply no possibility of a wholesale editing process whereby doctrines could be taken out of the whole corpus or other concepts read into the text. Alter a manuscript, or even a few manuscripts, in one geographical area and those will be seen to differ when compared with earlier manuscripts from another area. One would have to alter all manuscripts completely to be able to make any major textual change, and no one in the ancient world was ever in a position to pull that off.

The result of this uncontrolled production of the New Testament books is twofold. First, we can have complete confidence that what we possess today is what was written in the first century by the apostles of Jesus. Second, because the frequent copying was not always done by professionals (manuscripts destroyed by the Romans had to be replaced; church growth required more manuscript production), inevitable copyist errors appear in the manuscripts. *Any* handwritten work, no matter how carefully done, will contain these. But in the case of the New Testament, the *vast* majority of all variations do not impact the meaning of the text, being limited to vagaries of the Greek language, such as the "movable nu" or the spelling of arcane names.

If one has few manuscripts of a work from antiquity, textual variations can be a real problem. But the more manuscripts you have from a wide range of locations and from early on in the text's transmission, the better off you are. And all scholars agree that of all ancient documents, without doubt the single earliest, best, and most widely attested document is the New Testament.

Comparison of the New Testament to other documents of that age does not even seem fair. While the average work of antiquity has no witnesses until five hundred years after its production, the New Testament boasts numerous witnesses within the first hundred years, and many more within two hundred more years, from a wide geographical area. As noted, we have entire copies of the complete New Testament from as early as the start of the fourth century, and papyri fragments of individual books have been dated to the earliest years of the second century, an unheard-of treasure trove, historically speaking. As these earlier and earlier manuscripts have been found, they have shown that the text popular in the medieval period is not radically altered but is the very same primitive text of the New Testament.[4] No evidence exists of major alterations seeking to remove doctrines, insert beliefs, and the like.[5] Any fair analysis of the text's transmission reveals that its scribes sought to the very best of their ability to transmit it accurately.[6]

But what about the Qur'an? How was it transmitted? Was it a controlled or uncontrolled transmission? And if controlled, do we have early enough manuscripts to detect any later controlled editing or recension of the text?

A Startling Set of *Ahadith*

The *hadith* literature encompasses thousands of sayings from Muhammad and his Companions, collected into many written volumes. Critical scholars may dispute the mechanisms derived by early Muslims by which these statements are judged, but the fact remains that they provide a vital light upon the early period of the Islamic faith. And though the Qur'an's textual history surely is not a major focus of the *ahadith*, there are still key texts that assist us greatly.[7]

Without question, and thankfully, the most important set of *ahadith* for our study here is found in the most authoritative collection of such materials, *Sahih Al-Bukhari*. We refer to volume 6, numbers 509 and 510.[8] This section gives us the earliest Islamic version of the story of the Qur'an's collection, who was involved, and what motivated the project. It is startling because it is far more directly honest and frank than one might expect from a few centuries after the fact. It traces its origin to one of those directly involved with the process that has become known as the "Uthmanic Revision."

Muhammad has died. The Prophet's living voice has been removed, and in the days after his death, divisions began to take shape with ramifications for the Islamic world up to our very day. There is no written Qur'anic text. While some *ayat* have been written on various available items—parchment, shoulder bones of camels, smooth rocks—the only truly authoritative versions exist in the minds of particular men, the Qurra, who have memorized all of, or at least parts of, the Qur'an. Muhammad had pointed to them as its best reciters, and thus they held a high place in the hearts and minds of the faithful:

> Narrated by 'Abdullah bin 'Amr: Allah's Apostle neither talked in an insulting manner nor did he ever speak evil intentionally. He used to say, "The most beloved to me amongst you is the one who has the best character and manners." He added, "Learn the Qur'an from (any of these) four persons. 'Abdullah bin Mas'ud, Salim the freed slave of Abu Hudhaifa, Ubai bin Ka'b, and Mu'adh bin Jabal."[9]

So at first there was no rush to codify the Qur'an into a single volume, a *mus'haf*, manuscript, that would have final authority. There were bigger concerns, such as who would lead the Muslim people, and how this would be decided. But it did not take long for problems to arise.

> Narrated Zaid bin Thabit: Abu Bakr As-Siddiq sent for me when the people of Yamama had been killed (i.e., a number of the Prophet's Companions who fought against Musailama). (I went to him) and found 'Umar bin Al-Khattab sitting with him. Abu Bakr then said (to me), "Umar has come to me and said: 'Casualties were heavy among the Qurra' of the Qur'an (i.e., those who knew the Qur'an by heart) on the day of the Battle of Yamama, and I am afraid that more heavy casualties may take place among the Qurra' on other battlefields, whereby a large part of the Qur'an may be lost."[10]

Abu Bakr was the first "rightly guided Caliph," from the Sunni perspective. A battle had taken place a few months after Muhammad's death against a "false prophet" (Musailama) and his followers. That such a battle could flare so quickly showed how fragile was the very early Muslim coalition. A number of the learned men who had memorized portions of the Qur'an were killed, so Umar had a rightful and serious concern: If more of the Qurra died, might unrecoverable material become lost?

The Arabic does not admit to any other meaning: "whereby a large part (*kathirun*) of the Qur'an may be lost." It is not possible, as later writers would try to read these words and conclude that at this point, the Qur'an already existed as a unified, agreed upon (or written down) body of revelation. Plainly it existed primarily in the minds of those who had memorized major portions during Muhammad's lifetime. And even the fact that he could point to certain men as its best reciters shows there were variations of skill and memory among his followers.[11] It was a genuine danger that another battlefield loss of the Qurra could result in irretrievable damage. And, in fact, that is exactly what others said happened, as we will see below.

> "Therefore I suggest, you (Abu Bakr) order that the Qur'an be collected." I said to 'Umar, "How can you do something which Allah's Apostle did not do?" 'Umar said, "By Allah, that is a good project." 'Umar kept on urging me to accept his proposal till Allah opened my chest for it and I began to realize the good in the idea which 'Umar had realized."

Note the words, "something which Allah's Apostle did not do." Yet *in the minds of most Muslims today, that is exactly what Muhammad did!* The direct assertions of this sound *hadith* are turned upside down by the passage of time.

Zaid bin Thabit initially is overwhelmed with the project's magnitude. After some urging and coercion, though, he begins to warm to the idea.

> Then Abu Bakr said (to me). 'You are a wise young man and we do not have any suspicion about you, and you used to write the Divine Inspiration for Allah's Apostle. So you should search for (the fragmentary scripts of) the Qur'an and collect it in one

book." By Allah if they had ordered me to shift one of the mountains, it would not have been heavier for me than this ordering me to collect the Qur'an. Then I said to Abu Bakr, "How will you do something which Allah's Apostle did not do?" Abu Bakr replied, "By Allah, it is a good project." Abu Bakr kept on urging me to accept his idea until Allah opened my chest for what He had opened the chests of Abu Bakr and 'Umar.

Note the need to "search for the fragmentary scripts." If a search must take place, then everyone knew the Qur'an was a fragmentary, orally transmitted, only partially written document that did not yet exist as one book. Also, the *hadith* repeats the direct assertion that Muhammad had left this task undone.

So I started looking for the Qur'an and collecting it from (what was written on) palmed stalks, thin white stones and also from the men who knew it by heart, till I found the last Verse of Surat At-Tauba (Repentance) with Abi Khuzaima Al-Ansari, and I did not find it with anybody other than him. The Verse is:

"Verily there has come unto you an Apostle (Muhammad) from amongst yourselves. It grieves him that you should receive any injury or difficulty . . . (till the end of Surat-Baraa' (At-Tauba). (9.128–129) Then the complete manuscripts (copy) of the Qur'an remained with Abu Bakr till he died, then with 'Umar till the end of his life, and then with Hafsa, the daughter of 'Umar."

Note Zaid's sources, written ones first: palmed stalks and thin white stones. Other sources mention the bleached shoulder bones of camels. But the written material is insufficient and fragmentary—he must rely upon men's memories. He gives precious little information about how he collated materials, put them together, or dealt with the inevitable differences of recollection. To many outside the Muslim faith, the Qur'an's organization looks tremendously haphazard, and even Islamic *tafsir* literature notes how one *surah* can contain materials Muhammad gave at very different times in his life. Many Muslims assume he was behind this organization, but there is little reason to believe it. Zaid and his committee are far more likely to have been responsible.

The last verse Zaid finds in his search (Surah 9:128) is one of the last to have been given, if tradition is correct. But note what he says: He found it with only one person. He does not say whether it was written or memorized, yet no one else had any memory of this *ayah* but Abi Khuzaima Al-Ansari. Does this not raise an obviously relevant question? If only one man knew this *ayah, could there not have been others lost when the Qurra died at Yamama?* How could anyone know? And if that verse is found in the Qur'an on the basis of one man's testimony, possibly one man's memory, what was the basis for the insertion of Surah 4:157? Is there not just as much reason for concern about parts of the Qur'an being inserted as there would be for parts being lost?

Note below a non-Muslim recitation of much the same tradition. Interestingly, it picks up with the later Uthmanic recension and makes only an indirect mention of this stage of the Qur'an's collection, coming as it does so close to Muhammad's death. And it does seem strained for the text to insist that this one *mus'haf* was then in the possession of Abu Bakr, and then Umar, and finally Hafsa, when in the next *hadith*, this one *mus'haf* is going to function in such an odd fashion. We cannot be blamed for wondering if this portion shows concern for what the entire narration could be taken to mean regarding the collection of the Qur'an.

The next *hadith* moves us forward to the days of Uthman, around AD 650, about eighteen years after the previously noted events. The Islamic state is spreading in all directions, leading again to problems regarding the Qur'an. This time the concern expressed is not about the loss of the Qur'an as an entire document, but about differences and disagreements among the faithful.

> Hudhaifa bin Al-Yaman came to 'Uthman at the time when the people of Sham and the people of Iraq were waging war to conquer Arminya and Adharbijan. Hudhaifa was afraid of their (the people of Sham and Iraq) differences in the recitation of the Qur'an, so he said to 'Uthman, "O chief of the Believers! Save this nation before they differ about the Book (Qur'an) as Jews and the Christians did before."[12]

The impetus for Uthman's revision, and the production of a finalized version, is said to be concern about division coming from the Muslims differing "about the Book as Jews and the Christians did before." That disputing was seen as a source of division, and if the Islamic nation were divided, its future would be uncertain. The concern is focused on "differences in the recitation of the Qur'an." Many Muslims today limit this to issues of pronunciation, but that would hardly be sufficient as a reason for fearing debilitating divisions. But if there were more major differences, differences in wording that would impact belief and hence unity, then the concern would be understandable.

It would seem the problem would be easily solved in light of the preceding production of a *mus'haf* by Zaid bin Thabit during the days of Abu Bakr. Just ask for the manuscript, make some copies, and send them out. Is that what happened?

> So 'Uthman sent a message to Hafsa saying, "Send us the manuscripts of the Qur'an so that we may compile the Qur'anic materials in perfect copies and return the manuscripts to you." Hafsa sent it to 'Uthman. 'Uthman then ordered Zaid bin Thabit, 'Abdullah bin AzZubair, Said bin Al-As and 'Abdur-Rahman bin

> Harith bin Hisham to rewrite the manuscripts in perfect copies.
> 'Uthman said to the three Quraishi men, "In case you disagree
> with Zaid bin Thabit on any point in the Qur'an, then write it in
> the dialect of Quraish, the Qur'an was revealed in their tongue."

Clearly this committee is going to be undertaking something
more than the mere copying of the already collected, already
established Qur'anic text. Why would they need to worry about
the dialect of the Quraish? Wasn't that dealt with eighteen years
earlier? Hadn't Abu Bakr thought of such a thing? But Uthman
had something far more extensive in mind.

> They did so, and when they had written many copies, 'Uthman
> returned the original manuscripts to Hafsa. 'Uthman sent to
> every Muslim province one copy of what they had copied, and
> ordered that all the other Qur'anic materials, whether written
> in fragmentary manuscripts or whole copies, be burnt.

No information about how long this work took—simply, "They
did so." Did *what*? As the *hadith* will go on to note, Zaid even
found another *ayah* he had missed almost two decades earlier,
so clearly this was not a mere copying out of the *mus'haf*. Behind these words' brevity is an obviously lengthy and involved
process, one that other sources seem to indicate Uthman himself was involved with. We would be negligent not to note that
this is the very period when the birth pangs of Islam's deepest
division already were beginning. Uthman would be murdered,
and in Ali's ascension to Caliph, the split that would create the
Sunni and Shia branches would come into view. Can anyone
truly think the sacred text of Islam would not be central to the
power struggle taking place? We shall return to this point.

The committee made copies for distribution to the Muslim
empire's key centers. There are two contradictory statements,
however. On one hand, the "original manuscripts" were given

back to Hafsa. On the other, Uthman ordered that all "the other Qur'anic materials, whether written in fragmentary manuscripts or whole copies, be burnt." Why would this not include the earlier manuscript from Abu Bakr, which was missing, at the very least, one *ayah*? Further, what about where the men had disagreed with Zaid and rendered the text in the Quraishi dialect? Once again, we are left wondering about this earlier manuscript.

What we are *not* left wondering about is that, according to this *hadith*, Uthman sought to make this new recension, this now official version, the supreme authority. All others are to be destroyed. Why? The concern was already expressed. But he is taking a major step, and in so doing determining that only he, as Caliph, has been able to determine the actual Qur'anic text.

Before considering what all that means, let's finish this *hadith*:

> Zaid bin Thabit added, "A Verse from Surat Ahzab was missed by me when we copied the Qur'an and I used to hear Allah's Apostle reciting it. So we searched for it and found it with Khuzaima bin Thabit Al Ansari. (That Verse was): 'Among the Believers are men who have been true in their covenant with Allah'" (33.23).

Yet another *ayah*, missed in the original collation, is added. Such an honest admission raises no end of questions regarding what might have been lost with the death of every Qurra before the first collation, and even since then during the intervening eighteen-plus years.

The Uthmanic Revision, recorded here in *Sahih Al-Bukhari* 6:510, is without a doubt the *hadith* literature's most important statement about the Qur'an's history. While we still have other statements to examine, this one puts us in the position of considering some of the most important issues. Of course, many scholars question this story. Many feel the dating for this collection is far too early and that external information points rather to a final collation much later, around AD 705.[13] While these theories are intriguing, and the actual manuscript information too scant to make final decisions on them, for the purpose of the Christian/Muslim dialogue, we can look at what Bukhari has provided and make at least one substantial observation.

The Uthmanic Revision places the Qur'an in a completely different classification than the New Testament. The latter had multiple smaller books by multiple authors from multiple locations, each starting out with its own transmission history, first brought together into smaller collections (like the Gospels or Pauline Epistles), and finally coming together as a single body in free, uncontrolled transmission. There is never a Christian Uthman, never a Zaid bin Thabit. The Qur'an had one author (according to Islamic orthodoxy), one compilation, then two decades later, a revision, followed by the concerted central-government effort to destroy any competing textual form.

With revision and a controlled transmission, one would expect a much "cleaner," more unanimous text. Combine governmental propagation with the Qur'an being shorter than the New Testament and undergoing around six hundred years *less* time in pre-modern transcription, and the result should be obvious: a very stable text with few textual variants. And by and large, this is what we find with the Qur'an. Muslims see this as a great advantage, even an example of divine inspiration and preservation. In reality, just the opposite is the case.

When a text has a major interruption in transmission—as with Uthman, his committee, and the effort to suppress competing versions—one's certainty of being able to obtain the original text becomes limited to the materials that escape the revisionist pen. For the Muslim, Uthman had to get it right, because if he was wrong, there is little hope of ever undoing his work. Yes, we have evidence, as we will see below, of other text types, but not enough to have a sound basis, at least at this point in history, of re-creating a pre-Uthmanic text. So if Uthman was at all biased, at all influenced by the debates and struggles of his times, the resulting text could be altered forever. And how would anyone know? This is the danger of a controlled transmission: You have to have ultimate trust in the controller. If there is any reason to distrust those who control the form and content, the resultant trust you can place in the text is commensurately reduced. We will see that one such textual variant is directly related to the struggle for power in the Islamic state. How can we determine the original reading? Unlike the New Testament, the Qur'an had no wide variety of freely reproduced texts from all over the Islamic state to draw upon to determine the earliest text. With every one of those early manuscripts destroyed at Uthman's command, the light dims on the original Qur'anic text.

We have further light to shed on this situation from a Christian apologist less than two hundred years after Muhammad's death.

The Earliest Christian Commentary on Qur'anic Corruption

We have had previous occasion to refer to the work of Al-Kindi, one of the earliest Christian apologists responding to Islamic claims whose works remain extant. We noted above that he provides vitally important verification of the tradition, recorded by Bukhari, relating to the Uthmanic Revision, collation of the Qur'an, etc. But in his correspondence with his Muslim interlocutor he shows an amazing knowledge of Islam's early history, especially given that he wrote when the earliest *hadith* collections were only starting to appear. We provide here an extended portion of his apology for a couple of reasons.

First, his statements prove beyond doubt that these matters were public knowledge, known to both Muslims and Christians, within two centuries of Muhammad. *Second,* by listening to this ancient voice, we not only honor that long-ago dialogue but also see that our effort in this study reflects the ongoing defense of the gospel that has been undertaken by Christians for many centuries. We are connected to al-Kindi because the issues that matter have not changed, even if our language, dress, and culture have.

We begin with al-Kindi's recitation of the same tradition found in Al-Bukhari's narration of the Uthmanic Revision. It is tremendously important to recognize how this account verifies, from a perspective of opposition, the core elements of Uthman's revision and sheds further light. Note as well the references to the tensions not only between Ali and Abu Bakr (the seeds of the eventual Sunni/Shia split) but also in reference to Ibn Mas'ud.

> But to return, when 'Ali, still paying homage to Abu Bakr, con-
> fessed that he was collecting the sacred writings, they replied:
> "You have some passages, we have others, why should not the
> sacred book be compiled?" So they united their efforts and put
> together the fragments which had been preserved in various
> quarters, e.g., the Sura Barat, which they wrote down from the
> Arabs of the desert, and other portions gathered from scattered
> tribes, as well as what they found written on white stones and
> the leaves of palm trees, on shoulder bones and so forth. They
> did not combine these in a single volume, but wrote them on
> loose leaves and rolls, after the manner and at the instigation
> of the Jews. Thus it came about that different texts were in use.
> Some read the text of 'Ali, and to this day they swear by him.
> Others read the version whose origin we have just described.
> Others read according to the text of the Arabs who came from
> the desert saying: "We to (sic) have a verse more or less, and
> someone wrote it down, without inquiry as to its history or

authority. A select circle read the Qur'an of Ibn Mas'ud." You remember your master's words: "If you wish to read the Qur'an pure and undefiled, as it came from heaven, read the Qur'an of Ibn Umm Mahad." He himself perused it every year and in the year of his death he read it over twice. Some read the Qur'an of Ubayy b. Ka'b, as it is said: "Ubayy is the best reader of you all." The Qur'an of Ubayy and that of Ibn Mas'ud very nearly correspond.[14]

The disunity danger is seen again here, the lines of division being more starkly drawn. Al-Kindi's account has close connections to other *hadith* we will examine below, and this only increases its importance to our study. He places the initial responsibility for gathering fragments on Ali (Abu Bakr joining together with him). The result was not a single, unified volume but a series of different texts: from Ali, from Abdullah ibn Mas'ud, one from Ubai ibn Ka'b. Even these versions were based upon fragmentary recollections from "desert tribes" and others. So according to al-Kindi's research and sources, the initial collection under Abu Bakr, resulting in a single *mus'haf,* is too simplistic a story. The original haphazard collation was undertaken by men who did not necessarily agree. This fits perfectly with our observation that Bukhari's account of the Abu Bakr manuscript seemed a little forced and anachronistic. Both Ubai ibn Ka'b and Abdullah ibn Mas'ud were renowned as experts in the Qur'an according to later *ahadith,* so it is easy to see why they would take the lead in producing their own texts in answer to queries presented to them.

> The result was that in the Caliphate of 'Uthman it was discovered that there was no consent as to the true text. Meantime 'Ali was conspiring against 'Uthman and aiming at his overthrow. Undoubtedly it was his purpose to kill him. One man, then, read one version of the Qur'an, his neighbor another, and differed.

> One man said to his neighbor: "My text is better than yours," while his neighbor defended his own. So additions and losses came about and falsification of the text.

Clearly the issues went far beyond matters of vowel pointing or pronunciation. These touched upon what is called the *rasm*, the actual wording of the consonantal text. And the divisions between versions were related not just to theology but to politics as well.

> 'Uthman was told that various versions were in use, that the text was being tampered with, and that strife, with all the mischief of party spirit, was being engendered. They said: "We do not believe that matters can continue as they are, it is an affair of urgency; they are slaying one another, the sacred book is corrupted, a second apostasy is imminent." So 'Uthman sent and gathered all the leaves he could secure and the various scraps, as well as the original text.

Notice the centrality of Uthman in the process. Evidently the "original text" refers to the original scraps gathered together, noted earlier.

> They did not interfere with the manuscript in the hands of 'Ali, nor with those who adhered to him. The new recension did not affect them.

This actually refers to the early Shiites, the followers of Ali over against Abu Bakr (today Shiites often refer to Sunnis as Bakrites).

> Ubayy (the) son of Ka'b was dead before it was made, while Ibn Mas'ud refused to give up his copy of the Qur'an, so they drove him from his post in Kufa, and appointed Abu Musa as governor in his place.[15] The next step was to commission Zayd (the) son of Thabit, one of the Helpers, and 'Abdullah (the) son of Abbas (but some say Muhammad, son of Abu Bakr) to carry

through the enterprise, compiling the Qur'an and rejecting what
was corrupt in the text. These two men were both young, but
they were told that if they disagreed on any point as to a letter
of a word, they must render it according to the dialect of the
Quraysh. Naturally they differed on quite a number of points,
e.g., the word "tabut" which Zayd pronounced "tabuh," while
the son of Abbas pronounced it "tabut"; so they adopted the
form in use among the Quraysh, and so on other occasions.

The direct parallel between this account and that of Bukhari,
even to the names on the committee, is good indication of both
having a common source in an earlier period. But al-Kindi seems
to have even more information than Bukhari did!

When the revision had been completed according to the various
manuscripts, four copies were made in large text, one of which
was sent to Mecca, a second remained in Medina, a third was sent
to Syria and is today in Malatya. The copy in Mecca remained
there to the days of Abu Saraya when in the year 200 A.H. occurred the last siege of Mecca. Rumor says that Abu Saraya did
not carry it away from the siege, but that it perished in the fire.
The copy at Medina was lost during the reign of terror in the
days of Yazid. A fourth copy was placed at Kufa, which was then
the capital of Islam and the center of the Refugees and friends
of the Prophet. This copy is said to be still in existence, but that
is not so; it was lost in the days of Mukhtar.

This is a fascinating account of the actual manuscripts, where
they were sent, and what became of them. We cannot confirm
al-Kindi's information, but the knowledge it gives of recent historical events (the siege of Mecca, the reign of terror in Medina)
all have the ring of truth. How useful it would be to have even
one of these manuscripts (and surely a number of them exist
today that claim to be from Uthman, though most scholars do
not think any of them are quite that old), but even if we did,

we still would be looking at an edited, altered text, one stream having a claim to being original but not the only one.

> Next, 'Uthman gave directions that the leaves and sheets of the Qur'an should be gathered in from the provinces. He ordered his agents to collect all that they could lay their hands on and destroy them till it should be certain that not a sheet remained in the possession of any private individual. Heavy penalties were threatened against the disobedient. All the leaves they could secure were shredded and boiled in vinegar till they were sodden, nothing remained, not even the smallest fragment that could be deciphered.

This portion gives us a much more in-depth picture of just how pervasive Uthman's actions were in seeking to destroy the preceding editions. The materials *from which* Uthman derived his version would be valuable to an analysis of how well he did, but those beyond his grasp—say, the *mus'haf* of Ibn Mas'ud, or copies of Ubai ibn Ka'b—would be the gold standard of textual material, vitally important to determining the original. So we see here the purposeful destruction of the most important witnesses the Islamic faith could ever possess *if* the goal is to know exactly what Muhammad said. But that is not Uthman's professed goal, even in Bukhari's version, let alone al-Kindi's. In Bukhari, his motive stems from the need to create *unity* so as to preserve the Islamic state. In al-Kindi, the added personal and political aspects are also seen. This led to the lamentable destruction of at least a large majority of the materials that would have provided a means of testing the revision.[16]

Al-Kindi continues with a catalogue of alterations and changes known to him from his research into the early history of the Qur'an:

> It is said that the Sura Nur was originally longer than the Sura Baqara, and that the Sura Ahzab in its present form is curtailed

and incomplete.[17] In the same way they say that the Sura Barat was not originally separated from the Sura Anfal, that they were not distinguished from each other by so much as the usual heading: IN THE NAME OF GOD: THE MERCIFUL. So of the two final suras which were included in his revision, Ibn Mas'ud said: "Add not to it what is not in it." On the other hand, 'Umar speaking from the pulpit said: "Let no man say that the verse about stoning is not in the sacred book, for I have myself read it. The man and woman who have committed adultery, stone them both. And if it were not that men would say that 'Umar had added to the Qur'an what was not in it, I would restore it with my own hands!" 'In another address he said: "I do not know how anyone can say that the ordinance of al-Mut'a is not in God's word; we have ourselves read it there, but it dropped out. God will not reward with blessing him who has omitted it. It was committed to him as a charge, but he was not faithful to the trust nor loyal to God and His Prophet."

Many of these direct allegations of alteration find echoes in the *hadith*.[18] But they surely go far beyond mere differences in pronunciation. For example, *Surah Nur* has only sixty-four *ayat* in the current Qur'an; *Surah Baqara*, over two hundred! If al-Kindi is correct, that is a very large amount of missing text. Controversies existed over whether the Qur'an's final two surat were canonical, and some rejected them. This is to be expected in the early period *unless* one holds to the view that the majority of Muslims espouse today.

> Much that had been added to the Qur'an was dropped, and so again 'Umar says: "God deals kindly with man and has sent Muhammad with an easy religion." Ubai b. Ka'ab said that there are two suras which they used to recite (he was speaking of the first recension and did not refer to the latter) these were al-Kanut and al-Witr, beginning with the words: "O God we ask Thy help, we invoke Thy pardon and guidance, we trust in Thee and commit

ourselves to Thee."—and so on to the end of al-Witr. And so
with al-Mut'a, which 'Ali caused to be dropped. It is said that
when he heard a man reciting it in his time, he had him scourged
with whips and commanded men not to read it. This was one of
the things for which 'Aisha reproached him on the Day of the
Camel. Among other things she said that 'Ali scourged men and
beat them because of it, and altered and falsified it.

Apart from the specifics of alleged changes, that this information
would be available *outside* the Islamic community is somewhat
startling. It is difficult enough in today's world to find such information; how al-Kindi did so in his day is thought-provoking.
Evidently the public nature of disputes, especially the open
warfare between the Sunnis and the Shiites, led to charges and
countercharges of corruption. This tumultuous period led to
such collections as Ahmad b. Muhammad al-Sayyari's *Kitab
al-qira-at,* which documented Shiite allegations of textual alteration and corruption by Sunni leaders.[19]

Let us finish hearing al-Kindi on this subject, for he still has
important concluding points to make to his Muslim friend:

> The copy of 'Abdullah (the) son of Mas'ud remained in his own
> hands and was bequeathed as an heirloom to the present day. In
> the same way the copy of 'Ali remains among his own people.
> Then followed the affair of Hajjaj who would not give up his
> material but put it together, omitting many things among which
> they say were verses concerning the sons of Umayya and the sons
> Abbas with names mentioned. Five copies were made of the ver-
> sion approved by Hajjaj, one of which was sent to Egypt, one
> to Syria, one to Medina, one to Mecca, one to Kufa and one to
> Basra. All copies of earlier additions (sic) on which he laid his
> hands he boiled in oil till they were sodden, and so made an end
> of them, following the example of 'Uthman. You are yourself
> witness to the truth of this. You have read the Qur'an and know
> how the material has been put together and the text corrupted,

a sure sign that many hands had been busy on it, and that it has suffered additions and losses. Indeed each one wrote and read as he chose, omitting what he did not like. Now, by the grace of God, are these what you consider the marks of an inspired book?

You know what happened between 'Ali, Abu Bakr, 'Umar and 'Uthman, how they hated each other and quarreled and corrupted the text; how each one tried to oppose his neighbor and to refute what he (had) said. Pray, how are we to know which is the true text, and how shall we distinguish it from the false (one)?

How does a Muslim today answer al-Kindi? Pointing to the Uthmanic codex does not suffice. It is self-evident that no matter how stable or even primitive the Uthmanic tradition is, *it is not the only stream that can claim direct connection to Muhammad and the primitive period of Qur'anic compilation.*[20] The greatest concern for any follower of Muhammad should be what he *said*, not what an uninspired Caliph later thought he *should have said*. So how does the controlled nature of the Qur'anic text's transmission allow for this?

A Few Other Voices From History

Additional witnesses lend insight on the Qur'an's historical transmission.[21]

It is well known that Aisha, Muhammad's youthful and favorite wife, told a story about an *ayah* that was lost because . . . it was eaten by a sheep. Yes, that happened.

It was narrated that Aishah said: "The Verse of stoning and of breastfeeding an adult ten times was revealed, and the paper was with me under my pillow. When the Messenger of Allah died, we were preoccupied with his death, and a tame sheep came in and ate it."[22]

But there is some confirmatory evidence of this interruption in the chain of divine revelation by domesticated animals in another sound narration:

> A'isha (Allah be pleased with her) reported that it had been revealed in the Holy Qur'an that ten clear sucklings make the marriage unlawful, then it was abrogated (and substituted) by five sucklings and Allah's Apostle (may peace be upon him) died and it was before that time (found) in the Holy Qur'an (and recited by the Muslims).[23]

This is plain reference to a portion of the Qur'an that had been recited by Muslims as divine revelation, but is no longer to be found in that text. And one *hadith* actually indicates that someone present when the revelation was given could impact its final form as well, showing how fluid was the Qur'an's process and form initially. Note this from *Sahih Al-Bukhari* 6:118:

> When the Verse:—"Not equal are those of the believers who sit (at home)," (4.95) was revealed, the Prophet said, "Call so-and-so." That person came to him with an ink-pot and a wooden board or a shoulder scapula bone. The Prophet said (to him), "Write: 'Not equal are those believers who sit (at home) and those who strive and fight in the Cause of Allah.'" Ibn Um Maktum who was sitting behind the Prophet then said, "O Allah's Apostle! I am a blind man." So there was revealed in the place of that Verse, the Verse:—"Not equal are those of the believers who sit (at home) except those who are disabled (by injury, or are blind or lame etc.) and those who strive and fight in the Cause of Allah." (4.95)

So the presence of a blind man asking how he could go on jihad resulted in further revelation that altered what had been given before.

Even widely published editions of the Qur'an contain information indicating variations in the very text. For example, in

Yusuf Ali's translation, at Surah 33:6 he acknowledges in the text note,

> In some Qira'ahs, like that of Ubayy ibn Ka'ab, occur also the words "and he is a father of them," which imply his spiritual relationship and connection with the words "and his wives are their mothers."[24]

Such statements indicate that Muslims must move beyond "This is our holy text, it is unquestionable and we need not concern with how it came to be in this form or whether it is accurate" and take a long, hard look at producing a meaningful, sound, critically researched edition of the Qur'an.[25]

A number of indications from both inside and outside the Islamic faith, point to the Qur'an's early history as far more complex than the vast majority of Muslims think. Of course, the Bible's early history was far more complex than most Jews and Christians think too. We all tend to accept what we have been given without appropriate examination and study. But as we have seen, there is a vast difference between the kind of evidence available concerning the New Testament and that of the Qur'an. A controlled (less complex) transmission does *not* mean "more trustworthy." Many Muslims make the mistake of joining simplicity and control with truthfulness and accuracy. Regarding the transmission of documents through time, the two are not synonymous.

A Few Specific Examples

Muslims often ask to see specific textual variations supporting our contention that the Qur'an has a textual history and has experienced textual corruption[26] like all other ancient documents. When we refer to textual variation, we are not dealing primarily with one peculiarity of the Qur'an's story, its revelation in seven "forms" (*ahruf*).[27] It is a universally recognized tradition that Gabriel recited the Qur'an in seven different forms to Muhammad, as noted in these words: "Allah's Apostle said, 'Gabriel read the Qur'an to me in one way (i.e., dialect) and I continued asking him to read it in different ways till he read it in seven different ways.'"[28] Islamic discussion of the *ahruf* and exactly how Gabriel could reveal the same divine text in seven ways would take us far afield; there also is great disagreement among Muslims on this matter. If the Qur'an was so revealed, do the seven *ahruf* still exist today? Some affirm, some deny. Add to this the fact that the various printed editions of the Qur'an have different readings[29] and one can see the topic can become quite complicated.

In 2007 Turkish Muslim scholars published a copy of the Topkapi Manuscript.[30] On pages 87 to 89 they reproduce a table with forty-four textual variants between the Qur'an's major *mus'haf*. Early *tafsir* literature mentions numerous variations involving consonantal structure. Here are a few.

Surah 3:158 reads, "If you should die or be slain, before Him you shall undoubtedly be gathered." But the great Paris manuscript of the Qur'an,[31] one of the earliest we possess, contains an extra Arabic letter that changes the entire meaning to "you shall not be gathered."

Surah 17:93 has a variation between "house of ornament" and "house of gold," "gold" being an Ibn Mas'ud reading adopted by many modern versions.

Surah 2:222 is an example of a variation that has a number of variant readings based on *palimpsest* readings of the most ancient manuscripts. One, the Fogg's Palimpsest manuscript,[32] gives Ibn Mas'ud's reading; it is at the top in the illustration. The Uthmanic reading is on the bottom, and a third found in the Sana'a palimpsest materials (not included) is a mixture of both.[33]

First Contrast: Text

Ibn Mas´ud and Surah 2:222 and the Fogg's Palimpsest Manuscript

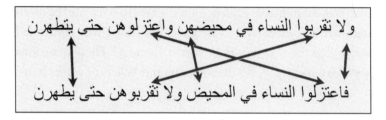

One need not be able to read Arabic to see this is not the result of random copyist error. Words being moved, grammatical terminations changed, verbal forms altered indicates purposeful copyist editing. At the least, this illustrates a verbal transmission coming into written expression in different ways, forcing a later recension and editing; but in any case, it shows beyond all possible question that the Qur'an was not written down in perfection in the days of Muhammad and never altered or changed in its transmission.

One last example: Surah 4:12[34] shows clear evidence of later tampering. Ultraviolet photography shows the rewriting of the term as *kalala* even more clearly. The text relates to offspring and family relationships, and given the controversies of the early Islamic period (both around Uthman's recension and later in the reign of Abd al-Malik, when many scholars see further recensional activity in the Qur'anic text) related to Muhammad's family relationships, it is highly relevant. A word that resulted in great confusion was inserted, and with high probability the alteration was purposeful, related to matters theological as well as political.

And so we conclude by observing once more that documents predating the modern period and transmitted by hand-copying inevitably underwent textual variation. The question for any truth-loving person is this: In the compilation of a work and in its transmission over time, was the process free or controlled? If free, is there sufficient evidence upon which to re-create the original text? If controlled, can we know that those who controlled it handled the text in a trustworthy manner? These questions must be answered honestly, no matter our beliefs or confessions.

Notes

1. I. A. Ibrahim, *A Brief Illustrated Guide to Understanding Islam* (Houston: Darussalam, 1997), 5.

2. Mazhar Kazi, *130 Evident Miracles in the Qur'an* (Richmond Hill, ON, Canada: Crescent, 1997), 42–43.

3. This also speaks to how the Christian view does not invest in the original languages a particular value outside of their being the original tongue; e.g., Greek is not a "divine" language because the New Testament was written in it. Contrast this with Islam's enshrined position of Arabic, in which even daily prayers are done and in which one must make one's confession of faith.

4. All that can be said about the later ecclesiastical text is that it seems to be "fuller" in using longer titles for deity and providing harmonization among the gospel accounts. That is, a scribe, accustomed to how, say, Matthew expressed a particular saying, would be liable to alter a shorter version in, say, Mark or Luke, either purposefully or, more often, because he was accustomed to the longer reading. With the wealth of early manuscripts, we are able to identify these later, natural accretions, and they represent a small fraction of the later text.

5. It has become popular in the past fifty years to emphasize allegedly purposeful changes. This comes after centuries of scholarly consensus that with very few exceptions, the variations in the New Testament represent scribal errors. But modern scholars, abandoning the task of establishing the original text itself, have wandered off into the "exegesis of textual variants," hoping to ascertain what certain scribes were thinking in their work, a task just short of fantasy. But even the most radical skeptics must admit that in general the scribes had one goal in mind: accurately reproducing the text. As even unbelieving skeptic Bart Ehrman has noted,

> Later scribes who were producing our manuscripts, on the other hand, were principally interested in copying the texts before them. They, for the most part, did not see themselves as authors who were writing new books; they were scribes reproducing the old books. The changes they made—at

least the intentional ones—were no doubt seen as improvements of the text, possibly made because the scribes were convinced that the copyists before them had themselves mistakenly altered the words of the text. For the most part, their intention was to conserve the tradition, not to change it. (Bart D Ehrman, *Misquoting Jesus* [New York: HarperCollins, Kindle Edition 2009], 215.)

6. Two of the most highly honored New Testament textual scholars of the past century were Kurt Aland (Germany) and Bruce Metzger (U.S.). Both had encyclopedic knowledge of the manuscripts of the NT textual tradition. Aland noted, regarding the tenacity of the NT text, that is, the fact that the original readings continue to persist in the manuscripts even when variations enter in,

The transmission of the New Testament textual tradition is characterized by an extremely impressive degree of *tenacity*. Once a reading occurs, it will persist with obstinacy. It is precisely the overwhelming mass of the New Testament textual tradition, assuming the ὑγιαίνουσα διδασκαλία of New Testament textual criticism (we trust the reader will not be offended by this application of 1 Tim. 1:10), which provides an assurance of certainty in establishing the original text. Even apart from the lectionaries . . . there is still the evidence of approximately 3,200 manuscripts of the New Testament text, not to mention the early versions and the patristic quotations—we can be certain that among these there is still a group of witnesses, which preserves the original form of the text, despite the pervasive authority of ecclesiastical tradition and the prestige of the later text. (Kurt and Barbara Aland, *The Text of the New Testament* [Grand Rapids, MI: Eerdmans, 1995], 291–292.)

Likewise, Dr. Metzger, toward the end of his life, was asked whether his study of the New Testament text had impacted his personal Christian faith. He replied,

Oh . . . it has increased the basis of my personal faith to see the firmness with which these materials have come down to us, with a multiplicity of copies, some of which are very, very ancient. . . . I've asked questions all my life, I've dug into the text, I've studied this thoroughly, and today I know with confidence that my trust in Jesus has been well placed. . . . *Very* well placed. (Lee Strobel, *The Case for Christ* [Grand Rapids, MI: Zondervan, 1998], 71.)

7. Later generations of Muslim writers invested much more interest in the Qur'an's compilation and transmission than did the first.

8. Given the plurality of numbering systems attached to Bukhari's work, and given the centrality of this portion to our examination, we note that aside from the volume: hadith form of citation we have followed, this reference also is identified as Volume 6, Book 60, Hadith 201 and 202; the Arabic references are Book 65, Hadith 4725 and 4726. In the Arabic/English text produced by Darussalam (trans. Dr. Muhammad Muhsin Khan [1997] in nine volumes), these *ahadith* are found in Volume 6, 424–426, numbers 4986 through 4989.

9. *Sahih Al-Bukhari*, 5:104.

10. Some translations include an expansion here, "unless you collect it."

11. Some *ahadith* reference Muhammad himself forgetting a portion of the Qur'an, only to say that section was abrogated anyway. Such *would* lead to

differences in remembrance and recitation among his followers, e.g., Aisha narrated that Muhammad said, "Allah's Apostle heard a man reciting the Qur'an at night, and said, 'May Allah bestow His Mercy on him, as he has reminded me of such-and-such Verses of such-and-such Suras, which I was caused to forget'" (*Sahih Al-Bukhari* 6.558). Who caused him to forget it? The next *hadith* says, "The Prophet said, 'Why does anyone of the people say 'I have forgotten such-and-such Verses (of the Qur'an)?' He, in fact, is caused (by Allah) to forget'" (559). Likewise,

> The Prophet said, "It is a bad thing that some of you say, 'I have forgotten such-and-such verse of the Qur'an,' for indeed, he has been caused (by Allah) to forget it. So you must keep on reciting the Qur'an because it escapes from the hearts of men faster than camels do" (550).

See as well *Sahih Al-Bukhari* 6.8, where the same concept is reiterated. Finally, Suyuti records a relevant story:

> Al-Tabarani reports in the work al-Kabir that Ibn 'Umar said: "Two men used to recite a chapter taught to them by the Prophet (s). One night they awoke to pray only to find that they were unable to recall even one letter of that chapter. The next morning they went to the Prophet (s) to inform him of what had transpired. He said: 'It is of those parts of the Qur'an that have been abrogated, so ignore it.'" (Jalaluddin Suyuti, *Al-Itqan fi Ulum al-Qur'an* [trans: Muneer Fareed], n.d., electronic version.)

12. *Sahih Al-Bukhari*, 6:510.

13. For a discussion of these issues, see Keith E. Small, *Textual Criticism and Qur'an Manuscripts* (Lanham, MD: Lexington, 2011). Also Powers, *Muhammad Is Not the Father of Any of Your Men*—in particular,

> That the Qur'an was collected or gathered on two separate occasions—first by Abu Bakr and then by Uthman—is widely known and accepted by Muslim and non-Muslim scholars alike. Less well known is the redactional activity which took place during the reign of Abd al-Malik b. Marwan (r. 65–86/685–705), who ruled from Damascus and, like all of the Umayyads, regarded himself as God's deputy (*khalifat allah*). . . . It is noteworthy, however, that Abd al-Malik is reported to have said that he was afraid to die in the month of Ramadan because inter alia that was the month in which "I collected the Qur'an" (160).

14. This portion of Al-Kindi's apology is found in Newman, *The Early Christian-Muslim Dialogue: A Collection of Documents from the First Three Islamic Centuries*, 455–459.

15. History records two very different streams of tradition relating to Ibn Mas'ud and his relationship to Uthman. One presents an amicable relationship, even presenting a kindly encounter between the dying Ibn Mas'ud and the Caliph. The other shows a much more fiery Ibn Mas'ud offended by Uthman's pretentious actions in thinking he could determine the text's final form (Muhammad had pointed to Ibn Mas'ud as one of the four from whom to learn the Qur'an). It seems the Sunni story favors the kindlier version; the Shiite, the other. Evidence seems to favor Ibn Mas'ud and Uthman being at odds. Numerous sources record Ibn Mas'ud refusing Uthman's demand that he give up his *mus'haf* of the Qur'an, and as the early *tafsir* literature records many examples of readings that came from Ibn Mas'ud, that is only explainable if he did not, in fact, give it up to destruction.

Some sources say the governor had Ibn Mas'ud beaten as a result and that he died from the wounds. J. C. Vadet puts it,

A public scene ensued between Ibn Mas'ud and the caliph, who had him ill-treated. It is not known whether he died in Medina, under a sort of house arrest, or at Kufa, where his teaching was highly esteemed. ("Ibn Masud" in *The Encyclopedia of Islam* [Leiden: Brill, CD-ROM edition, 2004].)

In any case, at least one *hadith* surely indicates a historical basis for a strong conflict here:

"O you Muslim people! Avoid copying the *Mushaf* and recitation of this man. By Allah! When I accepted Islam, he was but in the loins of a disbelieving man"—meaning Zaid bin Thabit—and it was regarding this that Abdullah bin Mas'ud said: "O people of Al-Iraq! Keep the *Musahif* that are with you, and conceal them." (*Jami at-Tirmidhi Hadith*, 3104)

16. It is possible that we *do* possess at least fragments of some pre-Uthmanic manuscripts of the Qur'an. These often come in the form of a *palimpsest*, a manuscript used to record a document, then washed clean, and another document written over it (a common practice when parchment, being made of animal skin, was valuable and often reused). We will note the reading of one particular *palimpsest* below. Some believe the Sana'a manuscript finds (1972) yielded sheets that contain pre-Uthmanic readings in the original text (which can often be seen using ultraviolet light or other techniques). Tests done at the University of Arizona indicated the parchment has a 75.1 percent probability of being older than AD 646. For further reading on the Sana'a finds and the current state of study into the early Qur'anic text, see Karl-Heinz Ohlig and Gerd-R. Puin, *The Hidden Origins of Islam* (Amherst, NY: Prometheus, 2010) and Behnam Sadeghi and Uwe Bergmann, "The Codex of a Companion of the Prophet and the Qur'an of the Prophet" in *Arabica* 57 (2010), 343–436.

17. He finds support for this accusation elsewhere. Abu Abaid's *Kitab Fada'il-al-Qur'an*:

A'isha . . . said, "Surat al-Ahzab (xxxiii) used to be recited in the time of the Prophet with two hundred verses, but when Uthman wrote out the codices he was unable to procure more of it than there is in it today [73 verses]."

18. One prime example is found in *Sahih Muslim*, 5:2286:

Abu Harb b. Abu al-Aswad reported on the authority of his father that Abu Musa al-Ash'ari sent for the reciters of Basra. They came to him and they were three hundred in number. They recited the Qur'an and he said: You are the best among the inhabitants of Basra, for you are the reciters among them. So continue to recite it. (But bear in mind) that your reciting for a long time may not harden your hearts as were hardened the hearts of those before you. We used to recite a *surah* which resembled in length and severity to (Surah) Bara'at. I have, however, forgotten it with the exception of this which I remember out of it:" If there were two valleys full of riches, for the son of Adam, he would long for a third valley, and nothing would fill the stomach of the son of Adam but dust." And we used to recite a *surah* which resembled one of the *surahs* of Musabbihat, and I have forgotten it, but remember (this much) out of it:" Oh people who believe, why do you say that which you do not practice" (lxi 2.) and that is recorded in your necks as a witness (against you) and you would be asked about it on the Day of Resurrection" (xvii. 13).

19. The English translation is in print. Etan Kohlberg and Mohammad Ali Amir-Moezzi, *Revelation and Falsification: The Kitab al-qira-at of Ahmad b. Muhammad al-Sayyari* (Leiden, The Netherlands: Brill, 2009).

20. The issue of the text's original reading is not solved by merely choosing one tradition based on authority. In the same way, Uthman's using the power of government to back his own text has no meaningful relation to its truthfulness or accuracy.

21. We are only charting the basics. So much work needs to be done in this field that truly the safest statement to be made about the text's collation and transmission is "We just don't know—yet." But this is theologically untenable for the believing Muslim, who must affirm something beyond the historical record, and while the vast majority of Muslims do not enter into this area of study (only slightly more Christians do), those who do almost always bring orthodox presuppositions with them. The best illustration we have encountered is M. M. Al-Azami's *The History of the Quranic Text from Revelation to Compilation: A Comparative Study with the Old and New Testaments* (Leicester, England: The UK Academy, 2003). Al-Azami tries to call for the very consistency of application of standards we call for but is thwarted by his presuppositions. The work relies heavily on later traditions and diminishes the importance of the *sahih ahadith*, but then when looking at the Old and New Testaments, relies upon very different methodologies while ignoring those documents' much greater age (relative to the Qur'an). Further, one need not embrace the naturalism of many Orientalists to make the criticisms we have above. Despite these (and other) observations, Al-Azami's seems the best modern work available to give the "other side" for comparison and contrast.

22. *Sunan Ibn Majah*, 1944. This *hadith* is marked as *hasan*, the level below *sahih* in the order of soundness.

23. *Sahih Muslim*, 8:3421.

24. Ali, *The Meaning of the Holy Qur'an*, 1057 n3674.

25. The currently ongoing project called *The Corpus Coranicum* is a major step in this direction, but many Muslims resist such a critical production.

26. Again, to say "a text has experienced corruption" is not the same as "we cannot know its original readings." Corruption just means textual variants have occurred in transmission. Of this there is no question regarding the Qur'an. As one noted scholarly source has said,

> In Sufyan al-Thawri's relatively short *Tafsir,* for instance, 67 variant readings—all introduced with *fi qira'at* ("in the reading of . . .") or *kana . . . yaqra'unaha* (" . . . they used to read it as . . .")—are mentioned, 24 of which have a different *rasm*. Most of these are synonyms that are attributed to Ibn Mas'ud (d. 32/652–3). On the whole, it appears that in the second Islamic century variant readings with a different *rasm*, especially from Ibn Mas'ud's codex, were still freely discussed and were called either *qira'at* or, less commonly, *huruf*. (Frederick Leemhuis, "Readings of the Qur'an" in *The Encyclopedia of the Qur'an* [Leiden: Brill, 2004], 4:354; see as well his discussion in 1:349.)

Once more, the *rasm* refers to the text's consonantal form, not merely to the vowel pointing, an issue we face when dealing with Semitic languages.

27. For an orthodox Islamic discussion of the Qur'an's readings and even of some of the textual variants, see Von Denffer, *Ulum Al Qur'an: Introduction to the Sciences of the Qur'an*, in particular, chapters 10 and 11.

28. *Sahih Al-Bukhari*, 4:442 (3219).

29. See Von Denffer, *Ulam Al Qur'an*, 199.

30. *Al-Mus'haf Al-Sharif Attributed to Uthman bin Affan* (Istanbul, Turkey: IRCICA, 2007).

31. Francois Deroche et Sergio Noja Noseda, *Sources De La Transmission Manuscrite Du Texte Coranique*, Vol. 1, Le manuscrit arabe 328 (a) de la Biblioteque nationale de France (Fondazione Ferni Noja Noseda Studi Arabo Islamici, 1998).

32. See Alba Fedeli, "Early Evidences of Variant Readings in Qur'anic Manuscripts" in *The Hidden Origins of Islam*, 311–334, with specific discussions of variants from Fogg's Palimpsest on 317ff.

33. See Sadeghi and Bergmann, *The Codex of a Companion of the Prophet*, 361.

34. For a rich and full discussion of the possibilities this text presents, see Powers, *Muhammad Is Not the Father of Any of Your Men*.

Conclusion

Surah 17:35 states, "Give full measure when you measure and weigh with even scales. This is better [now] and best in the end." It has been our goal to honor our Christian commitment and Christ's lordship by "weighing with even scales" in our analysis of the Qur'an and its teachings on the issues most vital to the Christian/Muslim dialogue. We confess our own weakness, and if in *any* way we have been unfair, we confess that we have fallen short.

We have examined information relating to Muhammad, the beginnings of Islam, and the key theological areas of disagreement and division between Christians and Muslims as they are touched upon in the Qur'an. We have looked at the Qur'an's history, the sources it drew from, and its own transmission over time. What then must we conclude?

Christians must judge Muhammad in the context in which he lived with fairness and equanimity. Muslims must allow an examination of Muhammad that is based upon all the facts and allows for conclusions that fall outside of historical Muslim orthodoxy. Muhammad should be judged on the basis of the claims he made for himself and the consistency of his teachings and actions.

The Qur'an itself should be understood within the context of seventh-century Arabia, and its teachings against polytheism, social injustice, and more should be acknowledged. At the same time, its elevation to ultimate authority, in light of its manifest and documented ignorance of the preexisting revelations, has been found untenable; it leads to confusion and contradiction.

Christians must understand and appreciate the emphasis of the best of Islamic theology upon *tawhid* and hear in confession of the *Shahada* an echo of our own emphasis on absolute monotheism. Muslims must realize, though, that Christians are no less committed to monotheism and must seek to understand our worship of Jesus first and foremost in the context in which we place it.

Christians must grasp the stumbling block that the idea of "saying three" is for Muslims. But Muslims must come to grips with the fact that their holy book misrepresents the Christian faith on this matter and attributes to us beliefs we never have confessed and do not now confess. The Qur'an's representation of the Trinity as "three gods" comprised of Allah, Mary, and Jesus is a complete canard and raises serious questions for the honest Muslim who wishes to believe the Qur'an truthful in all things because its author is Allah. How could Allah misrepresent beliefs as the Qur'an so clearly does?

The Christian must recognize that, for the Muslim, the cross of Christ is a scandal. How could Allah allow a cherished and righteous prophet to be treated in such a fashion? It is a fair question, yet one directly answered by the very Scriptures the Qur'an's author never encountered. Muslims must see that accepting the teaching of Surah 4:157 leaves them standing in direct opposition to the whole of history. These forty Arabic words, written half a millennium after the events in a faraway land with no firsthand connection to them, is utterly insufficient basis for overthrowing the mountain of testimony to the crucifixion of Jesus on a hill outside Jerusalem. Here Islam stands against the united testimony of the preceding Scriptures and of history itself.

Christians need to understand the Islamic emphasis upon the coming "Day of Judgment" and the freedom of Allah to forgive as he desires. But Muslims need to hear the Christian affirmation of the utter justice of God's law and character and answer the question of how arbitrary forgiveness without an eye to the vindication of divine justice can be appropriate or right. The Islamic call to submission fits well with Christian submission to the lordship of Christ, but the differences in our messages far outweigh the commonalities, for we begin with different views of sin and of how God displays His grace.

Christians need to be very familiar with the Qur'an's message directed to the People of the Book and need to understand the inherent distrust Muslims have for the integrity of the biblical text. Corruption of scriptural witness is a weighty matter indeed, but Muslims must recognize the inconsistent testimony of their own text at this point, at least in how modern orthodoxy handles it. The Muslim must answer how Christians can obey the command of Surah 5:47 if Injil *had* been corrupted prior to the time of Muhammad.

Muslims must recognize that if they were to follow the exhortation given to Muhammad in Surah 10:94, and if they were to ask the People of the Book about prophecies of Muhammad, we would unanimously and fervently disclaim the existence of any such prophecy. None of the major texts claimed by Muslims since the days of Muhammad withstand any fair analysis. If the Bible does not predict his coming, the Qur'an is in error on the matter.

Finally, the Muslim needs to recognize that the Qur'an has a history, in terms of its utilization of previous sources, which Islam seems intent upon denying, as well as a history of textual transmission.

One More Word to Our Muslim Readers

We cannot conclude our inquiry without coming to a firm conclusion on the matter. We cannot allow fear of offense to lead us to offend God. Just as you would say it is appropriate, if true, for the Qur'an to warn Christians of the dangers of unbelief and *shirk*, so too we in love must state the truth out of respect for God, for the Lord Jesus, for His gospel, and out of love for you.

When we obey the command of Surah 5:47 and test Muhammad's claims in the light of the gospel, of history, and of consistency and truthfulness, we find him, and the Qur'an, to fail these tests. The Qur'an is not a further revelation of the God who revealed Himself in Jesus Christ. The author of the Qur'an did not understand the gospel, did not understand the Christian faith, and as such cannot stand in the line of Moses → Jesus → Muhammad that he claimed. As much as we may agree with his stand against the polytheism of the tribes of Arabia, he likewise stood firmly against the gospel of Jesus Christ and therefore against the Lord, His apostles, and all the prophets who foretold His coming. If it is blasphemy to speak the truth about such matters, we can only say it is better to blaspheme a human authority than to dishonor God.

So if what we have said is true, what will you do? We know what it means to discover Muhammad is not who you thought he was. But if he wasn't, is it not appropriate for you to consider the truth of what he did not understand? We invite you to consider the claims of Christ. Read the Gospels for yourself, without prejudice. Consider the words of Jesus for yourself. Consider the prophecies that came hundreds of years before His birth. Read Isaiah 53 and consider well that those words were penned seven centuries before Messiah's birth. Read Psalm 22 in the same light. Then read Paul's epistle to the Romans and consider its message of sin, redemption, grace, and justification. It is our prayer, and the prayer of every believing follower of Jesus Christ, that by God's grace and mercy, you will see the light of the glory of Jesus Christ, and in seeing Him, will find forgiveness and eternal life.

Acknowledgments

My sincerest thanks and appreciation to the many fellow servants of the Lord Jesus whose support and encouragement has made this work possible. There are too many to list, but particular thanks go to R. P. and family, B. L. and family, my PRBC family, all those who support Alpha and Omega Ministries, and in particular V. L., R. P., and M. H. for their constant encouragement and assistance. Of course, I am so very thankful to my wife and children for their support, love, and patience. Special thanks to J. and N. W. for keeping me going and healthy! And a special thanks to T. A. E.

I wish to dedicate this book to Beau, Grace, and McKinley. Beau is a true "son in the faith," who was instrumental in directing my studies toward Islam. May God's blessings be yours!

Glossary

Please note: English spellings of Arabic terms vary greatly from source to source. The most often seen variation is the inclusion or non-inclusion of an "h" after a final vowel, such as dawa vs. dawah, umma vs. ummah, etc.

Ahl al-Injil—The Qur'anic identification of Christians in particular in opposition to Jews, "the People of the Gospel," Surah 5:47.

Ahl al-Kitab—The Qur'anic identification of the "People of the Book," which can refer to Jews, Jews and Christians, or Christians alone, depending on the context and usage.

ahruf—a mode in which the Qur'an was revealed, a different reading or pronunciation. Tradition claims the Qur'an was revealed in seven ways or modes.

al-Haqq—the Truth, one of the Ninety-Nine Beautiful names of Allah.

ayah/ayat—a unit of division, a sign, and as a result, a miracle. The verses of the Qur'an are individually called an *ayah*; *ayat* is the plural form.

Buraq—a small winged creature (smaller than a mule, bigger than a donkey) which is said to have transported Muhammad from Mecca to Jersualem, in the Isra, in approximately 619.

dawa—calling to Islam and the defense thereof. Islam combines into one what Christians normally call *evangelism* and *apologetics*.

dhimmi/dhimmitude—a dhimmi is a non-Muslim person who is subject to the Islamic state and pays the *jizya* tax. Some would limit its usage to Jews and Christians. *Dhimmitude* is the state of being subject. See Surah 9:29.

du'a—personal prayer, made in any language, in distinction from the salat, the formal prayers that are only performed in Arabic.

fitra—the original, innate spiritual condition of man that recognizes the existence of Allah. Theologically, the *fitra* is due to the taking of the *mithaq* (see below) from the descendants of Adam. See Surah 7:172–173.

hadith—plural, ahadith. The actions, statements, and teachings of Muhammad and his companions that forms the core of the Islamic tradition. The *hadith* literature comprises the essence of the Sunnah and is the primary lens through which the Qur'an is interpreted. An individual narration is determined to be "sound" (*sahih*), acceptable or good (*hasan*), weak (*daif*), or fabricated (*mawdu*). An *ahad hadith* is one that is narrated by only one source. *Hadith Qudsi* is a special kind of hadith wherein Muhammad quotes the words of Allah. The two most authoritative collections of hadith for the Sunni are *Sahih Al-Bukhari* and *Sahih Muslim*. Other important collections include the very early Muwatta of Malik ibn Anas, Sunan Abu Dawud, Sunan ibn Majeh, Sunan al-Nisaa, and that of Jami at-Tirmidhi.

Hajar al-Aswad—the "Black Stone" which is said to have fallen from heaven and is placed in one corner of the Kaaba in Mecca. Pilgrims attempt to get close to the Black Stone to kiss it during *hajj* or Umrah.

hajj—One of the five pillars of Islam, *hajj* is the pilgrimage to Mecca undertaken at least once in a faithful Muslim's life (if health and finances permit) involving reenactment of elements of Muhammad's life and the circumambulation of the Kaaba. It takes place in the twelfth lunar month of the Islamic calendar, Dhul-Hijjah.

halal/haram—Allowed (*halal*) and forbidden (*haram*), literally. *Halal* food, for example, is food permitted under the *sharia* (law) of

Islam. *Haram* is anything forbidden, but it also refers to the sacred house, the Kaaba, and the entire Grand Mosque around it.

Hijaz—the strip of land on the western border of present-day Saudi Arabia, which includes the Islamic holy cities of Mecca and Medina.

Hijra—literally "migration," but in particular, the migration of Muhammad from Mecca to Medina in AD 622, marking the beginning of the Islamic calendar.

howdah—a covered carrier placed upon an animal, such as a camel, for transport of a person. Aisha's *howdah* was placed upon a camel without her in it and the caravan left her behind in a famous incident in Islamic history.

iman—faith.

isnad—the chain of narrators of a tradition in the *hadith* literature. Study of the isnad chains in the *hadith* tradition is central to hadith sciences.

Isra—Normally noted in conjunction with the Mi'raj, the Isra is the night journey Muhammad took to Jerusalem in AD 619 upon the *Buraq*, the winged beast.

jahaliya—ignorance, specifically ignorance of Islam prior to the coming of Muhammad. Muslims speak of the period of "*jahaliya*" to refer to the time prior to the ministry of Muhammad among the Arabs.

Jibreel—The angel Gabriel.

Jizyah—obligatory tax placed upon the People of the Book who refuse to convert to Islam (Surah 9:29).

Kaaba—the cube-shaped building in the Grand Mosque in Mecca. Muslims believe it was initially built by Abraham and his son Ishmael. The Black Stone is embedded in a corner of the Kaaba, and it is toward it that the Muslims bow in prayer.

Kalima—the words of confession, specifically, the *Shahada*.

kufir/kafar—unbelief/unbeliever. The root in Arabic refers to "covering over," i.e., in unbelief.

La ilaha illa Allah—Arabic for "there is only one God worthy of worship," the first words of the *Shahada*. All prophets sent by Allah have been united by this one message.

Laylat al-Qadr—the "Night of Power." The entirety of the Qur'an was sent down on this night, though it was given piecemeal to Muhammad over the course of twenty-two years, the first portions given that night. Muslims believe prayers offered on this night are particularly efficacious and rewarded, and it is believed to fall on the twenty-first, twenty-third, twenty-fifth, twenty-seventh, or twenty-ninth night of the month of Ramadan.

Mi'raj—Muhammad's ascent into the heavens after his night journey.

mithaq—the covenant taken with the entire human race when Allah caused them to come forth from Adam, and then asked them if he (Allah) was their Lord. All of mankind confirmed their covenant with Allah. Man is born on the fitra due to this *mithaq*. See Surah 7:172–173.

mubinun—clear, perspicuous, easily understood. The Qur'an claims to be mubinun.

muhaymin—a guard or protector. The Qur'an is said to be a protector of the previous revelations (Surah 5:48), though most Muslims believe this means it corrects, or in most ways, supersedes, those previous revelations.

mus'haf—a copy of the Qur'an, historically, a handwritten manuscript such as the *mus'haf* of Ibn Mas'ud or Uthman ibn Affan.

Mutawaatir—a universally accepted *hadith*, reported by a large number of narrators at all stages of the isnad.

Mutazilite—an early branch of Islamic theology emphasizing reason and rational thought. *Mutazilites* believed the Qur'an to be a created thing (along with most Shiites). Abu Jafar Abdullah al-Mamun ibn Harun (813–833), Caliph, seemed to be of the *Mutazilite* view on this and other matters.

najas—impure, defiled.

qadar—literally power, but coming to mean Allah's divine decree concerning all things in time. The discussion of *qadar* is central to the Islamic understanding of predestination.

rasm—referring to the actual lettering of a mus'haf, over against the vowel pointing of the text. A difference in *rasm* is a difference in the actual orthography of the text, i.e., a textual variant, such as at Surah 2:222.

Salafi—the term *salaf* refers to the first few generations of Muslims after Muhammad, the great ancestors who are said to have been the "best" people. Hence, Salafi refers to one who follows after them, and holds to a very literal, conservative interpretation of the Qur'an and Sunnah. Salafi is often used as a synonym, in American usage, to the term *fundamentalist*. The Salafi are a major force in Egypt and Saudi Arabia.

Shahada—the confession of faith, spoken in Arabic, by which one becomes a Muslim. In English, the *Shahada* is "There is only one God worthy of worship, and Muhammad is His prophet."

sharia—Islamic law derived from the Qur'an and the Sunnah.

Shiite—a follower of Shi'ism, the second-largest sect in Islam, comprising 8 to 9 percent of world Muslim population. The conflict between Shi'ism and the Sunni sect goes back to the earliest decades of the Islamic movement and is centered, historically, in the succession of power in the Caliphate after Muhammad's death. Shiites believe the proper successor to Muhammad was Ali ibn Abi Talib (601 or 607 to 661), Muhammad's cousin and son-in-law, who eventually became Caliph from 656 to 661, but was preceded in that office by Abu Bakr as-Siddiq, Umar ibn al-Khattab, and Uthman ibn Affan. The succession struggle resulted in the Battle of Karbala in AD 680 in which Hussein, Ali's grandson, and more than seventy of his family were slain. The martyrdom of Hussein is central in Shiite lore and even theology and has led to many of the developments in theology that separate the Shiites from the Sunnis in belief, practice, and outlook.

shirk/mushrik—*shirk*, in secular Arabic, simply refers to "association," as in a corporation, a gathering of individuals. But in Islam, *shirk* is the sole unforgivable sin, for it involves association of anything or anyone with the one true God, Allah. *Shirk* is unforgivable because it is an essential negation of the central truth of Islam, that of *tawhid*, the oneness of Allah. A *mushrik* is one who practices *shirk*.

Sunnah—the Sunnah are the habits, customs, practices, actions, etc., of Muhammad, primarily communicated through the means of the collections of *ahadith*, that end up comprising the primary tradition of Islam. The Sunnah is the norm as it interprets the Qur'an through the life and teachings of Muhammad.

Sunni—the majority group of Islam, comprising approximately 90 percent of world Muslim population. Sunnis believe in the first four "rightly guided" Caliphs in opposition to the Shiites.

surah/surat—*surah* (singular) surat (plural), a chapter of the Qur'an, which contains 114 surat in its current form.

tafsir—commentary and explanation of the meaning of the Qur'an.

tahrif—the corruption of a written text, either in its interpretation or its actual written form. Corruption of meaning is referred to as *tahrif al-mana*, and the corruption of the actual text (removal of, or addition of, words, phrases, etc.) is *tahrif al-nass* (or *tahrif al-lafz*)

tawhid—the central affirmation of Islamic theology, enshrined in the first words of the *Shahada*, "There is only one God worthy of worship." *Tawhid* refers to the oneness of Allah, a oneness that Christians recognize to be unitarian in nature. Different forms of tawhid can be identified in Islamic thought, such as *tawhid ar-rububiyah*, tawhid of lordship; *tawhid al-uluhiya*, the *tawhid* of worship; and *tawhid al-Asma was-Sifaat*, the *tawhid* of Allah's names and attributes. The negation of *tawhid* is seen in the unforgivable sin of *shirk*.

Ummah—a community of people, and in particular, the entire body of Muslims.

Umrah—the lesser pilgrimage to Mecca outside the time of *hajj*.

Wahhabi—see **Salafi**. Wahhabi refers to a certain Sunni sect, often used interchangeably with Salafi. These are very conservative Muslims (the English equivalent in current usage might be *fundamentalist*) who follow the views of Muhammad ibn Abd al-Wahhab, a Muslim reformer who popularized the views of Ibn Taymiyya (1263–1328), who emphasized *tawhid* and a literal interpretation of the Qur'an and the Sunnah along the lines of the early Muslims, the *salaf* or pious ancestors, the first few generations after Muhammad.

Bibliography

Al-Azami, M. M. *The History of the Qur'anic Text From Revelation to Compilation: A Comparative Study With the Old and New Testaments*. Leicester, UK: The UK Academy, 2003.

Al-Mus'haf Al-Sharif. Attributed to Uthman Bin Affan. Istanbul, Turkey: IRCICA, 2007.

Al-Sadi, Allamah Abd Al-Rahman. *An Explanation of Muhammad Ibn Abd Al-Wahhab's Kitab Al-Tawhid*. Trans. Abu Khaliyl. Birmingham, UK: Al-Hidaayah, 2003.

al-Sayyari, Ahmad b. Muhammad. *Kitab Al-Qira'at*. Trans. Etan Kohlberg and Mohammad Ali Amir-Moezzi. Boston, MA: Brill, 2009.

al-Waqidi, Muhammad b. Umar. *Kitab Al-Maghazi, the Life of Muhammad*. Trans. Amal Ismail Rizwi Faizer, AbdulKader Tayob. New York, NY: Routledge, 2011.

al-Yahsubi, Qadi Iyad Ibn Musa. *Muhammad, Messenger of Allah, Ash-Shifa of Qadi Iyad*. Trans. Aisha Bewley. Inverness, Scotland: Madina Press, 2008.

Aland, Kurt and Barbara. *The Text of the New Testament*. Grand Rapids, MI: Eerdmans, 1995.

Ali, Yusuf. *The Meaning of the Holy Qur'an*. Beltsville, MD: Amana, 2001.

Ante-Nicene Fathers, The, Vol. VIII. James Donaldson and Alexander Roberts, eds. Grand Rapids, MI: Wm. B. Eerdmans, 1981.

Asad, Muhammad. *The Message of the Qur'an.* Bitton, Bristol, UK: The Book Foundation, 2003.

Crossan, John Dominic. *Jesus: A Revolutionary Biography.* San Francisco, CA: HarperSanFrancisco, 1994.

Dawud, Abdul Ahad. *Muhammad in World Scriptures.* Kuala Lampur: Islamic Book Trust, 2006.

Dawud, Imam Abu. *Sunan Abu Dawud.* New Delhi, India: Kitab Bhavan, 2007.

Deroche, Francois, and Sergio Noja Noseda. *Sources de la Transmission Manuscrite du Text Coranique Vol. 1 Le Manuscrit Arabe 328 (a) De la Biblioteque Nationale de France.* Fondazione Ferni Noja Noseda Studi Arabo Islamici, 1998.

Ehrman, Bart. *Did Jesus Exist? The Historical Argument for Jesus of Nazareth.* New York, NY: HarperOne, 2012.

———. *The Historical Jesus, Part 2, Lecture Transcript and Course Guidebook.* Chantilly, VA: The Teaching Company, 2000.

———. *Misquoting Jesus.* New York, NY: HarperCollins, 2009.

Ehrman, Bart, and Zlatko Plese. *The Apocryphal Gospels.* Oxford, UK: Oxford University Press, 2011.

Encylopedia of the Qur'an. Jane Dammen McAuliffe, ed. Leiden: Brill, 2001.

English Translation of Jami At-Tirmidhi. Trans. Abu Khaliyl. Riyadh, Saudi Arabia: Darussalam, 2007.

Gätje, Helmut. *The Qur'an and Its Exegesis.* Oxford, UK: Oneworld, 2004.

History of Al-Tabari: Muhammad at Mecca, The, Vol. VI. Trans. M. V. McDonald and W. Montgomery Watt. Albany, NY: State University of New York Press, 1988.

Holmes, M. W. *The Apostolic Fathers: Greek Texts and English Translations.* Grand Rapids, MI: Baker Books, 1999.

Ibrahim, I. A. *A Brief Illustrated Guide to Understanding Islam.* Houston, TX: Darussalam, 1997.

Ishaq, Ibn. *The Life of Muhammad: A Translation of Ibn Ishaq's Sirat Rasul Allah.* Trans. Alfred Guillaume. Karachi, Pakistan: Oxford University Press, 2006.

Jalulu'd-Din Al-Mahalli, Jalalud-Din As-Suyuti. *Tafsir Al-Jalalayn.* Trans. Aisha Bewley. London, UK: Dar Al Taqwa Ltd, 2007.

Kazi, Mazhar. *130 Evident Miracles in the Qur'an.* Richmond Hill, ON, Canada: Crescent, 1997.

Lings, Martin. *Muhammad: His Life Based on the Earliest Sources.* Rochester, VT: Inner Traditions, 2006.

Massod-ul-Hasan, S. *110 Ahadith Qudsi.* Riyadh, Saudi Arabia: n.d.

Metzger, Bruce Manning. *The Text of the New Testament: Its Transmission, Corruption, and Restoration,* 2nd ed. New York, NY: Oxford University Press, 1980.

Muhammad Muhsin Khan, and Muhammad Taqi-ud-Din Al-Hilali. *Interpretation and Meanings of the Noble Qur'an in the English Language.* Houston, TX: Darussalam, 1999.

Neusner, Jacob. *The Babylonian Talmud: A Translation and Commentary.* Peabody, MA: Hendrickson, 2011.

———. *The Mishnah: A New Translation.* New Haven, CT: Yale University Press, 1988.

Newman, N. A. *The Early Christian-Muslim Dialogue: A Collection of Documents from the First Three Islamic Centuries (AD 632–900) Translations with Commentary.* Hatfield, PA: Interdisciplinary Biblical Research Institute, 1993.

———. *Muhammad, the Qur'an, & Islam.* Hatfield, PA: Interdisciplinary Biblical Research Institute, 1996.

Nickel, Gordon. *Narratives of Tampering in the Earliest Commentaries on the Qur'an.* Leiden: Brill, 2011.

Ohlig, Karl-Heinz, and Gerd-R. Puin. *The Hidden Origins of Islam.* Amherst, NY: Prometheus, 2010.

Ozek Ali, Nureddin Uzunoglu, Tevfik R. Topuzoglu, and Mehmet Maksutoglu. *The Majestic Qur'an: An English Rendition of Its Meanings,* 4th ed. London, UK: Ibn Khaldun Foundation, 2000.

Powers, David S. *Muhammad Is Not the Father of Any of Your Men.* Philadelphia, PA: University of Pennsylvania Press, 2009.

Qadhi, Yasir. *An Explanation of Muhammad Ibn Abd Al-Wahhab's Kashf Al-Shubahat: A Critical Study of Shirk.* Birmingham, UK: Al-Hidaayah, 2003.

———. *An Introduction to the Sciences of the Qur'aan.* Birmingham, UK: Al-Hidaayah, 2003.

Sadeghi, Behnam, and Uwe Bergmann. "The Codex of a Companion of the Prophet and the Qur'an of the Prophet." *Arabica* 57 (2010): 343–436.

Sahih Muslim Arabic-English. Trans. Abdul Hamid Siddiqi. New Delhi, India: Idara Isha'at-E-Diniyat Ltd, 2001.

Schimmel, Annemarie. *And Muhammad Is His Messenger: The Veneration of the Prophet in Islamic Piety.* Chapel Hill, NC: University of North Carolina Press, 1985.

Small, Keith. *Textual Criticism and Qur'an Manuscripts.* Lanham, MD: Lexington, 2011.

Spencer, Robert. *Did Muhammad Exist?: An Inquiry Into Islam's Obscure Origins.* Wilmington, DE: Intercollegiate Studies Institute, 2012.

Strobel, Lee. *The Case for Christ.* Grand Rapids, MI: Zondervan, 1998.

Tafsir Al-Qurtubi. Trans. Aisha Bewley. London, UK: Dar Al Taqwa, 2003.

Tafsir Ibn Kathir. Trans. Shaykh Safi-Ur-Rahman Al-Mubarakpuri. Riyadh, Saudi Arabia: Darussalam, 2003.

Tanwir Al-Miqbas Min Tafsir Ibn Abbas. Trans. Mokrane Guezzou. Amman, Jordan: Royal Aal al-Bayt Institute for Islamic Thought, 2007.

Translation of the Meanings of Sahih Al-Bukhari, The. Trans. Muhammad Muhsin Khan. Riyadh, Saudi Arabia: Darussalam, 1997.

Wherry, E. M. *A Comprehensive Commentary on the Qur'an,* Vol. 2. London: n.p., 1886.

Biblical Reference Index

Page numbers in italic indicate the reference appears in a note.

Qur'an Reference Index

Page numbers in italic indicate the reference appears in a note.

303

Subject Index

Page numbers in italic indicate the reference appears in a note.

James R. White is the author of several acclaimed books, including *The God Who Justifies* and *The Forgotten Trinity*. The director of Alpha and Omega Ministries, a Christian apologetics organization, he is an accomplished and respected debater and an elder of the Phoenix Reformed Baptist Church. James also blogs at the Alpha and Omega Ministries site www.aomin.org. He and his family live in Phoenix, Arizona.

More From
James R. White

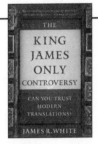

In this revised edition of a classic resource, James White traces the development of Bible translations old and new. Updated with the latest scholarship and packed with new examples, this book explains to the average layperson the differences between major Bible translations, and specifically addresses the claims and concerns of the King James Only camp.

The King James Only Controversy

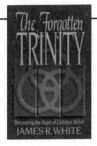

A basic teaching of the Christian faith, the Trinity defines God's essence and describes the ways in which He relates to us. In this concise, understandable explanation of the Trinity and its significance, James White reveals how a grasp of this important teaching leads to renewed worship and deeper understanding of what it means to be a Christian.

The Forgotten Trinity